The Marriage of
Maria Braun

Rutgers Films in Print

Charles Affron, Mirella Jona Affron, and Robert Lyons, editors

The Marriage of Maria Braun

Rainer Werner Fassbinder, director

Joyce Rheuban, editor

Rutgers University Press

New Brunswick, New Jersey

The Marriage of Maria Braun is volume 4 in the *Rutgers Films in Print* Series.

Screenplay by Peter Märthesheimer and Pea Fröhlich, from an idea by Rainer Werner Fassbinder; co-production, Albatros Film/Atlas Trio/WDR. Used by agreement with Verlag der Autoren. Stills on pp. 6, 75, 115, 120, 147, 149, and 212 courtesy New Yorker Films, New York. *The Marriage of Maria Braun* is distributed in the U.S. by New Yorker Films.

Library of Congress Cataloging in Publication Data
Main entry under title:

The Marriage of Maria Braun.

(Rutgers films in print; v. 4)
"Fassbinder filmography, 1965–1982": p.
Bibliography: p.
1. Ehe der Maria Braun (Motion picture)
I. Fassbinder, Rainer Werner, 1946–
II. Rheuban, Joyce.   III. Ehe der Maria
Braun (Motion picture)   IV. Series.
PN1997.E364M37 1986   791.43'72   85–2334
ISBN 0–8135–1129–1
ISBN 0–8135–1130–5 (pbk.)
Second paperback printing, 1991
Copyright © 1986 by Rutgers, The State University
All rights reserved
Manufactured in the United States of America

Chronology and "Strong Emotions" from press materials for *The Marriage of Maria Braun* courtesy *Hanns Eckelkamp/Trio Films.*

"Notes on Shooting Script" from the original script and "Letter to the Editor," courtesy Peter Märthesheimer. "The Decline of BRD," courtesy Hans-Jürgen Jagau/*Zitty.* "Responding to What You Experience: Interview with Fassbinder and Sirk," by Ernst Burkel, courtesy *Süddeutsche Zeitung.* "Primary Identification and the Historical Subject: Fassbinder and Germany," by Thomas Elsaesser originally published in *Cine-Tracts* (Montreal) v. 3, n. 3, pp. 43–52, courtesy of the author. "Six Films by Douglas Sirk," translated by Thomas Elsaesser from the original article by R. W. Fassbinder, "Imitation of Life," in *Fernsehen und Film*, February 1971, courtesy Thomas Elsaesser and Verlag der Autoren. "A German Actress Is Superb in Title Role of 'Maria Braun'," by Douglas Keating, December 22, 1979, p. 6, sec. A, © *The Philadelphia Inquirer.* "Cinema—High Camp: The Marriage of Maria Braun," by Frank Rich, © 1979 by Time Inc. All rights reserved. Reprinted by permission from *Time. Women's Wear Daily* review by Christopher Sharp, "Arts and People, The Marriage of Maria Braun," October 12, 1979, p. 14. *Cineaste* review by Ruth McCormick, vol. 10, no. 2, Spring 1980, pp. 34–36. "The Art of Stereo" from *Stuttgarter Zeitung*, March 30, 1979, translated by Joyce Rheuban, courtesy Hans-Dieter Seidel. "Before the Takeover," by Peter W. Jansen in *Die Zeit*, March 23, 1979, p. 52, translated by Joyce Rheuban, courtesy Peter W. Jansen. "A Star is Born," by Sheila Johnston in *New German Critique*, Fall/Winter 1981–1982, pp. 57–72, courtesy Sheila Johnston.

Acknowledgments

The editor would like to acknowledge several people and institutions for their generous assistance or support during the preparation of this volume. They are: Peter Märthesheimer; Hanns Eckelkamp of Atlas Filmverleih, Duisberg; John Montague of New Yorker Films, New York; Verlag der Autoren, Frankfurt, Germany; Heiner Ross, director of the Kommunales Kino, Hamburg; the library staff of the Deutsche Film-und Fernsehakademie, Berlin; the library staff of the Hochschule für Fernsehen und Film, Munich; the Research Foundation of the City University of New York; and the Mellon Foundation Community Colleges Project.

The editor is grateful to the authors and publishers of the reviews, essays, and interviews included in this volume for granting permission to reprint their work.

The editor especially wishes to thank Lindley Hanlon for her valuable advice and thoughtful comments, and Carole Pipolo for her generous assistance and expertise in the preparation of this volume. The editor is particularly indebted and deeply grateful to Tony Pipolo for contributing invaluable critical and creative insights on the topics presented in the introductory essay.

Contents

viii Contents

The Marriage of
Maria Braun

Introduction

The Marriage of Maria Braun

History, Melodrama, Ideology

Joyce Rheuban

I.

With *The Marriage of Maria Braun*, Rainer Werner Fassbinder achieved something he had not accomplished with any previous film—a great success with critics and public, at home as well as abroad. The film opened the 1979 Berlin Film Festival and later that year won the prestigious Federal Film Prize. Within one month of its release, *Maria Braun* had been seen by half a million viewers and had grossed three million marks (over a million dollars). A syndicated article in the *Westfälisches Volksblatt* bore the headline "People Are Coming Back to the Movies for Maria Braun,"[1] and credited Fassbinder's film, along with Volker Schlöndorff's *The Tin Drum*, also released that year, as the first postwar German films to enjoy wide popular success in Germany. With this triumph, Fassbinder for the first time gained full credibility as a commercial force in the German film industry.

In the United States, *Maria Braun* had a similarly enthusiastic reception, both critical and commercial. It was the closing night attraction at the 1979 New York Film Festival and on commercial release played for more than a year at its first-run house. It became the first postwar German film to surpass the one-million dollar mark in U.S. rentals. A full-page ad in *Variety* declared: "Fassbinder has

1. "Man strömt wieder ins Kino: In die 'Ehe der Maria Braun'." *Westfälisches Volksblatt* (Paderborn), 10 October 1979.

made a lot of movies—now he makes a lot of money." [2] The consequence of this success was that *Maria Braun* (again, together with *The Tin Drum*) opened the American film market to other German films, and introduced *Das Neue Kino* (New German Cinema), heretofore known to a limited number of American *cinéphiles*, to vastly larger numbers of American viewers.

While Fassbinder's success abroad led to some involvement in international productions (*Despair*, for instance, in 1977, and his last film, *Querelle*, 1982), his subsequent work remained intensely German—in subject, in script, in locations, and he continued to work with German technical crews and casts. This is not surprising when one considers that from the very beginning, his focus was largely confined to the individual, domestic, and social ills of West German society of his time. If anything, his ambitions and larger budgets with and after *Maria Braun* served to expand his compass with reference to those concerns. Thus, in 1981, he conceived a historical project whose object was to present German history of the last century and to delineate the social and cultural continuities that he believed connected his society with the German past. [3]

For this project, *The Marriage of Maria Braun*, subtitled *BRD* [Bundesrepublik Deutschland (Federal Republic of Germany)] *1*, was a crucial step. Fassbinder would directly link two other films about postwar Germany to *Maria Braun* through their subtitles: *The Longing of Veronika Voss: BRD 2* (1981) and *Lola: BRD 3* (1981). All three films dramatize the conditions of life within the prosperous bourgeois world of postwar Germany, and are further linked through their use of the experiences of individual women as the measure of the state of society. In addition, Fassbinder often repeats a motif or an historical reference to reinforce the milieu common to different parts of his trilogy. For example, the same soccer game that we hear over the radio in the last scene of *Maria Braun* is also heard in *Lola*, signifying both the chronological overlapping of the films and the socio-historical continuity which links their narratives. A fourth film, *Lili Marleen* (1980), though not officially a part of this grouping, nevertheless seems an appropriate "prelude" to the postwar trilogy. It is set during World War II and ends when the war does, thus overlapping with the beginning of *Maria Braun*.

Nor are these Fassbinder's only historical films. Before *Maria Braun*, he made *Bolwieser* (1977) and *Despair*, both set during the Weimar Republic of the 1920s, a period he was to return to for his fourteen-part television adaptation of

2. *Variety*, 2 May 1979, p. 43.
3. *Variety*, 2 September 1981, p. 32.

Alfred Döblin's important novel, *Berlin Alexanderplatz* (1980).[4] A most ambitious historical project was an aborted television series, undertaken in 1976 and based on the Gustav Freytag novel *Debit and Credit (Soll und Haben)*. The series was to trace the history of a family and their business firm from the mid-nineteenth century until the 1930s in order, according to Fassbinder, to "show that National Socialism wasn't an accident but a logical extension of the German bourgeoisie's attitudes, which haven't altered to this day."[5]

Fassbinder's remark indicates the significant links among all these historical films: whatever their period, they dramatize the circumstances and concerns of middle-class life, and stress the integral relationship between that life and the course of German history over the last one hundred years. While Fassbinder was generally regarded by the press and by his fellow Germans as anything but an average middle-class citizen, it was nevertheless as a member of the middle class that he perceived its problems and criticized its values. Like many others of similar disposition, he was convinced that middle-class existence was based on an exploitative capitalist economic structure and an equally exploitative patriarchal social structure. Though such convictions accord, in a general manner, with Marxist social theory, Fassbinder is hardly a simple expounder of political or ideological doctrine. This was true even in his early ventures. He first gained public recognition as an avant-garde artist in the German counterculture of the late 1960s, and his theater work reflected a radical sensibility. His Action Theater troupe was even threatened with the suspension of its license because of the subversive thrust of its productions.

Yet it became clearer and clearer that Fassbinder's importance lay in his paradoxical position vis-a-vis middle-class society. "I'm a German making films for German audiences," he once declared, asserting the persistent aim which drove him to become the most active and prolific filmmaker of his time. His unflagging energy thus pursued a double-edged purpose: to consistently criticize the assumptions and values of the middle class while continually seeking the means to affect and win over that very audience of "average" Germans who were the object of his criticism. A naive aspiration, perhaps, but not a disingenuous one.

4. Two more films were left uncompleted when Fassbinder died: "Rosa L.," whose subject was Rosa Luxemburg and the German revolution of 1918, and "Hurrah, We're Still Alive," a project based on a best-seller about the German "economic miracle" (the *Wirtschaftswunder* of the 1950s and 1960s).
5. Christian Braad Thomsen, "Five Interviews with Fassbinder," in *Fassbinder*, ed. Tony Rayns (London: British Film Institute, 1980), p. 95.

We can find the basis of this urgent project in Fassbinder's personal history. Born at the end of World War II, his cultural education reflected a typical bourgeois upbringing. He found the imprint of this upbringing, however vehemently he later repudiated it, to be indelible: "Bourgeois life is what one deals with in one's films . . . you can't crawl out of your own skin." [6] Yet, if Fassbinder could not completely separate himself from his own past, he was able not only to feel the potency of bourgeois values but to sense those values as delusive and ultimately destructive. As a filmmaker, he saw his task to be the awakening of his middle-class audience to the destructive implications of their own unexamined values. By the time he made *Maria Braun*, Fassbinder had found the means to engage his audience with such material without openly attacking their values. This development helps to explain the popular success the film enjoyed.

In his exploration of middle-class society, Fassbinder, while never hesitating to denounce patent evils like fascism and racism, concentrated primarily on the underlying "sentimental idealism" that he believed helped to foster such evils.

6.　Craig Whitney, "Fassbinder: A New Director Movie Buffs Dote On," *New York Times*, 16 February 1977, sec. C, p. 17.

Sentimental idealism can be thought of as a debased version of values associated with nineteenth-century German Romanticism. It includes such vague and unquestioned notions as "the virtue of personal sacrifice," "the ennobling power of love," "freedom of the individual will," along with indulgence in sentiment for its own sake and a belief in the ostensible moral simplicity and heroic glories of a mythicized past. Because these values so pervade German society—and, indeed, middle-class society in general—Fassbinder maintained that in the collective mind of the public they are equated not with a particular ideology, but with universal truth. For him, this assumption is reinforced by the artistic productions of bourgeois culture that continually manifest these values and thus support the foundations of the bourgeois world—capitalism, patriarchy, and economic individualism. Fassbinder sought to encourage audiences conditioned by this culture to recognize that their attitudes, their assumptions, and their aspirations grew directly from this reinforced socialization process, not from any "inherent nature." As he said: "I try to illustrate . . . that we have been led astray by our upbringing and by the society we live in. . . . When I show people, on the screen, the ways that things can go wrong, my aim is to warn them that that's the way things *will* go if they don't change their lives." [7]

Fassbinder wanted his audience to see their own predicament in the dilemma of characters who are misled by sentimental illusions. In his films, characters frequently waste their lives for the sake of a great love (*Maria Braun*, *The Merchant of Four Seasons*, *In a Year of Thirteen Moons*), or come to a tragic end when the illusions that nurtured them conflict with their own instincts and the material realities of life in middle-class society (*Effi Briest*). The costs of false idealism emerge again in Fassbinder's last films, those he identifies as part of his historical project. Willie, the heroine of *Lili Marleen*, and Von Bohm, the naive building commissioner in *Lola*, are, like Maria Braun, victims of their own dreams of romantic fulfillment. Willie's devotion, like Maria's, is betrayed by a conspiracy of men while her other sentimental illusion, that of a glorious show business career in Nazi Germany, goes down with Hitler and the Fatherland. Von Bohm's great love for Lola is betrayed by Lola herself and a cabal of small-town opportunists who symbolize *Wirtschaftswunder* capitalism and culture. The predicament of the characters in *Lola*—the moral confusion, the feeling of a loss of stability and direction, and the search for something to substitute for a discredited idealism—is, in fact, the same predicament experienced by the charac-

7. Thomsen, p. 93.

ters in Fassbinder's contemporary melodramas filmed somewhat earlier in his career (*Why Does Herr R Run Amok?*, *The Merchant of Four Seasons*, *Fox and His Friends*, *Fear of Fear*, *I Only Want You to Love Me*, among others).

These similarities suggest that Fassbinder's interest in historical context lies less in exploring the distinctive qualities of a particular period than in stressing the continuity between past and present. In this enterprise, Fassbinder was contradicting the commonly accepted view of twentieth-century German history, which defined German life as being marked by a series of significant ruptures, most notably that which occurred in 1945. That year, which saw the nearly total destruction of Germany at the end of World War II, is known as Germany's "*Stunde null*" or "zero hour"—a moment to mark a void or a new beginning. The customary assessment of postwar German history found its "economic miracle" to be a testament to the country's democratic transformation and saw a different society from the one that marched under the banner of Nazism. But Fassbinder transforms the meaning of 1945 by linking it to another date significant for the development of his historical films—1977, the year that marked the height of the German government's anti-terrorist campaign. The political events of 1977 (the Mogadishu hijacking, the Schleyer kidnapping, the supposed suicide of three imprisoned Baader-Meinhof terrorists) demonstrated for Fassbinder how quickly and with how little resistance what he regarded as fascist oppression could again emerge in Germany. To Fassbinder, "Year Zero" was not the beginning of a new German society, but merely a temporary setback, during which time the old order renewed itself with financial aid and military support from its new American partners before continuing on in the old familiar way.[8]

Thus, Fassbinder sees 1945 as crucial for understanding the 1970s, but also sees the 1970s as crucial to an understanding of 1945. That year can be taken to represent the end of a Romantic tradition that had been drained of meaning, partly through cultural exhaustion, and partly through the open acknowledgement of the perversions of the Nazis, who had exploited the vague hallmarks of sentimental idealism for their own ideological purposes. But in Fassbinder's view, it was

8. Fassbinder observed: "Germany in particular finds itself in a situation in which there is very much that is very reactionary. In other words, I would say that the opportunities that Germany had in 1945, when the war and the Third Reich came to an end, were not taken advantage of. Instead . . . the structures and the values on which this country, now as a democracy, ultimately rests have remained essentially the same." Peter W. Jansen, "Exil würde ich noch nicht sagen," *Cinema* (Zurich) 2(1978):12.

not until the 1970s that the significance of 1945, the end of such idealism as a viable ideology, could finally be understood. The parents of Fassbinder's generation had been too busy with the war, reconstruction, and the economic miracle to reexamine their beliefs; as a result, the burden of this confrontation with a bankrupt idealism fell on their children. Fassbinder turns to history because the unresolved problems of older generations are still unresolved; through history, he can show his audience how the present status quo came to be.

Since Fassbinder was obviously not primarily interested in recreating earlier decades for their nostalgic appeal, his method of making a "period film" is not the conventional one of invoking historical events (battle scenes, vignettes of important historical figures making momentous decisions, public acts of bravery or treason) to lend credibility to the narrative. In fact, such momentous events are never depicted in a Fassbinder film and are rarely even referred to in a direct way. The most important "historical" event featured in *Maria Braun* (and then only through a radio broadcast) is a soccer game; in *Lili Marleen*, it is Willie's command performance for the Führer.

The catastrophic or triumphant occurrences emphasized in Fassbinder's films are private experiences. (And even these are often presented in terms of a character's reaction to news of an event—Maria is *told* of the pact between Oswald and Hermann—rather than depicting the event itself.) The significant moments for Maria Braun occur in her personal life: the report of Hermann's death, Bill's actual death, the meeting with Oswald, her husband's return. These private events are played out against the background of the war, reconstruction, and growing prosperity. Germany's astonishing economic recovery is evoked through the persistent background sound of a pneumatic drill and through the signs of the Braun family's gradually improving lifestyle—the changes in their clothing and their physical surroundings.

Fassbinder's disregard for the direct representation of public events does not mean that he disregards history; instead he creates a different kind of historical reconstruction, composed as a mosaic of iconic details. In one long tracking shot, Maria and her friend Betti walk through the city streets, talking of their personal lives. But the streets are devastated and the two women are wearing their "Suchschilder"—cardboard signs with a missing husband's or sweetheart's photograph and bold lettering asking for his last known whereabouts. As they walk and talk, a U.S. Army truck rumbles by, and they pass a group of women picking through the rubble—the "women of the ruins" (*Trümmerfrauen*) who, in the absence of men, began the reconstruction of Germany. This densely packed image forcefully provides the historical context, even though it is neither observed nor commented on by the two characters.

Immediately before this shot of Maria and Betti, there is a brief sequence in which two young boys playing in a bomb crater set off firecrackers when a man stops his truck to strip a fence for firewood. The driver ducks, as in a reflex action, then shouts at the boys and drives away. During this entire seemingly inconsequential sequence, the truck radio is heard on the soundtrack: a voice in English from American Armed Forces Radio describes a U.S. proposal to turn Germany into an agrarian breadbasket for Europe. Throughout the film, as here, the ambient sounds from Fassbinder's sound track are as significant as the details of his images in evoking particular moments in German history. In the Braun apartment immediately after the war, the radio is constantly playing in the background, providing the latest pop songs intermingled with the roll call of the names of missing servicemen. In later and more prosperous times, radio broadcasts carry quotations from Chancellor Adenauer's speeches to the Bundestag, the new German parliament, during debates on rearmament. The characters once again do not attend to these voices, not even to register the way Adenauer reverses his position in the course of time. Often in Fassbinder's films, the sights and the sounds that constitute the most recognizable signatures of a period are so familiar to the characters themselves that they go unheeded. In *Maria Braun*, the cumulative force of these details of image and sound give a powerful impression of its being immersed in history. In fact, the film was praised in Germany for its historical accuracy.

Nevertheless, the macrocosmic events of official history—the benchmarks of the transformation of postwar Germany—take place off-screen and have no immediately perceptible impact on the daily lives of Fassbinder's characters. Consider Maria Braun's marriage: she and Hermann continue to live apart under three different political regimes: Nazism, the American occupation, and the Bundesrepublik. Through and despite all this, Maria herself remains faithful to her ideal of one true love. Historical change only serves to heighten our awareness of how things remain the same, both in Maria's own life and, by extension, between the old and the new Germany.

Fassbinder's most emphatic assertion of this continuity is expressed in the final sequence of *Maria Braun*, once again through a radio broadcast that the characters ignore. The voice of sportscaster Herbert Zimmermann is heard counting down the remaining minutes of the 1954 world championship soccer match between West Germany and Hungary. His voice continues throughout the reading of Oswald's will and finally counts down the seconds to the end of the game, an end that coincides with the gas explosion at the end of the film. Even as the explosion blows Maria's house to bits, Zimmermann's voice hysterically proclaims victorious Germany as *Weltmeister*, literally "Master of the World."

II.

Beginning with *The Merchant of Four Seasons* in 1971, Fassbinder learned to control the erratic and eclectic tendencies that basically were the driving forces behind his first eleven films. These works, all made in a period of two years (1969–1970), gave ample expression to his many interests: they reveled in experimental uses of lighting, editing, camerawork, and mise-en-scène, much of it in loving imitation of his favorite Hollywood directors; but at the same time, the very anarchic quality of these films expressed a radical departure from the aims and conventions of Hollywood narrative cinema. However much they satisfied his immediate needs to explore cinema as an alternative form to the theater, the films themselves failed to engage social issues in a manner that could reach beyond the limited audience interested in their idiosyncratic style. As Tony Pipolo has observed, "Clearly, Fassbinder's subsequent desire to reach a large audience necessitated relinquishing such a ['reflexive' avant-garde] posture and the adoption of a mimetic style consistent with the priorities of narrative cinema."[9]

Among the newfound approaches to which Fassbinder adapted his social and historical concerns was the Hollywood "family" or "domestic" melodrama. Through the appeal of this traditionally popular genre, he proposed to place before a much wider audience the analysis of contemporary German society that his earlier films had carried to the restricted public of the art houses. Fassbinder's exploitation of the conventions of melodrama was to serve the ends of his "good myth," a salutary myth which, unlike the others that had molded the national consciousness, would effect a cure rather than spread a disease.[10]

In using the melodrama in this way, he was not breaking entirely new ground. He had already perceived in the melodramas and "women's films" made by Douglas Sirk in Hollywood the possibilities for criticizing the unquestioned

9. Tony Pipolo, "Bewitched by the Holy Whore," *October* 21(Summer 1982):95.
10. Wilfried Wiegand, "Interview with Rainer Werner Fassbinder," in *Fassbinder*, Peter Iden, et al. (New York: Tanam Press, 1981), p. 77.

values of a middle-class culture within the framework of a popular genre with admitted entertainment aims. In an essay on Sirk's films written in 1971 (and included in this volume),[11] Fassbinder praised their cinematic qualities and Sirk's uncanny ability to sympathize with his characters while turning the mise-en-scène into social commentary. It was this quality that made him realize the subversive potential in the genre and that it was by no means a capitulation to bourgeois values if one could question and contradict the system on which those values depend.

But since Fassbinder, unlike Sirk (and other American directors of domestic melodrama like John Stahl and Vincente Minnelli), was not working within the Hollywood studio system and therefore not subject to industry strictures, he was not obliged to resort to the subterfuges made necessary by official and unofficial censorship. And because he was responsible for his own scripts, he was also not bound to "tack on" a superficial happy ending or falsely reassuring resolution to the problems raised in the film. Even Sirk's films often have some version of these conventions in which the death or self-sacrifice of one of the characters leads to a highly emotional cathartic ending that often overwhelms the viewer and displaces his or her attention from the original focus on to an oceanic feeling of redemption (recall, for example, the denouements of *Written on the Wind*, *The Tarnished Angels*, *All I Desire*, *All That Heaven Allows*, and *Imitation of Life*). Fassbinder therefore took some of melodrama's cherished conventions—the predominance of a female protagonist, the obligatory happy ending, the profusion of coincidence—but employed them in his own unique way, opting more for irony and detachment over immersion and catharsis. In accentuating these conventions, his films reveal the potentially subversive dimension of the genre, even in the more pedestrian examples of it that proliferated in Hollywood.

An examination of how these conventions often unwittingly exposed the rifts in social and domestic structures is useful here. For example, the female protagonist of many Hollywood melodramas manages to dominate the narrative by competing successfully, for a time at least, in a male world. Sexual roles are reversed and thereby put into question. Michael Curtiz's *Mildred Pierce* (1945), a film that American critics have compared with *Maria Braun*, serves as an example. When the men in her life prove weak or irresponsible, Mildred is forced to assume the duties of the breadwinner, raises her child alone, and finally be-

11. Rainer Werner Fassbinder, "Six Films by Douglas Sirk," trans. Thomas Elsaesser, in *Douglas Sirk*, ed. Laura Mulvey and John Halliday (Edinburgh: Edinburgh Film Festival, 1972).

comes a successful businesswoman. (Though in the end, typically, she is punished for her ambitions.) In such family melodramas, the problems and contradictions of middle-class life are central to the plot. The family, most sacred of middle-class institutions, is the locus of the dramatic conflict; the home is not an idealized haven but rather the scene of disharmony. Family members fall victims to emotional isolation, exploitation at each other's hands, and sexual frustration. Their suffering is sublimated into silent despair or violent outburst. And the spectators are encouraged to recognize that the contradictions and defeated aspirations displayed on the screen are in fact their own.

The second of the conventions—the happy ending—offers a resolution that proves far more complex than is immediately apparent and is often disturbingly ambiguous, sometimes even overtly ironic. In the Hollywood domestic melodrama, the happy ending returns the woman to a place, *her* place, from which she can no longer threaten society's sexual equilibrium. But whether the central conflict is truly resolved is open to doubt. The closure—the neat tying of all narrative threads, the explaining away of all aberrations from the "natural" order—leaves unattended those desires which once expressed cannot be unsaid. The effect of an ostensible happy ending that through ambiguity or irony denies satisfactory closure is to leave the spectator with a sense of incompleteness. This dissatisfaction leads the audience to question an ideology that proposes the home as the peaceful retreat of the male worker and the sole workplace appropriate to the ambition of a woman; it also suggests that sexual roles are a product of ideology, not an immutable function of human nature. In Fassbinder's more blatant version of the ambiguous Hollywood ending, the conflict between the individual and bourgeois society often ends with the death of the protagonist. Even where the character survives and becomes reconciled to his or her milieu, the conflict takes its toll in the form of psychosomatic illness, depression, nervous breakdown, or violence against the self and others. However, in Fassbinder, such dire conclusions are not excuses for a sudden upsurge of pathos, or for cathartic resolution, but remain distanced from the viewer in the Brechtian tradition.

A third convention of melodrama—the reliance on coincidence as the basis of plot development—tends to undermine one generally recognized objective of fiction: the suspension of disbelief. The accumulation of coincidence, its outrageous nature, its implausible regularity, has the effect of arousing doubt in the most receptive spectator, thus undermining the simple identification of viewer and protagonist. What the character regards as chance, the viewer may indeed come to regard as the fulfillment of the characters' desires. And these desires, however unconscious, are shaped by social reality—a social reality grounded in bourgeois culture. Fassbinder will use the melodramatic devices of coincidence and an ending that denies satisfactory closure to heighten his audience's consciousness of the unseen psychological and ideological forces at work in the story, and, through the story, in their own lives.

III.

The special kind of causality at work in *Maria Braun* can easily be seen even in a skeletal outline of the film's narrative, in which, if we take it at face value, Maria's spectacular rise and fall are brought about by a series of lucky and unlucky coincidences. From the opening sequence depicting Maria's and Hermann's wedding amidst an aerial bombardment, itself an example of melodramatic hyperbole, to their "reunion" in the final sequence, the narrative is dependent at every turn on the fortuitous and the coincidental. At one point, believing Hermann to be dead, Maria has an affair with Bill, a black American soldier, and in the midst of an intimate love-making scene, Hermann suddenly appears. In the confusion, Maria accidentally kills Bill, but Hermann insists on taking the blame and is sent to prison, thereby separating the married couple for the second time. This particular plot contrivance precipitates Maria's subsequent involvement with Oswald and her concomitant rise to prosperity and success. The last scene provides the final twist. After a ten-year absence, Hermann appears unexpectedly at the door of her villa and announces that he has made his fortune in Canada and has returned since now he is a proper husband for her. Coincidentally, on the same day, Maria also receives the executors who have come to read the will of the recently deceased Oswald. The reading reveals that Hermann had agreed to go away and make a new start in life, financed by his rival, so that the ailing Oswald could continue as Maria's sponsor and lover for the remaining years of his life. Shortly after the will is read, Maria lights a match at the gas stove, which she had not completely switched off after lighting a cigarette there some time earlier. In the ensuing explosion both she and Hermann are killed.

This ending seems at first to conform to the familiar modes of melodrama. For example, the reading of a will is a conventional prelude to closure, a way of distributing rewards and of solving economic problems, thereby legitimizing emotional bonds. Oswald's will serves this conventional function, bestowing wealth on the people he values and seemingly guaranteeing their future happiness and security. However, this traditional function of the will is quickly discounted. Hermann and Maria do not react to the disclosure of the will with surprise and elation: he is stolid, since he already knows its contents—it confirms his agreement with Oswald; she is distracted at first and obviously bothered, for through the will she discovers that she has been deluded about the degree of control she assumed she had always had over her own life. Both Maria and Hermann offer to renounce their share of the legacy, a characteristic gesture of sentimental self-sacrifice, yet at the same time, an ironic reminder that they both are now so prosperous that they don't need the money.

This final convergence of events triggers the unexpected and ambiguous conclusion and ultimately inverts the axioms of melodrama on which the film has relied. The "reunion" of the "lovers" does not resolve the various lines of tension as in a conventional melodrama. And the disaster that follows does not merely close the narrative. On the contrary, it reopens the narrative and places under suspicion the mechanisms of illusion and sentimental idealism that have motivated the characters' actions and led them to this moment—the very mechanisms, in fact, that traditionally support the established conventions of melodrama itself.

In this crucial final sequence, the revelation of the pact is less important than the revelation that the characters' actions and the final outcome have been brought about not by coincidence but by the psychological forces and ideological factors at work, and often in conflict, throughout the course of the film. It is not by coincidence that Hermann appears at Maria's door immediately after Oswald's death or that the executors of Oswald's estate follow right after him. From this perspective, the characters' conscious and unconscious desires are seen as the causal connections between the day's events. It is also apparent that the behavior of the men has been influenced by the same sentimental idealism that dominated Maria's thoughts and actions. The cruel "twist of fate" that sends Hermann away from Maria again after Bill's death is therefore explained by the fact that Hermann's image of himself as women's protector requires him to take the blame and punishment for his wife's deed. Similarly, his long separation from Maria after prison is a consequence of his belief in an ideal of male self-sufficiency. Hermann can accept money from Oswald, but not from Maria. He accepts Oswald's offer and goes away because he cannot allow himself to be dependent on a woman. The inflated language of Oswald's will in which he justifies buying Hermann off by praising his humility and noble self-sacrifice also suggests that the two men are bound by their common adherence to the ideology expressed in Oswald's sentimental rhetoric.

The understanding between Oswald and Hermann fully revealed through the reading of the will confirms the existence of an underlying value system that permits those generally in charge of that system (in this case the men in Maria's life and the essentially male-dominated culture in which they act) to decide things for those in a subordinate position (in this case Maria, and by extension, the women of that culture); to in fact, predetermine a course of events which secretly governs the lives of others and renders their individual ambitions and actions virtually ineffectual. The contents of the will constitute documentary proof of the working of such a system and a palpable example of how embedded the cultural values are, since both Oswald and Hermann have somehow taken the premises of the contract for granted and thus reveal their own subservience to the prevailing ideology and authoritarian value system.

Fassbinder's use of camera movement in the final sequence, together with Maria's "suicidal gesture" in leaving the gas burner on prior to the will's revelation, are typical strategies through which he undercuts the significance of the will as closure and emphasizes its actual significance to her as proof of something she has feared and resisted throughout the film. The erratically circling camera movement in which Maria's frantic last moments prior to the reading of the will are presented is a translation of her restless energy, using itself up in repetitive, aimless, and agitated movement around the house. In the final moment of recognition Maria clearly sees herself for the first time as an object of exchange between the two men.

If we reexamine Maria's role in the film, we can now clearly see the fatal contradictions on which her life is based and which she has worked so hard throughout the film to deny. We can also see that Fassbinder's characterization of Maria also involves some modifications of domestic melodrama's model of the female protagonist that make it easier for the audience to trace the psychological and ideological forces that have influenced Maria's fate. In accordance with this model, Maria has always possessed the courage and independence usually associated with male characters. Because of her cleverness and initiative, the Braun family survives the war and flourishes during peacetime. Maria enjoys playing the active male role, not only by being the family provider, but by presenting Hermann with a gift of a checkbook while he sits in prison and by reversing social roles when she asks Bill if he would like to dance. She preserves an emotional control as well, refusing to commit herself fully to Bill or Oswald, and exercising her power over Oswald by establishing that the time he has with her depends entirely on her mood. Maria enjoys the prerogative which, outside melodrama, is usually allowed only to male protagonists, namely the separation of romantic love and sexual satisfaction. It is Maria who tells Oswald that she will sleep with him, but that her true love will always be Hermann, while Oswald must accept the traditionally feminine role of devotion and silent suffering.

However, Maria's pleasure in playing the male role and in succeeding in a man's world is gained by the compromising of her own identity. She has "made it" because she plays by society's rules, and in this society, the rules have been made by men. Maria must sometimes deny her own conscious and unconscious desires, those which are not approved for women in a bourgeois milieu; she must continually justify her ambition and desires with the rationale of "selfless love," openly declaring that whatever she does is for her husband's sake and their future life together. Her insistence on an artificial separation of romantic love and sexual pleasure is therefore a prerequisite to her fulfillment of her sexual needs.

In fact, the way Maria first gains entry into the man's world of money and power is by offering herself as a sexual object. In exchange for sex, Maria gets from Bill and the other American soldiers she serves in the bar, not only cigarettes and nylon stockings; she also learns their language. It is her knowledge of English and the aggressive language of men that first impresses Oswald in Maria's handling of a drunken soldier on the train, and these are the very qualities, combined with her sex appeal, that lead to her success in the business world of men as Oswald's private secretary; it is her sex appeal, for instance, that succeeds where the men have failed when she proffers sexual favors to persuade an American businessman to make a crucial deal. Maria's reward is an important position in Oswald's textile firm and a salary that assures economic security.

In the course of her rise, Maria gradually discovers that, quite beyond any "ideal" or "selfless" goal, she does derive pleasure and satisfaction from her relationship with Oswald and from her new-found authority. But because society does not endorse these as legitimate goals for women, she cannot consciously pursue these desires fully and freely, nor embrace their satisfactions as legitimate rewards. The double standard by which Maria lives eventually begins to take its toll. Her cherished myths: her confidence in her own autonomy and her ideal of selfless romantic love begin to give way. The rift between her illusions and reality gradually widens under pressure from suppressed inner tensions and growing threats from the world outside. The effect on Maria as these pressures build can be seen in her growing dissatisfaction and frustration. She becomes increasingly irritable, hard to please and distracted: alternating shouting at her secretary with outbursts of laughter, screaming at a furniture mover, arguing with her mother, absentmindedly putting her purse into a flower vase, then, fatally, leaving the gas burner on after lighting a cigarette.

While Maria clearly suffers from the contradiction and denial that dominate her life, she never confronts this on a conscious level. Nevertheless, Fassbinder has been confronting the audience with it all along through his distinctive adaptations of melodramatic devices and through his mise-en-scène. Fassbinder's goal in general is to make it easier for the audience to see the latent meanings that the prevailing ideology needs to hide. As the discrepancy between the ideal and the real becomes more and more difficult for Maria to reconcile, the audience becomes increasingly aware of the underlying significance not only of Fassbinder's melodramatic devices, but also of his bold camera movements and formal framing strategies, all of which converge in the ending—our sense of discovery coinciding with Maria's—to show how the unconscious mind deals with a contradiction the conscious mind cannot bear.

As the moving camera in the final sequence unmistakably implies, and the reading of the will subsequently confirms, it is not chance or coincidence, but the conflict between cultural and ideological constraints and Maria's unconscious defenses against them that bring about her downfall. In addition to the melodramatic contrivances Fassbinder uses to undermine Maria's sense of controlling her life and actions, the contrivances of Fassbinder's mise-en-scène have similarly prepared the way for Maria's unconscious suicidal gestures (leaving the gas on prior to the disclosure of the pact and, afterwards, going into the bathroom to run water over her wrist) and the explosive ending which results. Generally, Fassbinder's framing of characters in doorways, windows, stairwells and mirrors is the trademark of his formal style. This detached perspective is manifested in a type of "point of view" shot that is not identified with any particular character, but presents Fassbinder's own insight into the predicament of his middle-class characters. The audience sees what the characters do not see: that they are confined by their everyday, middle-class surroundings, the unsuspecting victims of psychological and social forces that control and condition their behavior. Fassbinder's framing devices and distanced perspective permit the audience to momentarily look in on the action from outside the framework of the narrative, and herein lies the educative function of his mise-en-scène.

For example, though Maria asserts in her first visit to the doctor for a health certificate that she is going to sell beer and not herself, in her next visit to see if she is pregnant, she is conspicuously framed by a doorway which dominates the foreground. Even before this, Maria's figure is enclosed in the silhouetted entrance to a courtyard where she goes to meet the black market dealer, then is seen through the curtained entrance to Bronski's "office" in the bar while she waits to be interviewed by him. During her visits to Hermann, she is seen through prison bars. She is also seen surrounded by an unidentified frame-within-a-frame, which turns out to be the interior of Oswald's car as he watches her one day leaving her apartment to go to the prison. She is often seen tightly framed in the doorway of her own office. Just before the crucial final sequence, there is a shot of Maria with her head down on the kitchen table with a liquor bottle beside her. Prior to this shot, which Fassbinder films from the adjacent living room through the kitchen door, the audience's sympathy has been channelled toward Oswald, who has just died, a slave to his love for Maria. In conferring sympathy on Maria, the shot clearly hints at the reversal that is about to unfold when Oswald's will is read.

Though Fassbinder confirms the film's latent "message" in the disclosure of the pact and Maria's reaction to it, he never makes it clear to the audience whether Maria's act of lighting the match that sets off the explosion is an accidental or deliberate one. This element of ambiguity was introduced by Fassbinder in the only major modification he made in the plot developed by his screenwriters. (In the screenplay, Maria's and Hermann's deaths are clearly the result of a deliberate act: she drives the car in which they are riding over an embankment.) It is important to Fassbinder that the ending remain ambiguous, not because it makes a difference in the plot or characterization, but because for Fassbinder an unconscious act is as much the result of a specific cause as a conscious one. Maria's act remains ambiguous in order to raise questions in the audience's mind: can it be that a woman would rather kill herself than live with the husband for whom she had waited so long? Is it possible that Maria is not really happy with her new home, her status, the inheritance, and now her beloved husband—the only thing that has been missing from this idyllic picture? Why would a woman do such a thing? These questions encourage the audience's active rethinking of everything that has gone before, a necessary step toward discovery of the message conveyed in Oswald's will: that Maria has been playing a role in someone else's scenario—one composed by the men.

The obvious parallel between Maria and German women of the wartime and postwar period extends this notion to the film's historical context. Fassbinder's comparison suggests that these women, too, were exploited and betrayed by a male conspiracy when, after beginning the reconstruction of Germany in the absence of men, they were put back in their places in the home or returned to unskilled or menial tasks on the soldiers' return. The culture born of the economic miracle is criticized throughout Fassbinder's work. Here, by showing the victories of Maria and the "women of the ruins" to be hollow, he also shows up the hollow victory of the economic miracle, which is parodied in sportscaster Zimmermann's voice hysterically screaming, "*Deutschland ist Weltmeister!*" over the image of the smoldering ruins of Maria's new house.

This linking of past and present that is found in all of Fassbinder's historical films is perhaps most boldly and blatantly reasserted in the film's postscript: a montage of portraits, in negative, of the German postwar chancellors from Adenauer to Helmut Schmidt (but excepting Willy Brandt, whom Fassbinder regarded as a progressive figure). The portrait of Schmidt—chancellor when the film was made—is the film's final image. As it fades from negative to positive, it corresponds to the portrait of Hitler (also nominally a German chancellor) that opens the film and is *followed* by an explosion. Through this circular structure, Fassbinder inscribes in the film the notion of a vicious cycle, thereby asserting another important connection—that between individual and national destiny, and the real impact of ideology on individual lives.

A Chronology
of the Years
1943–1954

July 1943	The last German offensive on the Eastern Front fails.
June 1944	The Allies land on Normandy.
July 1944	Von Stauffenberg's ill-fated assassination attempt upon Hitler.
September 1944	In Germany, all men between the ages of 16 and 60 are conscripted into the so-called *Volkssturm* (People's Army).
April 25, 1945	American and Soviet forces meet at Torgau on the Elbe River.
May 7, 1945	General Jodl signs the unconditional surrender of the German Reich in Reims, and repeats this act two days later at Soviet headquarters in Karlshorst.
August 1945	The U.S.A. drops the first atomic bombs in history on Japan.
January 1947	The American and British Occupation Zones are unified into a common market.
March 1947	A conference of foreign ministers in Moscow reaches agreement for the return of German prisoners of war held in the Soviet Union by the end of 1948, at the latest.

From the press materials for *The Marriage of Maria Braun.*

April 1949	Ten European nations join with the U.S.A. and Canada to form NATO.
May 1949	Constitution of the Federal Republic of Germany.
May 1949	Constitutional proclamation of the German Democratic Republic.
1950–1953	War in Korea.
1952	The third stanza of the "Deutschlandlied" is proclaimed by President Theodor Heuss to be the national anthem of the Federal Republic of Germany.
June 1953	Workers' uprising in East Berlin.
1954	The rearmament of West Germany is agreed upon in the Paris Accords.

Rainer Werner Fassbinder:

A Biographical Sketch

The death of Rainer Werner Fassbinder at the age of thirty-seven on June 10, 1982, was not unanticipated by most of those who knew him personally or professionally. According to Kurt Raab,[1] who worked with Fassbinder more closely and for a longer period than most of the director's collaborators, it had long been apparent that Fassbinder was expending his energies with life-threatening intensity.

Fassbinder was born on May 31, 1945, in Bad Wörishofen, Germany. His father, Hellmuth, was a physician who also had substantial real estate holdings. His mother, who later acted in her son's films under the names of Liselotte Eder and Lilo Pempeit, was a translator of literary texts. After his parents' divorce in 1951, Rainer lived with his mother, attending first the "progressive" Rudolf Steiner School and later public schools in Augsburg and Munich. He left school in 1964, before graduating, and held a series of minor jobs before enrolling in the Fridl Leonhard acting studio.

In 1967, along with classmate Hanna Schygulla, Fassbinder left the studio to join the Action Theater, founded on the model of Julian Beck's controversial, experimental Living Theater. (Other members of the Action Theater who would later become known through Fassbinder's films included Raab, Peer Raben, Ursula Strätz, Irm Hermann, and Ingrid Caven.) Fassbinder soon asserted himself as the dominant personality of the group, and two months after joining became the company's co-director.

1. "My Life with Rainer," *The Village Voice*, 3 May 1983, p. 4.

The Action Theater reorganized in 1968 under the name of "anti-teater" with Fassbinder as its leader. In a move characteristic of the communal tendencies of the late 1960s, the group entered a period of not only working but living together in a house outside Munich. The anti-teater performed in a variety of settings before adopting the back room of a Munich night club as its theatrical headquarters from 1968 to 1969.

But Fassbinder conceived of the theater, with its relatively low production costs and high prestige, as a means towards his goal of making films. (He had been an active filmgoer since childhood; his fare consisted mostly of Hollywood films. In 1965 he had applied—unsuccessfully—for admission to the prestigious Berlin Film and Television Academy.) During the anti-teater period, he made ten feature films, from *Love Is Colder Than Death* (1969) to *Beware of a Holy Whore* (1970). In these productions, Fassbinder drew upon the anti-teater for his actors and gathered a technical team that soon became accustomed to his working methods. It was, to a considerable degree, the cooperation of these actors and this crew that enabled Fassbinder to work with such astonishing speed and economy, often bringing his films to completion well ahead of schedule and under the prescribed budget.

The films of the anti-teater period were experimental and idiosyncratic in technique and rather esoteric in content. *Love Is Colder Than Death*, for example—a film dedicated to Claude Chabrol, Eric Rohmer, and Jean-Marie Straub, directors whom, along with Jean-Luc Godard, Fassbinder particularly admired at the time—was a kind of contemporary fable drawing upon elements of French and American gangster films. Though such films as these proved generally less popular with the wide moviegoing public than with certain critics, Fassbinder was nevertheless successful in competing for German government film subsidies. Indeed, by 1972 Fassbinder could confidently rely on government support to subsidize his filmmaking activities.

Also by 1972, Fassbinder's style had undergone considerable transformation. "In *Holy Whore*," he asserted, "something old comes to an end and something new begins and in [*The*] *Merchant* [*of Four Seasons*] (1971), that new thing is there. . . . I would say that the films have become more universal, . . . no longer just films for myself and my friends." [2] The transformation was due in large part to Fassbinder's attendance in the winter of 1970–1971 at a retrospective of twenty films by Douglas Sirk, the UFA-trained director of Hollywood domestic melo-

2. Wilfried Wiegand, "Interview with Rainer Werner Fassbinder," in *Fassbinder*, Peter Iden, et al. (New York: Tanam Press, 1981), p. 76.

dramas of the 1940s and 1950s. Shown simultaneously in theaters and on television in 1971, *The Merchant of Four Seasons* was the first in the series of Fassbinder's own domestic melodramas in which Sirk's influence is manifest.

Meanwhile, Fassbinder's reputation outside Germany was growing dramatically. *Fear Eats the Soul* (1973), roughly modeled on Sirk's *All That Heaven Allows* (1955), tied Robert Bresson's *Lancelot du lac* for the International Critics Prize at the 1974 Cannes Film Festival. By the mid-1970s, Fassbinder, Werner Herzog, and Wim Wenders were widely recognized as key figures in *Das Neue Kino* (the New German Cinema); their films, introduced to New York audiences in a series at the Museum of Modern Art in 1972, were by 1975 among the principal attractions at the New York and London film festivals. When *Mother Küsters' Trip to Heaven* opened a twelve-film Fassbinder retrospective at the New Yorker theater in 1977, it set a new one-day attendance record. In the same year, Vincent Canby's tribute to Fassbinder in the *New York Times* appeared under the headline "The Most Original Talent Since Godard." [3]

On the strength of such successes, Fassbinder officially entered the high-finance world of international co-production with *Despair* (1977). Budgeted at $2,500,000 (an amount nearly equivalent to the cost of Fassbinder's first fifteen films combined),[4] starring Dirk Bogarde, scripted by the English playwright Tom Stoppard after a novel by Vladimir Nabokov, and shot in English, *Despair* was the first Fassbinder production to be distributed by a major American firm, United Artists.

Nonetheless, even as his international renown burgeoned, Fassbinder's films, with rare exceptions (such as *Effi Briest* [1974], based on Theodor Fontane's classic German novel), seemed to make relatively little impression on the German market; even *Mother Küsters* was not a commercial success in Fassbinder's homeland. Although he admitted that some of his films, such as *Satan's Brew* (1976) and *In a Year of Thirteen Moons* (1978), were made for a small audience of the initiated, Fassbinder proclaimed at the same time that his target was a broad audience of middle-class Germans—the very audience that by and large declined to attend his films.

But even if German moviegoers did not flock to Fassbinder films, they could hardly have been unaware of Fassbinder as a public figure. Thanks to his work in television and radio, and to innumerable articles and interviews in the German

3. *New York Times*, 6 March 1977, sec. D, p. 1.
4. Wolfgang Limmer, *Rainer Werner Fassbinder, Filmemacher* (Hamburg: Spiegel Verlag, 1981), p. 11.

press, Fassbinder was a celebrity; and thanks to his straightforward expressions of his personal and artistic beliefs, he was always a controversial figure.

He was, first of all, openly homosexual. (Following his 1972 divorce from Ingrid Caven, whom he had married in 1970, he lived in succession with two men, El Hedi Ben Salem and Armin Meier; both appeared in his films, and both ultimately took their own lives.) Perhaps more significantly, his films in their outspokenness were politically volatile. The gamut of charges raised against him encompassed anti-Semitism, anti-Communism (after *Mother Küsters*), pro-terrorism (after *The Third Generation* [1979]), and the trivialization of labor unions (after the television series *Eight Hours Are Not a Day* [1972]). The controversies that Fassbinder provoked were not without their consequences for his career. Several projects to which he was seriously committed were cancelled or aborted because of enmity from one group or another.

With *The Marriage of Maria Braun*, however, Fassbinder finally attained wide popular acceptance from German audiences. His budgets were now large by any standard, from $1,000,000 for *Maria Braun* to twice that for *Lola* (1981) to $5,000,000 for *Lili Marleen* (1980) to well over $6,000,000 for the mammoth fifteen and one-half hour television film *Berlin Alexanderplatz* (1980). But whether working on a shoestring, as in the anti-teater days, or providing richly endowed productions for a wide audience, Fassbinder's creative energies never flagged. As director, he made no less than forty-three films from 1969 to 1982, in addition to his work as an actor in films directed by others and his work in theater and radio. Whether a film was completed in three days, like *Katzelmacher* (1969), or, like *Alexanderplatz*, required first a year of pre-production and then a full year of shooting, Fassbinder's working schedule remained truly staggering.

Heavy doses of drugs and alcohol seemed to have become necessary to sustain his ferocious creative impulses. But for his admirers, the tragedy of his early death could at least be set against the unprecedented range of his achievements. Whatever the cost, he had succeeded in proving himself, in Canby's words, "probably the most important filmmaker of the immediate post-World War II generation." [5]

5. "Fassbinder—The Movies' First Great Satirist," *New York Times*, 20 June 1982, p. 21.

The Marriage of
Maria Braun

The Marriage of Maria Braun

The *Marriage of Maria Braun* bears the dedication "For Peter Zadek." Fassbinder worked with Zadek in the founding of the Bochum Ensemble in 1972–1973. Their professional relationship during this enterprise was a rather stormy one. Fassbinder rebelled against what he perceived as Zadek's authoritarian attitude. This eventually led to the departure of Fassbinder and his company. Fassbinder later came to respect Zadek, as he explained in an interview in the *Frankfurter Rundschau* (20 February 1979):

When I dedicate a film to someone, I'm not saying the film directly relates to the person to whom it is dedicated. Though, in the case of *Maria Braun*, for example, I will say that Zadek has become someone who broke out of this hardened attitude that is described in *Maria Braun*. From a certain moment on, Zadek became an important person for me and someone to talk with. It made me feel a little more encouraged to know that here was a person, already past fifty and fully matured, who yet was able to change so completely. And I find that very positive and hopeful. Five years ago he was all wrapped up in himself and who he was, and then he changed completely.

The continuity script that follows was prepared from the film, the transcript of the German dialogue, and the transcript of the English dialogue for the English-dubbed version. Since the sound track and such elements as camera movement and visual composition are such a vital dimension of this, as of any Fassbinder film, an attempt has been made to provide as careful a description as possible of the film's audio/visual images.

X C U	extreme close-up
C U	close-up
M C U	medium close-up
M S	medium shot

The abbreviations used to describe camera distance follow the usual conventions:

¾ S	three-quarter shot
F S	full shot
M L S	medium long shot
L S	long shot

Credits and Cast

Direction
Rainer Werner Fassbinder

Producer
Michael Fengler

Script
Peter Märthesheimer and Pea
Fröhlich, from an idea by Rainer
Werner Fassbinder

Dialogue
Pea Fröhlich, Rainer Werner
Fassbinder, Peter Märthesheimer

Cameraman
Michael Ballhaus

Assistant Cameraman
Horst Knechtel

Editors
Juliane Lorenz, Franz Walsch [Rainer
Werner Fassbinder]

Sound
Jim Willis, Milan Bor

Music
Peer Raben

Art Direction
Norbert Scherer, Helga Ballhaus,
Claus Hollmann, Georg Bergel

Costumes
Barbara Baum, Susi Reichel, Georg
Hahn, Ingeberg Pröller

Sets
Andreas Willin, Arno Mathes, Hans
Sandmeier

Makeup
Anni Nöbauer

Production Direction
Martin Häussler

Editorial Assistance
Volker Canaris

Musical Collaboration
David Ambach, Kurt Maas

Assistant Editor
Christine Kolenc

Sound Assistant
John Salter

Assistant Director
Rolf Bührmann

Script Girl
Helga Beyer

Technicians
Hans-Jürgen Höpflinger, Raimund
Wirner

Grip
Karl Willim

The Organization
Michael Fengler, Robert Busch,
Thomas Wommer, Harry Zöttl [Baer],
Dieter Dubine, Christine Fall, Jochen
Losse

Locations
Coberg, Berlin

Process
35 mm Fuji Film

Running Time
120 minutes

Production Time
35 days, January–March 1978

Cost
1,975,000 DM

Distributor
United Artists

German Premiere
February 20, 1979
Berlin Film Festival

Release Date
March 30, 1979

American Premiere
October 14, 1979
New York Film Festival

Maria
Hanna Schygulla

Hermann
Klaus Löwitsch

Oswald
Ivan Desny

Willi
Gottfried John

Mother
Gisela Uhlen

Wetzel
Günter Lamprecht

Bill
George Byrd

Betti
Elisabeth Trissenaar

Vevi
Isolde Barth

Bronski
Peter Berling

Nurse
Sonja Neudorfer

Frau Ehmke
Liselotte Eder

Conductor
Volker Spengler

Interpreter
Karl-Heinz von Hassel

Lawyer
Michael Ballhaus

Madame Devoald
Christine Hopf-de Loup

Senkenberg
Hark Bohm

Man with Truck
Dr. Horst-Dieter Klock

American on the Train
Günther Kaufmann

American Businessman
Bruce Low

Black Market Dealer
Rainer Werner Fassbinder

Doctor
Claus Holm

Grandpa Berger
Anton Schirsner

Registrar
Hannes Kaetner

Reporter
Martin Häussler

First Guard
Norbert Scherer

Second Guard
Rolf Bührmann

Third Guard
Arthur Glogau

The Continuity Script

1. MCU: *a portrait of Adolf Hitler.*

   Superimposed title: An Albatros Production. Produced by Michael Fengler and Trio Film, Duisberg with the Westdeutscher Rundfunk.

   A voice reading marriage vows. The Hitler photo falls toward the camera at the end of the shot as the whistle of an aerial bomb is heard.

2. *The whistle sound culminates in an explosion as part of a brick wall falls toward the camera. Hermann and Maria are seen through a hole in the wall.*

   Superimposed title: Rainer Werner Fassbinder Film.

   The two come into focus as they turn to look through the hole toward the camera. They are framed by the ragged edges of the blasted wall. The sound of explosions, rubble falling, aircraft engines, and antiaircraft is heard.

3. LS: *the exterior of the registrar's office as parts of the building come crashing down. The sound from 2 continues.*

4. MCU: *the couple are looking out the hole in the wall as the sound from 2 continues. Hermann is in a Wehrmacht uniform and Maria is wearing a bridal dress and veil.*

   HERMANN (*looks away from the camera again*): I do.
   MARIA: I do.

5. *As 3. Smoke is coming from the windows of the registrar's office. An explosion blows out another window.*

6. XCU: *the marriage license, upside down. The sound from 2 continues.*

7. *As 3. Windows crash down from above as people flee from doors and windows. Another window is blown out.*

Superimposed title: with Hanna Schygulla.

MARIA (*standing in a window frame*): I can't get out.
MAN (*comes out of a cellar door pulling a woman after him*): Looks bad.
HERMANN (*appears in a window as the registrar appears in the doorway*): Hey, come back here! Don't run away!

Hermann jumps out of the window and tackles the registrar who is running out the door.

REGISTRAR: Let me go, please!

Hermann holds the registrar as Maria comes out. Zoom in to a CU of the sign over the door, "Marriage License Bureau 3," just as the sign falls off. A slogan painted on the building says, "The enemy is listening."

8. *The street in front of the building is littered with paper. Maria dives into the frame in MS. The sound from 2 continues and Beethoven's Ninth Symphony begins.*

REGISTRAR: Please let me go! Let go!

9. MLS: *people in the street are scrambling for safety. Hermann is holding on to the registrar. A shower of leaflets flurries down from above as the sound from 8 continues.*

10. *As 8. Maria is face down on the ground and grabs the marriage license as the sound from 8 continues.*

11. *As 9. Hermann wrestles the registrar to the ground and the sound of a baby crying is added to the music and sounds of bombardment.*

12. *As 11, from a reverse angle. People rush for cover.*

MARIA (*pops up into frame*): Hermann! Hermann! What is it?

FS: *the camera pans with her as she rushes to Hermann with the marriage license.*

HERMANN: Come here!

Maria dives down beside Hermann and the registrar. They duck their heads at the sound of a blast, followed by a woman screaming as the sound of a child crying continues. Flyers flutter down over them.

HERMANN: Sign here.
MARIA: Sign it . . . Stamp it.

The registrar signs, gets up and rushes off-screen, yelling; then Hermann signs.

13. *The sounds of an explosion, aerial bombardment and nearby antiaircraft guns are heard with low music and a baby crying. There is a single frame lap-dissolve from an amorphous red glow to . . .*

14. *Fiery sparks in a black field which fade away to smoke as the sound from 13 continues.*

15. *Superimposed title fades in: The Marriage of Maria Braun.*

   The smoke and black background clear to reveal a FS *of Hermann and Maria on the ground as papers continue to flutter down and the sound from 13 continues.*

   The shot is frozen for the remainder of the superimposed titles as battle sounds continue: You see: Hanna Schygulla, Klaus Löwitsch, Ivan Desny, Gisela Uhlen, Elisabeth Trissenaar, Gottfried John, Hark Bohm, George Byrd, Claus Holm, Günter Lamprecht, Anton Schirsner, Lilo Pempeit, Sonja Neudorfer, Volker Spengler, Isolde Barth, Bruce Low, Günther Kauffmann, Karl-Heinz von Hassel, Cristine de Loup, Hannes Kaetner. The team: Ballhaus, Baum, Berling, Bührmann, Fassbinder, Häussler, Klock.

   The sounds die down to only a siren.

   Script: Pea Fröhlich and Peter Märthesheimer from an idea by Rainer Werner Fassbinder. Dialogue: Pea Fröhlich, Rainer Werner Fassbinder, Peter Märthesheimer. Camera: Michael Ballhaus. Art direction: Norbert Scherer. Costumes: Barbara Baum. Sound: Jim Willis, Milan Bor.

The siren sound ends; low music continues, and the sound of the last plane flying away, then a church bell is heard. Then there is the sound of a truck coming to a stop, then only music.

Makeup: Anni Nöbauer. Music: Peer Raben. Editing: Juliane Lorenz, Franz Walsch. Production manager: Martin Häussler. Editorial staff: Volker Canaris. Grip: Karl Willim. A film by Rainer Werner Fassbinder.[1]

16. *Fade to white as the final title from 15 fades out and a new title—for Peter Zadek—fades in. The music continues.*

17. *Fade in on* MLS: *Maria's mother is in a small kitchen as the music continues. The foreground is framed by an indistinct dark outline.*[2]

18. CU, *point of view shot: Mother's hands are seen as she pours some water over a dry piece of bread. A photo of Hermann is on the kitchen counter. Low music continues through 22.*

19. *As 17.*

20. CU: *Mother's head wrapped in a scarf is seen from behind as she eats the bread and turns at the sound of a door opening and closing.*

   MOTHER: Is that you, Maria?

21. *As 18. Mother's hands put down the water pitcher.*

22. *Mother enters the frame from the left in* ¾S *preceded by her reflection in a mirror in the background.*

   MOTHER: I was worried to death about you. I thought something happened to you.

   As the camera tracks right to follow Mother, Maria enters with a rucksack full of kindling wood.

   MARIA: Wedding dresses aren't much in demand at the moment. Too many brides—not enough men.

Maria is dressed stylishly despite her moderate means. She empties the contents of the pack onto the kitchen table. As Maria takes out some scraps of food, Mother comes forward from the background and greedily pounces on it, knocking over a chair in her excitement. The music ends.

MARIA: That's all I got for it.

23. CU, *high angle: Mother's hand takes a shaving set from Maria's hand. Very low music is heard.*

MARIA: There's plenty of shaving brushes on the market too.

24. MCU: *Mother and Maria as Maria turns and catches sight of . . .*

25. CU: *Hermann's picture seen behind a pile of dishes as very low music continues.*

26. *As 24. Maria starts to cry as Mother puts her arm around her.*

MOTHER: My baby.

The camera revolves to reframe them in MS as a low voice comes from the radio.

MARIA: Let's make some potatoes with bacon.

The radio catches Maria's attention and the camera now continues to revolve and dolly out to a ¾S as Maria goes to turn up the sound on the radio. The camera continues to follow and reframes her in MS as she listens.

RADIO: We have brought you the Ninth Symphony by Ludwig van Beethoven, and now have messages for the following persons: 5821, Adler, first name unknown . . .

Maria leaves the frame, leaving Mother at the stove in the background with Mother's reflection in a mirror on the wall behind her.

27. *The radio announcer's recitation of the names of the missing continues on the sound track. People leave a train station coming toward the camera along a wooden fence that has been ravaged for firewood. Maria walks against the crowd toward the train in the background. She is wearing a handmade sign on her back with Hermann's picture that says "Who knows about Hermann Braun?" and gives information on his last known whereabouts. A sign on the station wall warns, "Restricted zone. Danger of typhus."*

28. *The sound of the radio continues low. The camera now tracks along the fence from the opposite side with Maria in* CU *walking through the crowd. Others are wearing signs and photos.*

29. MS: *people come toward the camera, passing Maria. The camera pans past Maria and dollies through the crowd past men in Wehrmacht coats and hats without insignia, and circles around another soldier from behind in* MCU. *Then a young girl passes into and out of the frame in* CU *looking for someone. The shot is filmed by a hand-held camera moving through the crowd at eye level, as if from the subjective viewpoint of a character looking around in all directions, searching the faces in the crowd.*

RADIO (*low*): . . . serial number 7510, Wilhelm Burmeister from Dresden . . .

30. *As 27. An old man in a Wehrmacht uniform with only one leg passes the camera on crutches as Maria looks on from midground, where she is talking with a Red Cross nurse in* FS.

MARIA: It still makes me sick to see some of them. Could I have some tea?
NURSE: The medics say that a diagonal hit isn't the worst. (*She hands Maria a cup of tea.*) It's the symmetry. If you get hit all on one side, you can't even hold your own crutch. (*Another soldier wearing a fur-lined hat with ear flaps passes them on a crutch.*) I've been looking at them for six years, five of those I've been a widow. He'd still suit me fine if he was only coming back. How long were you married?

People leaving the train station continue passing them.

MARIA: I still am married.
NURSE: Yes, but I mean you didn't get much out of your marriage, did you?
MARIA: Yes I did. Half a day and a whole night.

31. MCU: *Maria is seen from behind. The camera tracks with her as she walks along the fence, looking at the handwritten signs and photos tacked to what remains of the fence. The signs offer cigarettes for sale and include offers to "take any kind of work" and to sell personal belongings. The sound of the train engine gets louder. As Maria turns away from the fence and stops, the camera pans past her to the train as people board. The pan continues to circle and now takes in a woman, also wearing a sign, with her daughter and a group of former soldiers. At the end of a complete revolution, the camera discovers Maria again in the spot where she was talking with the nurse. As Maria and the nurse walk away from the camera, it comes to rest on the fence where the sequence started.*

32. *Inside the train station. A slogan on the wall reads, "Wheels must roll for the . . . ," with the last word scratched off. A Red Cross worker is serving soup as the nurse and Maria enter and get in line. People can be seen through a doorway, sitting at tables in a back room.*

NURSE: He got killed right at the beginning, in Norway. He was in the
   Navy . . .

33. CU, *low angle: a man's profile is seen from over his shoulder. Smoke is
   coming from his cigarette as the nurse's voice continues.*

   NURSE (*off*): . . . until his ship was sunk.

34. *As 32. The one-legged man seen in 30 passes Maria and the nurse as they
   stand and talk by the soup vat. The train whistle is heard.*

35. *As 33. The man throws his cigarette butt over his shoulder.*

36. *The camera is at floor-level looking through a dense foreground of table
   and chair legs. A dozen men dive for the cigarette butt as it hits the floor,
   with the noises of tables and chairs being pushed around in the scramble.*

37. *The noise from 36 continues.* MCU: *the nurse and Maria, who has her
   back to the camera. Maria turns to look over her shoulder at . . .*

38. *As 36. The men are scrambling for the cigarette butt.*

39. *As 37.*

   NURSE (*to Red Cross worker*): Two soups please. But he survived it and
   swam through ice cold water covered with burning oil. (*Maria
   continues to look over at the men.*)

40. *As 36. The men return to their seats in unison. It's not clear which one
   got the butt.*

41. MLS: *Maria and the nurse stand beside the soup vat. Two former German
   soldiers sit silently eating their soup at a table in the right foreground.
   Maria turns back toward the nurse after watching the men take their seats
   again.*

   NURSE: And then he had to fight on land. And he fell into a crevasse and
   was killed.

Someone off-screen starts to whistle.

42. MCU, *reverse angle from 37: Maria and the nurse. The whistling continues.*

MARIA: Why didn't you get married again to somebody else?

43. *As 41. The whistling continues.*

NURSE: As a consolation they sent me a plaque. It had waves painted on it and there was a wreath with a ribbon floating on the water (*they move into foreground left and sit at a table with their mugs of soup*) that said, "They died that Germany may live." Can you believe that?
MARIA: "They died that Germany may live"—and he's dead.
NURSE: They sent me a picture of the ocean and he fell into a crevasse.

Another crippled soldier enters in the background for soup.

MARIA: The ocean used to be where the mountains are now—before the last ice age.

Off-screen noises of another scramble for a cigarette butt. Maria turns at the sound.

44. *As 40. Whistling, and scrambling noises.*

45. CU, *low angle: the man smoking in 33 is now seen from the front to be an American serviceman who is expressionlessly watching the men scramble.*

46. MS: *Maria and the nurse at the table.*

NURSE: What makes you so sure that your husband isn't dead too?
MARIA: Because I want him to come back. (*Maria has a faint smile on her face and looks toward the back room.*)[3]

47. *Reverse angle from 46. Maria is in the foreground, the crippled soldier is at right on the opposite end of Maria's table. In the back room in LS, a*

group of American GIs are sitting around a table. The one who threw the butts away turns toward Maria and the camera.

GI (*in English*): You should see mine honey, you'd love it.

He turns back to other GIs at the table. They all laugh.

MARIA (*to nurse*): What did he say?
NURSE (*shrugging her shoulders*): Something not very nice.

Maria gets up from the table and walks into the other room.

MARIA (*in English*): Mister . . .

48. MCU: *Maria.*

49. MCU, *slight high angle*: GI, *from behind, as he turns to face Maria.*

50. *As 48.*

MARIA: I don't know what you said, but you don't have any right.

51. *As 47. Maria returns to her place.*

NURSE (*mumbles into her soup*): You must be crazy.

GI (*from the background, in English*): What did she say?
SECOND GI (*in English*): She didn't like your joke.

Voices of GIs are heard in the background. The first GI walks over to Maria's table.

GI (*in English*): I'm sorry ma'am, I apologize.

He takes several packs of cigarettes out of his pocket, puts them down on the table, and goes back to his seat. Maria picks them up and starts to laugh. The GIs turn toward her and start to laugh.

52. MLS: *Mother, getting clothes out of an armoire, is seen from the kitchen through the ragged opening of a hole in the wall. The sound of the radio and Grandpa humming the "Horst Wessel Lied" gets louder as she goes off right while the camera pans right to Grandpa sitting in the kitchen in MCU. The camera continues to pan right to follow his glance toward Mother, now in MS, as she comes through the kitchen door. It continues to pan a bit further as Mother sets down an armful of clothes.*

RADIO: . . . Bauer, Georg, born . . . married in Worms. 5833, Feld, Paul . . .

MOTHER (*loud*): Come on, Grandpa Berger . . . (*Grandpa stops humming.*)

53. *Reverse angle from 52. Mother is in the foreground at ¾ S. Grandpa is sitting in the background.*

MOTHER: . . . let's try it on. (*Grandpa gets up and she tries a suit jacket on him for size.*) The problem with people, Grandpa Berger, is that they always have to give all their love to just one person. If you don't have potatoes, you eat turnips. When you don't have any more turnips, you eat oatmeal. But in love it always has to be the one and only, and then the husband goes to war. Five months later he's dead and you mourn for the rest of your life. (*She fits the jacket to him. He likes it.*) Now I ask you Grandpa Berger, does that make sense to you? (*Loud.*) Much too big!

The recitation of names continues low, and low music begins.

GRANDPA (*hasn't completely understood her*): That's right. It doesn't do a body good to be alone.

MOTHER: It was almost too small for Karl last time he was here in May of '41. The men still looked like something then. (*She goes through the pile of clothes on the kitchen table.*) Now they all look like they've shrunk. (*Loud.*) You can take the long underpants. (*She hands them to him.*)

54. ³⁄₄ S: *Mother from Grandpa's point of view.*

MOTHER: They're warm. Who's going to care if they're a little too big?
   (*Laughs, then loudly.*) Shall we say . . . three bundles of firewood?
   Hmmm?
GRANDPA: Alright.

She tosses him the rest of the clothes.

MOTHER: Just look at what happened to Maria. Engaged for three
   weeks, . . .

*The camera pans slightly to follow Mother as she goes through the door
with the jacket. Grandpa follows her to the door, then goes back across
the kitchen as the camera passes him. It settles on Mother seen through
the hole in the wall, as beginning of 52.*

MOTHER: . . . one day of marriage, and now she's out there with her
   sign. And shall I tell you why it is that it always has to be the one and
   only? (*She folds the jacket and puts it back in the armoire.*) Because in
   love there is only one, that's why. I don't know how Maria knew that
   already—at her tender age. . . . She's back! (*Mother rushes through
   the hole in the wall as the camera dollies out to* MS, *two-shot.*) Quick,
   Grandpa, get your things. She has her pride you know. (*She takes the
   underwear from Grandpa.*)

The music stops and the radio voice continues low.

GRANDPA (*confused*): How much wood?
MOTHER (*annoyed*): I said pride [*Stolz*], not wood [*Holz*]. Quiet! (*The
   camera pans as Mother walks over to the kitchen table in* MCU.) There
   you are, finally. I was just going through your father's things again.

*Maria is seen in the background through the kitchen door hanging up her
coat in the hallway; then she enters the kitchen. The camera pans with
her and reframes Maria and Grandpa in* MCU, *two-shot.*

MARIA: Hello, Grandpa Berger. (*She gives him a kiss.*) It's nice to have a man in the house to come home to.

GRANDPA: A warm house, too.

MARIA: Yes . . .

55. MARIA (¾S): . . . a warm house, too. (*She turns to Mother, who is sewing at the kitchen table. Grandpa returns to his chair.*) Why do you have to do that now?

MOTHER (*dignified*): It's my way of remembering your father.

RADIO: And now we broadcast this week's list of missing servicemen . . . (*The recitation of names, home towns, and identification numbers continues throughout this sequence.*)

MARIA: Grandpa Berger can put them to good use. Father doesn't need them any more and we can use the firewood. (*She opens her bag and takes out a pack of cigarettes.*)

MOTHER (*acts surprised*): I thought of that too—but Father's things . . .

MARIA: Father is dead and we're alive.

She drops a pack of Camels onto the table. Mother picks them up in disbelief, stands up, rushes to the sink for matches, and excitedly starts to open the pack. Maria and the camera follow Mother. Grandpa looks on from his chair in the background. Mother strikes a match in ¾S. Maria leans over her shoulder and blows it out.

MARIA: What'll you give me for it—your brooch?

MOTHER (*excitedly*): My brooch . . . it's very valuable. (*She examines the pack of cigarettes.*) There's one missing.

MARIA: Then here. (*She drops a second pack over her shoulder onto the counter.*)

MOTHER: Oh, Maria! Wait, I'll go get it. (*Mother exits and Maria puts down a third pack.*)

56. XCU: *two packs of Camels as the recitation of names of the missing continues.*

57. *As at end of 54. The recitation continues. Mother comes through the hole into the kitchen. Maria stands by the sink, reflected in the mirror, and Grandpa is in his chair.*

MOTHER (*hands Maria the brooch*): There. (*She lights up and Maria examines the brooch.*)
RADIO: . . . Budschuss, Budschuss, first name, unknown.[4]

58. MLS: *pan to follow an old, noisy truck pulling up on the opposite side of a sparse wooden fence. In LS in the background, women are working to clear the rubble. An American Armed Forces radio broadcast is heard from the truck.*

RADIO (*in English*): Two years ago one saw things in a different light.

59. *Two boys in German army caps are playing in a huge shell hole.*

RADIO: In 1944, the then Secretary of the Treasury, Henry Morgenthau, Jr., . . .

60. MLS: *a civilian man in a black leather coat gets out of the truck, looks around nervously, and starts to pull slats from the fence.*

RADIO: . . . recommended that at the conclusion of the war, Germany should . . .

61. *As 59. The boys light a firecracker.*

RADIO: . . . be changed into a farmland.

62. *As 60. After throwing a slat into his truck, the man goes back for more, framed by the remaining fence slats.*

RADIO: In other words, the German nation should be broken up.

63. *As 59. The boys hold their ears as sparks start to fly and flare up into an explosion.*

64. *As 58. The man crouches in a wartime protective posture.*

65. *As 59. The boys look up.*

RADIO: To the contrary (*a dog starts to bark*) Herbert Hoover . . .

66. MLS: *a dozen women are clearing the rubble as a dog continues to bark.*

RADIO: . . . following his visit to Germany . . .

67. *As 59. The boys stand up and laugh at the man.*

68. *As 58. The man shakes his fist at them.*

RADIO: . . . voices the opinion that the industry must remain . . .

(*The barking continues.*)

MAN: Nazi pigs! Snot-nosed brats!

69. *As 59. The boys point at him and laugh. The radio is heard, low, through 73.*

70. *As 66. Some of the women look.*

71. *As 69. The boys continue to point and laugh.*

72. *As 58. The truck pulls away.*

73. *As 69.*

74. *The truck passes through the frame in the foreground to reveal Maria and Betti standing in ³⁄₄s before a ruined building. Women are at work in* LS. *Their humming continues throughout the shot.*

MARIA: Men just aren't the same.
BETTI: What difference does it make if you're a man or a woman if you're freezing?

The two, each wearing signs, walk past the women working in the background. The camera tracks with them.

MARIA: Something's got to change.
BETTI: What is it you want to change?
MARIA: I don't know. But something's got to.

75. *As 69. The humming continues as the boys in the shell hole look on.*

FIRST BOY: Have you seen Hermann Braun?
SECOND BOY: No.

76. LS: *a devastated landscape with meager remnants of a fence in the foreground and women at work, humming, in the background is seen as Maria and Betti exit at frame right.*[5]

77. ¾S, *very low lighting: Maria is having her hair done by Betti. A low, bluish light from a curtained window in the background illuminates the scene. Their faces are illuminated from candles on the dressing table.*

BETTI (*sings*): "Don't cry, baby. There's more than one man on earth. (*Maria hums along.*) There's more than one, more than one . . ." (*They laugh.*)[6]

78. CU: *Maria's dressing table with Hermann's photo, amidst hair curlers and makeup.*

79. CU: *Maria sits with Betti behind her, fixing Maria's hair. The background is very dark and the shot is of a reflection in a mirror. They are both heavily made-up.*

MARIA (*studying her new hairdo*): I look like a poodle.
BETTI: You think so? But it's the latest thing.
MARIA (*laughs*): I'll bet the Americans are crazy about poodles.

80. *As 78.*

81. CU: *Betti is seen left of center frame in the candlelight.*

BETTI: Willi would definitely not approve.

82. MS: *Maria is in the foreground. Betti is behind Maria, with a double reflection of Betti in the background and a row of candles in the left foreground that illuminate the shot. The entire shot is a reflection.*

MARIA: Hermann would.
BETTI: They won't hire you anyway.
MARIA: We'll see about that.
BETTI: What'll you wear?[7]

83. MLS: *a jeep with American MPs crosses the frame, seen from inside an entrance to an alleyway. Maria enters the frame and turns into the alleyway. The camera precedes her at MCU as she walks by a row of people who are buying and selling all kinds of goods on the black market. A woman offers Maria something wrapped in newspaper. Maria passes them all without acknowledgement. She appears to know exactly where she is going.*

FIRST MAN (*off-screen*): What am I supposed to do with this?
SECOND MAN (*off-screen*): Play music. Want me to play something for you? Got any requests?

FIRST MAN (*comes briefly into view*): Sure. Play the national anthem. (*He sings.*) "Deutschland, Deutschland, über alles" . . .

Maria passes the camera, which now follows her in FS to the end of the alley. The camera pivots to show Maria turning to go through another silhouetted entranceway into an open courtyard. Sound of the "Deutschlandlied" played on a concertina. A dark-clad man comes up to her and she follows him out of the frame to the right, as the camera, still in the alleyway, tracks back along its path to include the man and Maria as they enter a building, seen through yet another silhouetted entranceway.

FIRST MAN (*off-screen*): Okay! Okay! Knock it off. For God's sake, stop with that. (*The concertina music stops.*) Damn thing can't even play the national anthem.[8]

84. ¾S: *Maria and the black market dealer, who is wearing dark glasses and a slouch hat [he is played by Fassbinder], hesitate at the building's entrance. The dealer whistles the opening theme from Beethoven's Fifth Symphony.*

85. *An open space next to the building.*

86. *As 84. The dealer nods toward the doorway.*

87. LS: *the alleyway, with many people and much activity.*

88. *As 84.*

DEALER (*to Maria*): Go on in. Be careful.

89. MS: *a man in a black leather coat and hat enters from the adjacent open space in 85.*

90. *As 84. Maria goes inside the building as the dealer looks inside before entering.*

91. FS: *the leather-clad man enters and goes to the dealer.*

DEALER (*to man*): Keep an eye out. (*The dealer takes a suitcase from the man and goes inside. The concertina starts to play the "Deutschlandlied" and continues throughout the black market sequence.*)

92. *As 87. A man exits from the alleyway stuffing something under his coat; a woman leaves with a bag.*

93. MS: *the dealer opens the suitcase in the dark interior of the building as Maria looks on.*

DEALER: I didn't think you were coming. I waited a long time. (*He takes off his jacket and hands it to Maria.*) Here, hold this a minute. (*He takes a dress out of the suitcase.*) Black, size 38, short sleeves, low-cut. Wasn't easy to get. Is it for you, or a gift?

MARIA: For work.

DEALER (*takes out a bottle of gin or vodka*): Yeah, we've all got to live somehow. And the booze?

MARIA (*laughs*): For my mother.

94. MARIA (MCU): It's to help her forget the troubles she has with her daughter and drown her sorrows. (*Tilt to the brooch in her hand as she looks down, then tilt back up to her face.*)

95. *As 93.*

   DEALER: That reminds me—I also have here a very valuable complete edition of the works of Heinrich von Kleist, 1907. Would it interest you?
   MARIA: Books burn too fast and don't give enough heat.[9] (*She takes the dress. He takes his jacket and puts it on as they exchange places in the frame.*)
   DEALER: Yeah, that's one way of looking at it.
   MARIA: It's my way.
   DEALER: At the moment, it's probably the best way. (*They come toward each other. She hands him the brooch. He gives it a quick once-over.*) Thank you. (*He kisses her hand.*)

96. MCU: *two-shot of the dealer and Maria.*

   DEALER: And good luck. (*She leaves the frame as he looks after her.*)

97. MCU: *Maria's foot is seen in a high-heeled shoe on the kitchen table as Mother's hand pours a drink. The radio announcer reads the names of missing soldiers through 99.*

   MOTHER: Don't count on me to sew it for you.
   MARIA: Just the hem. Mama, you know I can't sew.
   MOTHER (*lifts a glass as the camera tilts up*): Child, child.
   MARIA (*off-screen*): Come on and get started.

98. MLS: *Maria standing on the table, and Mother, are seen through a silhouetted doorway.*

   MARIA: Come on.

99. MS: *Maria's legs as Mother pins the hem.*

MOTHER: When you have such pretty legs, you really should show them off. (*She pins the hem up even higher as Grandpa looks on from the background.*) Your father would turn over in his grave, and I don't approve either. I just hope it doesn't do your soul any harm. (*She steps back to judge the length.*) At least see that somebody gives you a nice pair of stockings as long as you're doing this.[10]

100. CU: *sign: "Vocational School I-Gym," with "OFF LIMITS" (in English) stenciled over it.*

101. ¾S: *Maria enters, seen from inside the gym.*

102. MLS: *the camera pans around the interior of the gym from Maria's point of view to reveal a huge American flag on one wall, American Army jackets on a coatrack, gymnastic equipment, and windows on an opposite wall. Soft, wistful music is heard and continues through 106.*

103. CU: *reaction shot of Maria smiling.*

104. LS: *interior of the empty gym.*

105. *As 101. Maria enters, walking toward the camera as it tracks out in front of her. She stops at the parallel bars and runs her hand along them.*

106. LS: *Maria mounts the bars and swings between them. She is seen, in a shaft of daylight from the windows, from behind a curtain pulled aside across the upper foreground of the shot. Maria turns toward the camera in response to . . .*[11]

BRONSKI (*off-screen*): Amazing . . .

107. MCU, *reverse angle from 106: a fat, slovenly man emerges, wiping his nose, from behind a curtain that serves as a door to his makeshift office. Low music is heard as from a radio.*

BRONSKI: . . . really amazing.
MARIA (*off-screen*): I used to practice on these bars.

BRONSKI: Is that your way of applying for a job? (*The camera pans slightly to take in the man's reflection in a mirror behind him.*)

108. *As 106, but slightly closer at* MLS: *Maria is perched coyly on the bars. Radio music continues.*

MARIA: Not really, but if it was, I'd have found a job by now.

109. *Reverse angle of 108. Maria is in the foreground; Bronski is wiping his nose in the background.*

BRONSKI: We don't need anybody.
MARIA: Maybe once you've got me you won't need anybody else. (*He turns away. She jumps off the bars and goes to him. He turns toward her.*)
BRONSKI: Follow me. (*He gestures toward his office. They go in.*)

110. MARIA (MCU): We've still got doors at home.

111. ³⁄₄S: *Bronski from Maria's point of view as the camera pans to follow him to behind his desk. The final duet from* Der Rosenkavalier *is heard, low, from the radio.*

BRONSKI: We don't. Here. (*He lays a paper on the desk.*) I need your name, address, and age. Are you married? (*Maria is now included in the shot in* MCU, *then* MLS, *as she walks away from the camera toward the desk.*)
MARIA: Yes. (*Dolly in.*)
BRONSKI: Don't wear your wedding ring when you're working. And I'm going to need a health certificate. Cash or goods? (*The camera continues to dolly in on her hand.*)

112. *A woman sitting on a table in the doctor's examination room is seen through a doorway in the foreground. A Christmas tree is seen in the doctor's office beyond the examination room.*[12]

DOCTOR: You can get dressed now, Frau Binder.
WOMAN: Everything okay? Do I get the certificate?

DOCTOR (*goes to his desk in the background*): No, you're going to have to take three or four weeks off.

WOMAN: Have I got it?

DOCTOR (LS, *at his desk in the office*): You do, and bad. You're not going to be able to go back to work.

WOMAN (*almost whispers*): That's bad.

DOCTOR (*comes into the examination room*): Come back on Tuesday. Goodbye, Frau Binder. Would you ask the next patient to come in? (*He leans against the wall by the doorway in the foreground as if he were ill.*)

As Maria enters the examination room, foreboding music blares up on the sound track. A dark, vague reflection of Maria is seen in a full length mirror as she faces it with her back to the camera.

113. ¾S: *Maria stands beside an aquarium in the doctor's office as the doctor enters in* MLS. *Low background music is heard throughout the rest of the doctor's office sequence.*

DOCTOR: Maria? (*She turns toward him. She is now wearing her hair swept to one side.*) My little Maria.

114. MARIA (MCU): You used to give me a kiss on the forehead.

115. DOCTOR (*as 113*): Oh, did I?

116. MARIA (*as 114, coquettishly*): Yes.

117. DOCTOR (*as 115*): Then I must have forgotten, or learned to forget. (*He goes to his desk. She faces him from across his desk in* MLS.)
MARIA: That's sad.
DOCTOR: Yes it's sad. Tell me about yourself.

Maria turns toward the wall. The room is lit by the examination light which casts Maria's shadow on the wall behind her.

MARIA: I need a health certificate.

The low music rises to a higher pitch.

118. MCU: *the back of Maria's head.*

   DOCTOR (*off-screen*): Yes, of course. It's cold this year.
   MARIA (*turns*): I found a job in a bar.

   Cabaret-type music continues.

119. MCU: *the doctor is at his desk. Books and objects in silhouette clutter the foreground. Cabaret music continues.*

120. MARIA (MCU): I'm going to sell beer—not myself. (*Cabaret music continues.*)

121. DOCTOR (*as 119*): Even though I've learned to stop believing anybody here—you I believe. (*Low, soft background music begins and continues to the end of the sequence in the doctor's office.*)

122. MCU: *Maria.*

123. MCU: *the doctor at his desk.*

124. LS: *the doctor and Maria are in his office with the aquarium and Christmas tree.*

   DOCTOR: Well, you know what you're doing. Anyway, if anything happens to you, I'll get you penicillin. (*He goes behind a screen.*) I don't know how, but somehow I'll get some for you.
   MARIA (*goes behind another screen to undress*): Nothing's going to happen to me. What's this penicillin?

125. MS: *the doctor is enclosed by screens with the huge shadow of his head and hands on a screen behind him as he prepares an injection.*

   DOCTOR: Never mind, Maria. How's your mother?
   MARIA (*off-screen*): Well, the war didn't make her lose her sense of humor.

126. XCU: *the doctor's hand fills the hypodermic needle.*

MARIA (*off-screen*): She nibbles at my rations, cries my tears, lies my lies, but she leaves all the thinking to me so I don't have the time to be sad.

127. DOCTOR (*as 125, tests the hypodermic*): You can have my wife's bicycle if you want. (*He hastily pushes up his sleeve and injects himself.*) They dug it out of the rubble as good as new.
MARIA (*off-screen*): Thank you.

128. MARIA (¾S: *she comes out from behind the screen dressed only in her skirt*): Why don't you ask anything about Hermann?

129. *Vague shadow of the doctor's head on the screen from Maria's point of view. Low organ music takes on a sinister tone and continues through 132.*

130. MARIA (MCU): You must not think he's coming back.

131. MARIA (*as 129, off-screen*): But I do, and that's enough.

132. *As 130.*

133. MCU: *the doctor is seen in the small opening between a door molding and a screen. The music builds in volume and pitch as the doctor sighs from the rush of the drug and the camera booms down to the needle in his hand.*[13]

134. *As 27.* MLS: *a crowd of people are standing around the entrance to a train car. Maria's nurse friend is talking to someone in the foreground as Maria enters in the background and walks toward screen right past a fistfight and looks on indifferently. The sound of the train engine and the argument are heard throughout the station sequence.*[14]

FIRST MAN: My gloves are gone. You stole my gloves you bastard! Pig!

135. MCU: *Maria stands beside the fence and looks at . . .*

SECOND MAN (*off-screen*): Get out of here!
FIRST MAN (*off-screen*): Give them back to me!

136. *Two pairs of reunited lovers kissing, from Maria's point of view.*

SECOND MAN (*off-screen*): Leave me alone!

137. *As 135, reaction shot: Maria casts her eyes downward.*

FIRST MAN (*off-screen*): You better give them back to me. I saw you take them a minute ago.

138. MCU: *the nurse, in the foreground, and another Red Cross worker turn to look toward off-screen left.*

SECOND MAN (*off-screen*): Look, you'd better be careful what you're saying, or I'll call the police!

139. CU: *Maria's hand pulls Hermann's photo off the sign she is wearing.*

FIRST MAN (*off-screen*): You want to fight? Alright, come on. I'll teach you to steal from me.

140. *As 138.*

THIRD MAN (*off-screen*): Stop that, the train's going to leave any minute.
SECOND MAN (*off-screen*): Ow! Are you crazy, oh!

141. *As 134. The men are seen still fighting as Maria throws the sign under the train.*

THIRD MAN: That's enough now, you're blocking the way.
SECOND MAN: Come on, get up and fight . . .
THIRD MAN: Stop them, can't you see they're blocking the way for everybody?

142. *As 138.*

143. CU: *the sign lies on the tracks under the train as the train whistle signals its departure.*

144. *As 138. Nurse and Red Cross worker looking off-screen left.*

FIRST MAN (*off-screen*): I'll get even, you bastard!
SECOND MAN (*off-screen*): Will you shut up for God's sake!

145. *As 134.* MLS: *Maria stands in place as the train pulls out.*

FIRST MAN (*rolling on the ground with the second man*): Steal my gloves, will you? I'll teach you to steal, you . . .
SECOND MAN: Oh, kiss my ass!

146. *As 143. The train wheels run over the sign.*[15]

FIRST MAN (*off-screen*): Oh!
SECOND MAN (*off-screen*): Bastard!

147. LS: *dancers are now seen in the bar in soft blue lighting from behind the pulled-back curtain of Bronski's office, from Bronski's point of view. Glenn Miller's "Moonlight Serenade" is heard throughout the sequence in the bar.*

148. MCU, *reverse angle from 147: Bronski is watching with the shadow from the curtain across his eyes. He is smoking and wears gaudy jewelry.*

149. LS, *Bronski's point of view: Maria sitting at the bar. A black soldier sits at one end and Maria's friend, Vevi, stands behind the bar. Two candles in wine bottles are burning at both ends of the bar.*

150. MS: *the camera tracks with Bronski, who is wearing the same suit he had on for Maria's interview, as he crosses the room to the bar.*

BRONSKI: Business is slow.
VEVI: It's Tuesday.

151. LS: *the camera pans over the dancers as it follows a young black soldier who enters and crosses the room to the jukebox.*

152. BRONSKI (MS): You're probably disappointed.
     MARIA (MS): No, I'm satisfied.
     BRONSKI: Good. (*He takes a drink and the camera pans over the dancers to follow him back across the room to his office in* MLS.)[16]

153. VEVI (MS): If you ask me . . .
     MARIA (MS): Nobody asked you . . .
     VEVI: You're here, and he isn't . . . your Hermann. Anyway, he's somewhere else, maybe he's even dead already. (*The camera tracks along the bar, which is lined with lighted candle stubs, as Vevi makes herself a drink.*) Love's just a feeling, it's not real. (*The camera tracks back with her to Maria.*)
     MARIA: Of course love's a feeling. And a great love is a great emotion and a great truth.
     SOLDIER (*sitting in the dark at the end of the bar, in English*): A gin.
     VEVI: Truth. The only thing that's true is an empty stomach. And feelings! (*Vevi leaves the frame for a moment, then reenters behind the bar as the camera tracks to follow her while she makes the soldier's drink.*) Feelings are something you have between your legs. They're like an itch that you relieve by scratching it.
     SOLDIER (*off-screen*): Another one.

The camera tracks back again with Vevi as she hands the soldier his drink, then comes back out from behind the bar to Maria.

     VEVI: And to do that you need a full stomach and somebody that's here and not somewhere. Or nowhere. Your sweetheart over there . . . (*She nods toward the camera.*) He's here. (*Maria looks.*) And he sure isn't starving, you can see that.

154. MLS: *Bill, a mature, heavyset black soldier is sitting alone at a table surrounded by other black soldiers who are sitting at tables together or with the women who work at the club, seen from the point of view of the two women.*

VEVI (*off-screen*): And he's got a soft spot for you.
MARIA (*off-screen*): What sweetheart?
VEVI (*off-screen*): Your Bill, honey.
MARIA (*off-screen*): I don't know any Bill.

155. VEVI (*as end of 153*, MCU, *now behind the bar*): Don't tell me you
haven't noticed him. (*The camera tracks slightly to the right to reframe
Vevi and Maria and exclude the soldier at the bar.*)
MARIA: No. Which one is he?
VEVI: Over there. (*Maria looks.*)

156. *As 154. Bill, from Maria's point of view, looks up at her.*

VEVI (*off-screen*): He looks healthy and strong—so what if he's black.

157. *As 155.* MS *of Maria and Vevi.*

MARIA: Better black than brown. Braun. (*She laughs.*)
VEVI: He was perfectly normal until you came in . . .

158. *Reverse angle from 157. Maria is seen from behind in* MCU *in the right
foreground, looking at Bill in background left looking at her.*

VEVI: . . . and now he sits there like he's paralyzed. He asked me all
about you, put me through a real third degree. Look at him . . . (*Bill
stands up and bows toward Maria.*)

159. VEVI (MCU): . . . just like Willy Fritsch.

160. *As 158. Bill takes his seat again.*

MARIA (*turns to Vevi*): How do I look?
VEVI: Great, why?
MARIA: Because I want to look great right now. (*She smiles.*)

161. *Reverse angle from 160. Maria gets up from her bar stool in ¾s. The
camera dollies out in front of her as she goes over to Bill's table and bows
slightly.*

MARIA: Will you dance with me, Mr. Bill?

Maria's figure is reflected in a mirror high up on a wall in the background. Bill gets up. They start to dance just as "Moonlight Serenade" ends.

BILL: Thank you, ma'am.

162. MCU: *Bronski, frowning, watches from his office doorway.*

163. *Pan past a bare tree trunk as the camera follows Bill and Maria climbing steps up a wooded slope. Birds are singing. The two stop beside another trunk in* MLS.

   BILL (*in English through 165*): And this is a tree.
   MARIA (*in English through 165*): This is a tree.

164. BILL (MS, *as they continue up the slope*): And that which you hear—
   peep, peep, peep, peep, peep, peep—are birds. (*Birds are singing.*)
   MARIA (MS): And that which you hear—peep, peep, peep, peep, peep—
   are birds. (*Pan to follow them up the slope.*)
   BILL: I am black. You are white.
   MARIA: I am black. You are white.
   BILL (*laughs*): No, the other way around.
   MARIA: No, the other way around. (*Bill laughs.*)

165. MARIA (MCU, *from over Bill's shoulder. They laugh.*): You're black and
   I'm white. (*Birds are singing.*)
   BILL: Ja, ja. (*He touches her eye.*) These are your eyes.
   MARIA: These are me . . . my eyes.
   BILL (*touches her lips*): And these are your lips.
   MARIA: And these are my lips.

166. *Reverse angle from 165. Bill is seen over Maria's shoulder. Birds are singing.*

167. LS: *pan follows them as they walk through bare trees and bushes with dry leaves on the ground. Birds are singing. A broken window pane forms a*

line across the bottom part of the frame in the foreground. As the camera pans, we see, first, the left side of the window frame, then the right, as Maria and Bill leave the shot.

168. LS: *Maria and Bill cross a walkway between two old brick buildings. Then fade out as a harsh, repetitive rhythm comes in over the last few frames and the first few frames of the next shot.*[17]

169. *Fade in on* CU *of wringing hands in foreground left. Mother is at the kitchen table and Betti is standing in* FS *in the background. The radio is heard low and indistinct throughout most of this sequence.*

    RADIO: Bauer, Georg, serial number 4096 . . . married, Worms . . .
    MOTHER (*crying*): What are you crying about, you silly goose. Your
       husband isn't dead. He's standing right there in front of you—you can
       touch him. You ought to be glad you've got him and that you're not a
       widow like the others.
    RADIO: Baumfeld, Paul, Baumfeld, Paul, born in Mannheim . . .

    The camera tilts up to reframe the shot as Betti comes toward Willi, patting Mother on the shoulder as she passes her. She grabs Willi's coat and kisses him passionately. As the camera refocusses on Betti kissing Willi in MCU, *the outline of the hole in the wall, through which the camera has filmed the entire shot, becomes clear. Willi walks away into the background as Betti casts her eyes down and starts to cry.*

170. MCU: *Mother puts her head down on the kitchen table and cries. Willi, behind her, looks out the window, then is seen in profile as he turns toward Betti.*

    WILLI: Hermann didn't suffer at all. It was over fast for him and the
       others. They say nobody came through.

171. MCU: *Betti, from the reverse angle, crying.*

    MARIA (*off-screen*): It's me. Hello.

    Betti turns toward the doorway.

172. MS: *Maria in the doorway, from Betti's point of view.*

MARIA: You can't imagine what I've got. (*She hangs up her bag.*)

173. *As 171. Betti turns and rushes toward Willi as the camera tracks left with her.*

MARIA (*off-screen*): You're not going to believe it.
RADIO: Serial number 3280, a special message . . .

The camera tracks back again, fast, in an arc that takes in Mother, who jumps up from her seat while Betti grabs Willi violently and buries her face in his shoulder. As Mother tries to console Betti, Betti pushes her away, and Mother goes and hides behind a pillar at screen left.

174. MS: *Maria hangs her coat and scarf up and is reflected in the mirror on the coat stand. She turns toward the camera, standing in the doorway to the foyer, and starts to breathe excitedly.*

MARIA: Willi! You! You're back! Betti, you've got him back again. (*Maria comes into the room.*)

175. *Reverse angle from 174. Maria's back is seen in* MS *as she laughs and embraces Willi. Betti walks out of the shot at left. Maria turns toward her and Willi turns toward the two of them.*

MARIA: You've got him back!

Pan left to take in Mother and Betti hugging. They include Maria. Willi, at right, looks on. Mother goes to embrace Willi, Maria goes to Willi, Mother grabs and hugs Maria, then Betti crosses the screen to embrace Willi.

MARIA: It's so stupid for us all to be crying like this, but I'm so happy that we're together again and that Willi's safe.

A slow pan follows Maria, crying, across the room as Mother cries and Betti and Willi kiss.

MARIA: You didn't even get wounded.

Maria, at the kitchen sink, pours water over her hands. Mother reenters the frame in MCU *at left foreground with a painful expression on her face as Betti and Willi join Mother in the foreground.*

176. MCU, *reverse angle from the end of 175, three-shot. Willi and Betti turn toward Maria (off-screen) who continues to sob for joy.*

177. MCU: *Maria is at the sink with her back to the camera, seen from Willi and Betti's point of view.*

WILLI (*off-screen*): Hermann is dead.

Tilt down to the water running over Maria's hand. There is no sound except that of water trickling from the faucet.

178. *As 176. Betti and Willi look away from Maria. Mother turns toward her.*

179. *Reverse angle from 178, ¾s: Maria turns off the faucet as the others watch her from the foreground. Maria starts toward them as if in a trance, then suddenly turns away and goes out at frame right with Mother following her. Track left and dolly in as Betti goes to the window. Mother pursuing Maria is seen through the window on the right half of the frame and over Betti's shoulder. Betti is in the left half of the frame.*[18]

MOTHER (*off-screen*): Child! (*Maria stops. Mother enters the shot and grabs her arm.*)
MARIA: Leave me alone.
MOTHER: Where are you going?
MARIA: To the bar.
MOTHER: Child, please.
MARIA: I have to go someplace where I can be alone.

Willi reenters the shot, closes the window and embraces Betti in MCU. *Upbeat music from the bar—Glenn Miller's "In the Mood"—comes in over the last few frames of this shot as Betti and Willi kiss and Mother is seen through the window returning to the house.*

180. *Camera dollies out to precede Maria, opening up a corridor as she walks through the crowd dancing in the bar. Low, soft, blue lighting. The dolly now takes in Bill at a table with his back to the camera in* MCU.

MARIA (*bows slightly*): Will you dance with me, Mr. Bill?

The song ends.

181. *Reverse angle from 180,* MS: *the camera dollies back a bit as Bill comes around the table to embrace Maria.*

MARIA (*in English*): My man is dead.

"Moonlight Serenade" begins as if on cue. The two stand in place, with Bill's arms around Maria, swaying slightly as the camera dollies back, making a corridor through the dancers, at slightly below eye-level. The couple is then obscured as the dancers flow back into the open space.[19]

182. MLS: *a family picnic. Willi lies with his head in Betti's lap. Mother turns toward Bill.*

MOTHER (*in English*): Is it not beauty, Mr. Bill?
BILL: Wunderschön.
MOTHER: You must always correct me if I say something wrong.
MARIA (*in English*): Beautiful. (*To Bill.*) Come on. Let's go.
MOTHER (*in English*): Thank you for the good Essen, Mr. Bill.
MARIA (*off-screen, in English*): Dinner.
BILL (*off-screen, in English*): Lunch.

The camera pivots and dollies out slightly so that a window frame comes into view in the foreground. As it does, it obscures Maria and Bill at screen right. The dolly stops at MCU *of Grandpa inside the house. At the off-screen sound of a door opening, the camera tracks with Grandpa across the kitchen to the hole in the wall.*

MARIA (*off-screen, in English*): Give him a cigarette.
GRANDPA: Thank you.

Maria's hand passes Grandpa a cigarette through the hole in the wall. He exits through the hole as the camera returns to look out the window. Low music starts and continues to the end of this sequence.

BETTI (*to Willi*): What are you thinking? (*The camera dollies in past Mother to Betti and Willi in* MLS.) What are you thinking?

WILLI: Whether it's possible to think of nothing. (*Grandpa enters toward them.*)

BETTI: And?

WILLI: I don't think I can.

BETTI: I think I can. (*Grandpa takes a bottle of wine and exits as the camera dollies back out to include Mother and the window frame again.*) Do you think I would have gotten over it as quickly as Maria? (*Mother is eating as Grandpa sits near her and takes a swig from the bottle.*)

WILLI: I hope you would have, Betti.

BETTI: Why? How come?

183. CU: *Maria's hand caresses Bill's bare arm and shoulder.*[20]

MARIA (*off*): It's nice being with you, Bill. I was very happy just now. (*Low background music continues over the love scene.*)
BILL (*off*): Only, just now?
MARIA (*off*): I'm always happy when I'm with you.
BILL (*off*): So am I. Then it's simple . . .

184. BILL (*off, as his hand caresses the back of her naked body*): . . . if we're always together, then we'll always be happy.
MARIA (*off*): Maybe.
BILL (*off*): Not maybe, for sure. I have something for you.

185. MARIA (*off, as her hand caresses his abdomen*): You shouldn't give me so many presents.
BILL (*off*): It's something special this time and you have to promise me you'll take it.

186. CU: *Maria's head is on the bed with her hair falling over the side.*

MARIA: No Bill, I can't take your ring.

187. *Bill's head and shoulders are seen from behind.*

MARIA (*off*): I'm very fond of you and I want to be with you.

188. MARIA (*as 186*): But I'm never going to marry you. I'm married to my husband.

189. CU: *the doctor is washing his hands.*

MARIA (*off-screen*): Are you sure?
DOCTOR (*off*): Positive.
MARIA (*off-screen*): How positive?
DOCTOR (*off*): Maria!
MARIA (*off-screen*): Please, please, please, please . . .
DOCTOR (*tilt up to the doctor looking in a mirror, from over his shoulder*): Alright. You'll be noticing it soon.

190. MARIA (MCU, *left of center frame*): But you'll help me bring it into the world. Promise me you will. (*She is smiling.*)

191. *Reverse angle from 190. Maria, sitting undressed on a table, is seen from behind from an adjacent room, framed by the doorway as the doctor washes his hands in the background.*

> DOCTOR: I can't, Maria. I'm too old to live and too scared to die. (*He comes toward her, then past her and past the camera into the adjacent room as Maria turns in profile to the camera.*)
> MARIA: It scares me when you talk like that.

192. DOCTOR (MS, *lights a cigarette*): Then I'll say it another way.

193. *Maria, as 191.*

> DOCTOR (*off-screen*): I'm quitting. I'm going to live with my daughter in the Black Forest . . .

194. DOCTOR (*as 192*): . . . because my hands shake too much.

195. *Reverse angle from 194. Maria stands up. She is seen through the doorway with the doctor's back to the camera in the foreground.*

MARIA: Not for me! Or my little boy either. (*Maria gets up and goes off left as the doctor walks toward the Christmas tree at ³⁄₄s and plays with a decoration.*) I'll just come to you when it's time.
DOCTOR: Little Maria.
MARIA (*reenters in her slip, goes to the doctor*): That's just what I'll do. I'll come and you'll help me bring the boy into the world. It will be a boy won't it?
DOCTOR: Well, the chances aren't bad.
MARIA: Really?
DOCTOR: Well, about fifty-fifty.
MARIA: Oh, you're not taking me seriously.
DOCTOR (*moves toward the camera to* MS): No, I'm not. Do you have a father for the boy? (*He looks concerned.*)
MARIA: What do you mean? Can you have a baby without one? (*The doctor, facing the camera, smiles, nods, and raises a cigarette to his mouth. Maria is now off-screen.*) The father is black. (*He stops smiling, the hand with the cigarette stops midway to his mouth.*) And I'm going to name my boy Hermann.[21]

196. FS: *the hallway of Mother's apartment building as the front door opens. This is seen from a high angle with the camera on the stairwell. The banister and stairs cut across the right half of the shot.*

MARIA (*as they enter and Bill picks her up*): I'm not sick! I'm pregnant!

197. MLS: *the front door from inside the apartment and from the opposite end of a long foyer. Bill carries Maria toward the camera and through a door off the foyer.*

BILL: Pregnant!
MARIA: You can also say, I'm in good hope.
BILL: That's nice—I'm in good hope.

MARIA: Mama! Grandpa Berger! Nobody home. (*They pass the camera in* MCU.)

BILL: Alone at last. (*He puts her down. The camera pivots to show them kissing in the doorway at* MS. *Maria goes inside and Bill leans against the doorway and sighs from the exertion.*)

198. *Reverse angle from 197,* MCU: *Bill. A shadow pattern from the shuttered window (off-screen) falls across his face.*

BILL (*with a serious expression and tone*): Are you in good hope?

199. CU: *Maria turns toward him.*

200. *As 198.*

201. MARIA (*as 199*): Yes.
BILL (*off-screen*): I'm in good hope too. (*She walks out of the frame in his direction.*)

202. MLS: *Maria's bedroom. Maria starts to undress Bill as he leans in the doorway and staggers a bit as if he were slightly drunk. Soft shadows from the shuttered window fall across the room and their figures.*

MARIA: I'll speak German with him. How about you?
BILL: English. Then later he can marry either a German or an American girl.
MARIA: American girls are ugly. (*She pushes him toward the bed and throws his Army jacket on the floor.*)
BILL: German men are ugly. (*He takes her jacket off and drops it to the floor.*)
MARIA (*takes off his shoe and starts to unbutton his shirt*): I only know one American man who's handsome.

A man's figure appears in the slightly open doorway. He stands there looking in, in MLS *as Maria takes off Bill's tie and they kiss.*

BILL: I only know one German woman who's beautiful. (*He unbuckles her belt. She unbuttons his shirt.*)

MARIA: And strong.

BILL: And rich.

MARIA: And brave. (*She takes off his undershirt and tosses it over her shoulder. Bill slides her dress back and kisses her shoulder as she lets down his pants.*) And tender.

BILL (*lifts her up again by the arm*): And tender.

MARIA (*pushes him playfully down onto the bed and takes off his pants, then sits on the bed beside him*): Guess who I mean.

203. BILL (MCU, *from over her shoulder*): Me? (*He kisses her shoulder and looks up at . . .*)

204. MS: *Hermann, expressionless, from Bill's point of view. He is standing behind the bedroom door. He is dressed in old civilian clothes with short-shaven hair.*

205. MARIA (*as 203, turns toward the door, stares, blinks, then low*): Hermann? (*She turns back to Bill.*) Look, Bill. It's Hermann. (*Both turn toward Hermann. Maria smiles.*)

206. *As 204.*

207. MARIA (*as 203, low*): Ohhh . . .

208. *As 202.* MLS: *Maria rushes, laughing, to the door. Bill, who is naked, stands up. Maria opens the door and Hermann smacks her. She falls to the floor.*

BILL: Maria! (*He goes to her.*) Maria! Maria! Maria! (*He looks up at Hermann, who is still standing in the doorway.*)

Hermann looks down, then across the room, and suddenly rushes across the room as the camera pans to follow. He grabs a cigarette from the night table, greedily lights it, and inhales deeply.[22]

209. MCU: *Bill looks from Hermann (off-screen) to Maria and lifts her up from the floor. Both look at . . .*

210. ¾s: *Hermann, from their point of view. He is taking long, deep drags from the cigarette.*

211. *As 209. Hermann's shadow passes over them.*

212. *As 210. Hermann is seen in profile as he sits on the bed, smoking and staring into space.*

213. *As 209.*

214. MCU: *Hermann smokes.*

215. *As 202.* MLS: *Hermann starts to pull at the bed covers, then tears at the sheets. Bill runs over to restrain him. They struggle. The camera shifts slightly to the left as Maria gets up and picks up a bottle. Hermann seems to be subdued and starts to cry when Maria crosses the room deliberately,*

as the camera pans slightly, then hits Bill over the head with the bottle.
Hermann backs away as Bill falls on the bed.

216. MCU: *Maria, slightly left of center frame looks up with a confused*
expression. There is a shadow across the lower half of her face.

217. *Reverse angle from 216.* MCU: *Hermann, seen from Maria's point of view,*
turns toward her and blinks.

218. *As 216. Maria breathes a sigh, and smiles slightly.*

219. *The camera tilts down over the stars of an American flag.*

> JUDGE (*off-screen, in English*): So you met the deceased in the
> Moonlight Bar?
> INTERPRETER (*off-screen*): (*He repeats the line in German.*)
> MARIA (*off-screen*): Yes.
> JUDGE (*off-screen*): Would you tell us more about this bar?
> INTERPRETER (*off-screen*): (*Repeats.*)

220. MLS: *an American military court of inquiry is set up in a former factory.*
In the audience are Vevi, Willi, Betti, and Mother. The torso of an Army
MP is seen in the left foreground. Another stands beside Maria in ¾S.
She is facing the camera and an unseen person on the panel. She is
stylishly dressed, as usual.

> MARIA: It's a bar like any other.
> INTERPRETER (*off-screen*): (*He repeats the line in English.*)
> JUDGE (*off-screen*): Wouldn't you say that this was a very special bar?
> INTERPRETER (*off-screen*): (*Repeats.*)
> JUDGE (*off-screen*): Private, bring up Mr. . . .

221. MS: *two-shot of an American military judge and a German interpreter at*
his left. The stripes of a huge American flag can be seen behind them.

> JUDGE: . . . Bronski.

222. FS: *MP stands at attention as the floor suddenly jerks beneath him and takes him down while the camera tilts down to follow. We now see that he has been standing on a freight elevator.*

JUDGE (*off-screen*): A bar exclusively for . . .

223. JUDGE (*as 221*): . . . members of the American occupation forces?
INTERPRETER: (*Repeats.*)

224. MARIA (MCU, *left of center frame*): Sure, it was off-limits. Germans weren't supposed to go there.
JUDGE (*off-screen*): Exactly, Germans are not allowed to go there.

225. INTERPRETER (*as 221*): (*Repeats.*)

226. JUDGE (*as 224, off-screen*): Except for the girls who work there.
INTERPRETER (*off-screen*): (*Repeats. Maria giggles.*)
JUDGE (*off-screen*): And that in this role, you attached yourself to the deceased . . .

227. LS: *the entire scene from the rear of the "court room."*

INTERPRETER: (*Repeats.*)

The camera tracks laterally across the back of the room, showing Hermann getting up from his chair. He is wearing a long khaki coat and hat and has his hands in his pockets. The shot becomes MCU *as the camera pivots around Hermann, who is standing behind a booth in the back of the room. His hat brim shadows his eyes.*

JUDGE (*off-screen*): . . . and allowed yourself to be kept by him.
INTERPRETER (*off-screen*): (*Repeats.*)
JUDGE (*off-screen*): While your husband was a Russian prisoner of war, you, for low, egotistical reasons, entered into relations . . .
INTERPRETER (*off-screen*): (*Repeats.*)

228. JUDGE (*as 224, off-screen*): . . . with a man who could pay for your services with chocolate and silk stockings.

229. INTERPRETER (*as 221*): (*Repeats.*)

230. MCU: *Mother sits, expressionless, as loud, pounding music punctuates the interpreter's last line. There are abrupt pans from one face to another in the audience—Willi, with moist eyes; Betti, expressionless; Vevi, with a blank expression; and Mother. The pounding rhythm of the music blares with a sinister intonation throughout shot.*

231. JUDGE (*as 221*): And as soon as your husband . . .

232. MARIA (*as 224*): I was very fond of him.
     JUDGE (*off-screen*): Oh well, you seem to have a big heart.
     INTERPRETER (*off-screen*): (*Repeats.*)
     JUDGE (*off-screen*): Didn't you also just say the same thing about your feelings for your husband?
     MARIA: No.

233. JUDGE (*as 221*): No? (*He picks up the transcript.*)
     MARIA (*off-screen*): You don't have to look.

234. MARIA (*as 224*): You wouldn't understand the difference anyway. I was fond of Bill and I love my husband.

235. *As end of 227.* MCU: *Hermann puts his hand to his mouth quickly as if he were about to vomit.*

     INTERPRETER (*off-screen, in English*): You needn't look into the papers because you wouldn't understand it.

236. *As 221.*

     INTERPRETER (*in English*): She loved Bill and she loves her husband.
     JUDGE: Well . . .

237. *As 222.* FS: *the camera tilts back up as the freight elevator brings the MP and Bronski up into view.*

JUDGE (*off-screen*): . . . that is really a very fine difference.
INTERPRETER (*off-screen*): (*Repeats.*)

238. *As 235.*

JUDGE (*off-screen*): Oh, there's Mr. Bronski.

Bronski gets out of the elevator in LS *in the background as Hermann,* MCU, *turns around to face the dais. The camera pivots in the reverse direction from the end of 227.*[23]

HERMANN: You can stop your questioning.
JUDGE: I beg your pardon. (*He leans over into view to try to see Hermann.*)

239. HERMANN (*frontal* MCU): I killed the negro. (*To himself.*) Yes.

240. MLS: *the visitors' room in the prison. Hermann and Maria sit at tables separated by bars. On either side sit other prisoners facing their visitors. The camera is on Hermann's side of the bars. A guard paces in the background. The loud noise of all the visitors and prisoners talking at the same time is heard throughout the prison sequence.*

241. *Reverse angle from 240.* MS: *Hermann is seen from over Maria's shoulder; she is at* MCU *in the foreground. A guard also paces on Hermann's side of the bars. Hermann is dressed in a brown prison uniform. Maria is stylishly dressed.*

242. *Reverse angle from 241.* MS: *Maria is seen from over Hermann's shoulder; she is at* MCU *in the foreground.*

MARIA (*seen through the bars, yells*): The baby will be our baby and we'll explain everything to him later.

243. HERMANN (*as 241*): (*He says something that is indistinguishable over all the noise.*)

244. MARIA (*as 242*): What did you say?

245. HERMANN (*as 241, yells*): Later is a long time off.

246. HERMANN (*to Maria, as 242*): What are you going to do until then?

247. *As 241. Hermann strains to hear her answer.*

248. MARIA (*as 242, mouths words loud and clear*): I'll wait for you.

249. LS: *an overhead angle of the scene from Maria's side with the sharply defined shadow of the barred gate across the floor.*

    HERMANN: You're a young woman. You're a beautiful woman.

250. MARIA (*as 242*): I'm your wife.

251. HERMANN (*as 241*): (*His answer is unintelligible.*)

252. *As 242. Maria turns her ear toward him to hear better.*

253. HERMANN (*speaks up and repeats*): How are you going to (*the noise suddenly stops*) live?

254. MARIA (*as 240, continues yelling though all is now quiet*): Since I never learned how to do anything, the first thing I have to do is learn a job.

    They all turn to look at her. Hermann looks around from one side . . .

255. *As 241. . . . to the other.*

    MARIA: Then I'll go to work. Our life . . .

256. MARIA (*as 242, still yelling and sounding out each word though it is quiet*): . . . will start again when . . .

257. MARIA (*as 241*): . . . we're together again. (*Hermann smiles.*)

258. *As 240.* MLS: *Maria looks around her at everyone in the visitors' room watching and listening. They start to laugh.*

259. *As 242.* MS: *Maria, as Hermann laughs.*

260. *As 241.* MS: *Hermann, as Maria laughs.*

261. *As 249.* LS: *overhead angle, all continue to laugh.*

262. *As 260. Maria laughs.*

263. *As 259. Hermann laughs.*

264. LS: *Maria and the doctor walk away from the camera down a long, empty pedestrian tunnel. A loudspeaker announces train departures.*

   MARIA (*to the doctor, who is carrying her suitcase*): Shall I take it?

265. FS: *lateral tracking shot accompanies Maria and the doctor through the tiled corridor. Their shadows are cast on the wall behind them. Low music is heard and continues through 268.*

   DOCTOR: No, no. Things are hard enough for you as it is, Maria. I know how hard it is for a mother.
   MARIA: And it was a boy, too.
   DOCTOR: The Lord giveth and the Lord taketh away. Who knows—maybe it's better this way. The poor little thing wouldn't have had it easy in life anyway—or you either. (*They stop as Maria starts up the stairs to the platform.*)
   MARIA (*turns to face the doctor*): I never said I wanted to have it easy.

266. DOCTOR (MCU, *from Maria's point of view*): But with a black baby. Now he's a little black angel.

267. *Reverse angle from 266. Maria,* MCU, *is seen over the doctor's shoulder.*

   MARIA (*laughs*): A little black angel. That's nice. And will he always have flowers on his grave?

DOCTOR: I promise.

268. DOCTOR (*as 266*): What are you going to do when you go back home?

269. MARIA (*as end of 265*, MLS): I don't know yet. But I have a lot to do. I have to go now.
    LOUDSPEAKER: Attention, attention. Express train 309 to Heidelberg will be leaving shortly.

    Maria takes her suitcase and goes up the stairs as the doctor looks after her, leaning against the wall in a shaft of daylight.[24]

270. CU: *the back of Maria's head in the crowd inside a second-class car. A cacophony of train announcements, people yelling, and babies crying is heard through 272.*

271. MLS: *higher angle view of the crowded car.*

    LOUDSPEAKER: Attention, attention. Express train 309 is now leaving.

272. *As 270. Maria turns toward the camera with a wearied expression as a man rudely pushes past her.*

273. *Reverse angle from 272.* CU: *Maria is surrounded by the faces of other passengers who are also standing in the tightly packed car. She looks upwards at . . .*

274. CU: *. . . the sign: "To First Class."*

275. MARIA (*as 273, calls*): Leni!

276. *As 271. The cluttered car as Maria pushes her way through the crowd holding her suitcase above her head.*

    MARIA: Leni! Leni! Let me through. Leni! I have to find my little girl. Leni!

277. MCU: *Maria closes the door of the second-class car behind her. She is seen through a window that has the number "1" painted on it, seen from inside the first-class car.*

MARIA: Leni!

As she closes the second-class car door behind her, the noise abruptly stops, leaving only the sound of the train engine, which continues throughout the train sequence. She stands between the cars, leans back, and breathes a sigh of relief.

278. MLS: *the interior of the nearly empty first-class car is seen from Maria's point of view. The number "1" on the glass is prominent in the foreground.*

279. CONDUCTOR (*as 277, off-screen*): You don't need to look here. There's no little girl in here.
    MARIA (*turns*): What?

280. MCU: *the conductor is dressed in an elaborate uniform and has a black patch over one ear and another over one eye.*

CONDUCTOR: Your Leni, Madam.

281. *As 277, but from slightly deeper inside the first-class car. The conductor and Maria talk. The frame is divided by a door panel. Maria is seen through the window at right of center frame and the conductor is seen through the half-open door at left.*

MARIA: Oh. It's a boy, not a girl.
    CONDUCTOR: Then, why did you name him Leni?
    MARIA: I want a ticket for first class. How much is it?
    CONDUCTOR: It depends on how far you're going.
    MARIA (*hands him money*): That depends on how far I can get. (*The train whistle signaling departure is followed by the chugging sound of the train getting underway.*) I can go in now, can't I? (*She is juggling her suitcase in her arms.*)

CONDUCTOR: That takes care of it.

MARIA (*leaning her head on her suitcase so that only her head is now seen through the window in the door*): I don't travel first class very often.

CONDUCTOR (*making out her ticket*): Well, times change . . .

282. *As 278, but slightly closer, from Maria's point of view. Someone's elbow is now seen jutting into the empty aisle of the first-class car. Light plays across the floor as the train gets underway. The train whistle is heard.*

283. *As 277.* MCU: *Maria looks into the first-class car. The whistle is heard.*

CONDUCTOR: Take him for example. He's French, but his factory is here.
MARIA: French?

284. CONDUCTOR (*as 282, off-screen*): Well, half French anyway. Somebody like that can have whatever he wants. (*The rhythmic clatter of the train in motion continues throughout the remainder of the train sequence.*)

285. *Reverse angle from 284.* FS: *Maria and the conductor are seen at the end of a corridor from inside the first-class car.*

> MARIA: Hold this a minute. (*She hands the conductor her suitcase and goes through the door to the bathroom.*) Open the suitcase and turn around (*from off*).
> CONDUCTOR: Now?
> MARIA (*comes back into view in her bra and slip and takes a dress from her suitcase*): You can close it up now.

She goes back into the bathroom. He closes the suitcase, puts it on a rack, and opens his fare book.

286. CU: *the conductor's finger runs down a column in his fare book.*

> CONDUCTOR: Ever since I've lost one eye I can't read this anymore. Now is it 23 or 33 kilometers she has to pay for?

287. *Reverse angle from 285, as 282: a man's foot protrudes into the empty aisle.*

> MARIA (*off-screen*): Did you ever notice how tiny these restrooms are?

288. CU: *Maria's foot in black mesh hose slips into a platform slipper.*

> MARIA (*off*): I always thought that in first-class the bathrooms would have to be bigger since the people are fatter.

289. CONDUCTOR (*as 285*): Yeah. I didn't have any passengers until the currency reform, and now I even get people like you.

290. *As 282. Interior of the first-class car.*

291. MARIA (*as 289, reenters in the low-cut black dress she wore at the bar and with her hair swept to one side*): So?
> CONDUCTOR: Hey! Looks good to me. (*Maria kisses him.*) This doesn't happen to a guy every day.

292. MARIA (MCU, *from over the conductor's shoulder*): Now just put this dress back in the suitcase, and don't forget my purse. And then just . . . Thanks a lot. (*She winks at him as she turns away.*)

293. MCU: *Maria walks away from the conductor toward the camera as he watches her intently.*

294. FS: *Maria walks down the aisle of the first-class car as seen from the conductor's point of view. She stops at Oswald's seat and turns to face him.*

     MARIA (*in English*): I beg your pardon, Mister.

295. MARIA (*off-screen, in English*): May I ask you a question?
     OSWALD (MCU, *looking up*): Excuse me?[25]

296. ¾S: *Maria is seen from behind Oswald's seat. His leather coat is hanging in the foreground.*

     MARIA (*laughs*): Oh, you speak German. Since I heard you were French, I thought you'd speak English. I don't speak French myself.

297. OSWALD (*as 295*): Yes. I don't speak English, but I do speak German. What can I do for you?

298. MARIA (*as 296*): Just answer a question—a very simple question. Is this seat taken?

299. *As 295.* MCU: *Oswald, with an amused expression.*

300. OSWALD (*as 294,* FS *of Maria*): I don't think so . . . (*He stands.*)

301. *Reverse angle from 300.* MCU: *Oswald is seen from over Maria's shoulder.*

     OSWALD: . . . doesn't seem to be . . . (*congenially*).

302. *Reverse angle from 301.* MCU: *Maria is seen from over Oswald's shoulder as she smiles at him.*

303. *Reverse angle from 302.* MCU: *Oswald from slightly further away than 301.*

OSWALD: . . . please . . . (*He offers her his seat.*)

Tilt down slightly as she takes his seat and he sits opposite her.

MARIA: Thank you. That's very kind of you. I don't like to ride facing forward. (*She leans her head on her arm and closes her eyes as he resumes reading his book.*)

304. OSWALD (MCU, *looks up from his book at her*): Haven't we met somewhere before?

305. *Reverse angle from 304.* MCU: *Maria is seen from over his shoulder.*

MARIA (*her eyes are closed, indifferently*): I'm sure we haven't.
OSWALD: Sometime?
MARIA: Definitely not.

306. OSWALD (*as 304*): So. (*He looks down at his book, then up again at Maria.*)

307. *As 305.* MCU: *Maria.*

308. *As 304. Oswald's eyes return to his book.*

309. MLS: *the interior of the car from the opposite end as the conductor enters toward the camera and goes to Maria, carrying her suitcase.*

CONDUCTOR: Your ticket, and your bag.

310. *As 304.* MCU: *Oswald.*

MARIA (*off-screen*): You can put my suitcase . . .

311. MCU: *the conductor looks over at Oswald.*

MARIA (*off-screen*): . . . up there please.

312. *As 304. Oswald looks from the conductor to Maria (both are off-screen) and smiles at her.*

313. *As 311. The conductor puts her bag on an overhead rack as Maria looks over at Oswald.*

314. *As 304. Oswald smiles at her.*

315. CONDUCTOR (*as 311*): Have a pleasant trip, Madam.

316. MS: *Oswald is seen at eye level from over Maria's shoulder. He is well dressed in a conservative but obviously well tailored and expensive three-piece suit. He is a mature, distinguished looking man.*

   MARIA (*seen from behind, turns to the conductor, whose torso is seen in foreground left, and says in a low, sexy voice*): Thank you, Herr Conductor.

317. *As 305. Maria looks at Oswald.*

318. *As 304. Oswald looks up from his book at her.*

319. *As 305. Maria settles back in her seat and closes her eyes again.*

320. *As 316.* MS: *Oswald, as the conductor's torso passes through the aisle.*

OSWALD (*smiles*): I'm Dr. Karl Oswald.
MARIA (*hidden by his coat, which is in the foreground*): How nice.
OSWALD: Oswald Textiles.
MARIA: How nice.
OSWALD: Cigarette?
MARIA: No thank you. I don't smoke.
OSWALD: Do you like taking the train?
MARIA: Sometimes.
OSWALD: Gives you time to think.

321. MARIA (MCU, *her eyes are still closed, slowly, as if annoyed*): How
true. That's just what I've been trying to do for some time now. (*She
sighs.*)

322. *As 304. Oswald takes a deep breath, returns to his book, looks up again,
then back down at his book. The sound of a car door opening and closing
is heard.*

323. LS: *a black GI enters and comes down the aisle toward the camera to
¾S. He carries a flask and his shirttail is hanging out. He tosses his
duffle bag on the rack above the seat behind Oswald.*

GI (*loud, boisterously, in English throughout*): Hello, guys and dolls!
Glad to meet you. (*He takes a seat behind Oswald and is now seen
from the front in MS.*) Hate being alone on this fuckin' old train . . .

324. CU: *Maria opens her eyes and closes them again as if annoyed.*

GI (*off-screen*): . . . and goin' through this fuckin' old country.

325. MS, *low angle: Oswald. The GI's arm is jutting out from the seat
behind him.*

OSWALD: Sorry, I don't speak English.
GI (*turns around in his seat to face Oswald*): You're a bloody old
German, but anyway you could be my bloody good friend. (*He slaps
Oswald on the shoulder.*)
OSWALD (*nodding toward Maria*): The lady's asleep . . . maybe you
could . . .
GI (*looks toward Maria*): Hey, you got a nice little . . .

326. GI (*as 324, off-screen*): . . . lady, boy. (*She smiles with her eyes still
closed.*)

327. MS: *Oswald and the GI at eye level.*

GI (*smiling slyly*): She's your little lady, buddy? (*Oswald looks annoyed.*)
I'm lonely Richard, as my friends call me, and I haven't had a girl

for the last two weeks. (*Oswald sighs and looks more and more exasperated as the GI gets louder and more obnoxious.*) She really is a beauty, isn't she? Tell me (*to Oswald, confidentially*), what about fucking?

MARIA (*off-screen, in English*): To answer your question, I'm really the best you could ever be fucked by . . .

328. MARIA (*as 324, her eyes are still closed*): . . . although I doubt that you'll ever get the chance after I've kicked you in your bloody old prick that your bloody old balls would just drop off. (*She opens her eyes.*)

329. ¾S: *the GI comes out into the aisle as Maria stands up to confront him. Her back is to the camera.*

MARIA: And now, sir, you'd better fuck off immediately, otherwise I would be forced to get the military police to get you bloody old son of a bitch in jail.

GI (*staring at her in amazement*): Aye, aye, sir! (*He stumbles off to take a seat in the next car as Maria takes a seat across the aisle from Oswald.*)

OSWALD (*from his seat, facing the camera, very impressed*): That was . . . What did you say to him?

Loudspeaker announcements, the sound of the train coming to a stop and of doors opening continue to the end of the train sequence.

330. MARIA (MCU, *with her eyes closed*): Oh, I said that you were Karl Oswald, textiles, that you like traveling and having the chance to think.

331. MCU: *Oswald at left of center frame. The aisle and entrance to the next car are seen out of focus in the right side of the frame.*

OSWALD: Where did you learn to speak English so well?

332. MARIA (*as 330*): In bed.

333. OSWALD (*as 331*): Oh. (*He smiles and clears his throat.*)

The conductor's voice is heard from off-screen.

334. As 330. MCU: *Maria. The sounds of the stationmaster's whistle and the train departing the station are heard.*

335. LS: *the interior of the car is seen from the doorway between first and second class, with the sound of the train in motion.*

OSWALD: May I invite you to the dining car?
MARIA (*gets up*): Yes, that's a good idea. (*She reaches for Oswald's coat and holds it for him as he gets up and puts it on.*)

As they walk away from the camera, the GI comes toward them. Piano music starts low, becomes louder, and continues over the next shot.

OSWALD: I'd like to discuss something with you—business.
GI (*salutes Maria as she and Oswald pass him*): Excuse me, sir, may I get my baggage?
MARIA (*in English*): At ease.

GI plops down into her seat with his bag and drinks from a bottle of liquor.

336. *The interior of an automobile seen through the front windshield. Senkenberg is driving. Maria is beside him at left. Oswald is in the back seat, seen between Maria and Senkenberg. It is night and their faces are illuminated by the soft glow from the dashboard. Low music from the previous shot and ambient sounds of passing traffic are heard.*

OSWALD (*with finality*): And after three months, if we find we don't get along, then . . .
MARIA: Is there anyone else I have to answer to?

Blue-green light from the highway lamps passes over the windshield as they drive.

OSWALD: No one—we've already discussed that. You'll get along fine with Senkenberg and the other men.

MARIA: Aren't there any women?

SENKENBERG (*in a monotone*): Not in the management. At least not until now.

MARIA: How nice. Then I'll be the first.

SENKENBERG: We've gotten along fine up to now.

The music ends.

OSWALD: Senkenberg, that's not polite.

MARIA: Let him talk. Forewarned is forearmed. (*She turns toward Senkenberg.*)

SENKENBERG (*turns to face her*): Right. (*He adopts a tone of pleasant banter with Maria.*)

MARIA: Thank you. And what is my official title?

OSWALD: Let's say, "personal advisor."

MARIA: How personal?

SENKENBERG: That depends on the initiative and skills of the personal advisor.

MARIA (*to Senkenberg*): Indeed it does.

SENKENBERG: Indeed it does.

OSWALD: I've already told you about our dealings with the Americans.

SENKENBERG (*interjects*): But never forget that it all has to do with money. (*He looks toward Maria as Oswald looks at him.*)

MARIA (*smiles*): Whatever you meant by that, dear Senkenberg, I'm sure it's true, one way or another. (*She faces Senkenberg as Oswald looks at her, then at Senkenberg, then back to her.*)

OSWALD: Let him talk. You'll find out that Senkenberg's basically a good fellow, and so am I. (*Oswald smiles at Maria.*)

MARIA: Well, I'm not.[26]

The low sound of traffic continues over the beginning of the next shot.

337. MS: *Betti and Willi sit at the kitchen table set for dinner. The dialogue and the voice from the radio overlap on the sound track throughout this sequence.*

RADIO (*up*): Dr. Konrad Adenauer, chairman of the parliamentary council of advisors, chairman of the CDU . . .

WILLI (*in suit and tie*): Hermann will be sad about the baby.[27]
BETTI: Maybe not.

Maria crosses the room in the background.

MOTHER (*enters from the opposite direction to put a bowl of potato salad on the table*): Yes, he will be sad, very sad.
WILLI: Maria is doing the right thing.

Grandpa comes to the table.

MARIA (*from the background, then from off-screen*): It's nice of you to say that. But I don't even know if I'm doing the right thing myself. I just know that I have to do something.

The camera pans and tracks to follow Mother across the room to the foyer.

RADIO: . . . it was solidly voted down. So, it was reported by the *Frankfurter Rundschau*, with the words, . . .
BETTI (*now off-screen*): But you don't know anything about this job.
WILLI (*now off-screen*): She'll learn.
MOTHER (*as she carries Maria's suitcase into the foyer, then from off-screen*): But you can't just move out. Who's going to take care of you . . . and whatever . . .
MARIA (*as she appears in the doorway*): I have to have my own apartment and my own life. I still have so much to do before Hermann comes back. (*She takes a booklet out of a drawer in the coat rack.*)
RADIO: . . . "I want no army. We want no part of any new war, like the last one which spilled so much blood onto the battlefield. We've had enough killed. Many too many young people have already fallen. One only need recall the fact that in Germany today . . .

338. *As beginning of 337. Betti, Willi, and Grandpa are at the table.*

BETTI: I just don't understand you.

Betti gets up from the table and leaves the frame as Willi looks up from eating.

WILLI: Maria is different than you.
RADIO: . . . there are 160 women for every one hundred men.

339. MARIA (MCU, *at the coatrack in the foyer, chewing*): Your potato salad is delicious.
RADIO: I must, publicly, once and for all make the declaration that I am on principle opposed to the rearmament of Germany . . .
MOTHER (*off-screen*): I should hope so! I used two egg yolks for the mayonnaise.

Betti goes to Maria in the foyer as the camera shifts slightly to include Betti's reflection in the mirror on the coatrack.

RADIO: . . . and I am therefore also opposed to the establishment . . .

340. MLS: *Mother is in the bedroom, seen through two doorways from Maria's point of view.*

MOTHER: You wouldn't believe what you can get again these days. Are you going to be making enough money?
RADIO: . . . of a new German Wehrmacht." And so again today Adenauer made another clear statement of his position on this question.

341. MARIA (*as 339, in the same clothes she wore on the train*): I think so.
BETTI: What's he giving you as starting pay?

The camera tracks out in front of Maria, and Betti behind her, as they walk through the foyer.

MARIA (MCU): I'm not going to discuss that with him until he knows what I'm worth.
BETTI: And is he married, your Herr Oswald?
RADIO: And now a quote from Konrad Adenauer's speech of today. (*A recording is played.*) "If the contention has been made that the

rearmament of Germany will be undertaken under my authority,
I can only respond by saying . . .

Betti stops, facing the camera at MCU *as the camera stops. Maria passes
by the camera and out of the shot. Grandpa and Willi, both nibbling from
the bowl of potato salad that Willi is carrying, enter the foyer in the
background.*

MARIA (*off-screen*): Believe it or not, I didn't discuss that with him either.

342. MARIA (CU, *reverse angle from the end of 341*): Betti, I'm sorry. I guess
I've changed a lot. (*Mother, out of focus in the background, nods
assent.*)
RADIO: . . . that such a contention is an unfounded fabrication." In a
conversation with one of our correspondents, the CDU chairman said
later . . .

343. MCU: *Betti is in the right third of the frame. Willi is holding the bowl and
Grandpa is eating from it in* MLS *in background left.*

BETTI: I don't think so. Nobody would know from looking at you what
you've just been through.
RADIO: . . . "Such a position should be understood as that of a Christian
party. Either . . ." (*The radio commentary trails off as music comes
in over the end of this shot and continues over the beginning of the
next shot.*)
WILLI: She didn't mean it that way. (*He comes toward the camera, past
Betti, as Grandpa follows with his spoon.*)

344. *Reverse angle from 343. Willi and Grandpa pass the camera, which
is now at the opposite end of the foyer. As they go through the door to
Maria's bedroom at the near end of the foyer, Maria and Mother can be
seen through the doorway, at screen left, packing Maria's suitcase. A wall
masks off the right half of the screen.*

MARIA: Leave it, I'll do it myself.
MOTHER: But maybe it's true, what Betti says.

WILLI: What?

MOTHER: That maybe he's really only after Maria.

MARIA (*to Willi, ironically*): Now do you understand why I have to move out of here?

Mother comes toward the camera and goes off. Maria goes off, right, leaving Willi looking after her, holding the bowl of potato salad while Grandpa dips into it with his spoon.

RADIO (*with music*): Good evening, dear listeners. I bid you warm welcome again to today's special request concert. Again we have just seventy-five minutes . . .

345. MCU: *Willi turns from facing Maria toward Betti (off-screen) as Grandpa eats from the bowl.*

RADIO (*with music*): . . . to fill as many of your requests as we can.

346. *As end of 343.* MCU: *Betti, seen from Willi's point of view, returns his glance.*

RADIO (*with music*): So, we'll start right off with . . .

347. *As 345.* MCU: *Willi, from Betti's point of view, looks up at her again.*

RADIO (*with music*): . . . the tune, "When the Bells Are Gaily Ringing" . . .

348. LS: *the same prison visiting room as before, without the tables. The sun streams through two windows in the background. Hermann and Maria embrace, then stand together on the far side of the floor-to-ceiling bars that divide the room. A guard is in the background, out of focus, and the camera looks in on the scene through the bars.*

HERMANN: Were you very sad?

MARIA: Yes, but it made me feel better to know you'd be sad too. (*She lights a cigarette for him.*) And because I can tell you everything and because I'm glad you don't ask me what you don't need to.[28] (*Hermann moves away from Maria toward the bars.*) And because I'm going to make a home for us like you would have done.

349. HERMANN (MCU, *smoking, in a brown prison uniform*): There's a word in Greek for somebody you let work for you. In German it's something like "man's foot."

350. *Reverse angle from 349.* MS: *Maria is seen through the bars and over Hermann's shoulder.*

   MARIA: I'm your man's foot. No, that's not right. I'm not the part you stand on. Just say, I'm your wife.

351. HERMANN (*as 349*): It was a stupid comparison. You're Maria. And you're my wife.

352. MARIA (*as 350*): And we're not Greeks.
   HERMANN (*laughs*): No . . . unfortunately . . . can't say we are. But you're brave . . . (*He embraces her. They are seen through the bars.*)

353. HERMANN (MCU, *from over Maria's shoulder*): . . . and you're beautiful and you're smart. And I love you.

354. MLS, *through the bars: Maria and Hermann take a few steps, arm in arm, toward the bars.*

   MARIA: Maybe I'll change in the next few years.
   HERMANN: You've thought everything out very carefully.
   MARIA: Yes, maybe that's just it.
   HERMANN: You'll never change for me. (*Maria puts her arms around him.*)
   GUARD: Your time is up.

   Hermann walks to the door at screen left. Maria exits at right.

   MARIA: No it isn't.

355. MCU: *Maria turns back toward Hermann.*

356. *As end of 354. Hermann hesitates, looks back toward her.*

357. MARIA (*as 355, beaming*): My time is just beginning.

358. ¾S: *the tastefully and expensively decorated drawing room of Oswald's home.*[29] *An American businessman, standing in a doorway at left turns to face the camera and Oswald, who is off-screen, but whose reflection is seen in a gilt-framed mirror on the wall beside the American. The camera pans to follow the American into the room. At the same time, Oswald, now at screen right, enters the shot from the doorway where he had been standing.*

> AMERICAN (*in English, emphatically*): Will you please tell your gentlemen that I'm not quite sure they understood—we are selling machines! (*Pan to follow him as he paces around the room. The pan takes in a second American in a chair, who is taking notes with his back to the camera, and Maria, who is facing the camera. Oswald and the American cross each other's paths.*) If they want to knit their stockings by hand they should do so, but that's not our business!
>
> SENKENBERG (*seated, taking notes with his back to the camera in the background*): What did he say?
>
> MARIA (*her appearance and attire have become increasingly sophisticated, tasteful, and expensive*): He emphasized again that Pency only supplies complete plant machinery and not individual parts.

A pan follows Maria across the room to the doorway where Oswald was originally standing. Oswald reenters the frame after her.

> SENKENBERG: I thought he said something about hand-work.
>
> OSWALD (MLS): Senkenberg, we've got enough problems as it is. (*He walks out of the room.*)
>
> SENKENBERG: I'm not trying to make problems. I'm just trying to make sure we don't have any. If we're going to be able to finance this, we can't afford more than two of these SE-machines. We're . . .

*The off-screen sound of the pneumatic drill is heard for the first time
and continues, low and occasionally, throughout this sequence. It sounds
very much like the antiaircraft gun heard during the bombardment in the
opening sequence.*

OSWALD (*as he reenters and crosses the room*): "We're a solid medium-
sized firm and we're not gamblers." I know that, Senkenberg. I already
know it by heart, but that's not getting us anywhere.

*Pan left to follow Maria to the doorway seen at the beginning of this
shot. The American leaves the adjacent room from which Oswald has
just reentered, passing Maria as he crosses the conference room from
the opposite direction.*

MARIA: Sometimes you have to take a risk.
SENKENBERG (*off-screen*): We're not at the racetrack here.
MARIA: Yes, yes, I know. (*She turns around at the door and walks back
into the room as the camera pans right to follow her.*) It's just that the
Americans are getting more and more nervous. We have to tell them
something. (*She leans over Senkenberg's chair.*)
OSWALD (*standing across from Senkenberg*): You're exactly right. Well,
Senkenberg.
MARIA (*in English*): Just a few seconds, gentlemen, we're just coming to
a decision. (*She crosses to the piano at right.*)
OSWALD (*walks to the left doorway with his hand on Senkenberg's
shoulder as the camera pans left to follow*): Senkenberg, now just try
for once in your life not to be Senkenberg, but Napoleon instead, or
Blücher if that suits you better.
SENKENBERG (¾s, *standing in the doorway with the mirror at screen
left*): Alright, three SE-machines—if we take out a loan on the stock,
and if the ERP credit is available, and if . . .
OSWALD (*impatiently*): If, if! Of course, if—that's our business. (*Oswald
moves off-screen.*) We're businessmen, not bookkeepers.
SENKENBERG: I beg your pardon, I am a bookkeeper! (*He walks out of
the shot as his reflection momentarily appears in the mirror.*)
OSWALD (*off-screen*): I'm sorry. I was just trying to say that taking a risk
. . . ach . . .

The American reenters the room through the doorway on the right as seen in the mirror. The camera pans fast from the American's reflection to the others and across the room as the American enters from the adjacent room through the doorway at right.

AMERICAN: Just to tell you the very truth, gentlemen, . . .

359. AMERICAN (¾S, *his back to the camera; he then turns toward the camera and the others, emphatically*): . . . we are getting tired of this!

360. *Reverse angle from 359. Now only the three Germans are seen from the American's point of view.*

SENKENBERG: What did he say?
MARIA: He summed up our previous negotiations and . . .
SENKENBERG: I heard something about him being tired.
MARIA: He said that too—he's fed up.

The camera dollies back a bit to include the American as Maria approaches him. MCU: *Maria, from over the American's shoulder.*

OSWALD (*in the background*): So what do we do now? Looks like we've bitten off more than we can chew.

Maria stands staring at the American with a flirtatious smile on her face.

OSWALD (*turns toward Senkenberg*): Maybe this deal really is too big for us. We have to forget about nylon, and just offer German women woven stockings. (*He crosses the frame in the background.*)
MARIA (*still staring coyly at the American*): Do you mind if I say something?
OSWALD: Of course, go ahead.

361. *Reverse angle from 360.* MCU: *the American is looking at Maria with interest.*

MARIA (*turns her head toward Oswald*): You go on into the kitchen, have a cognac, and give me half an hour in here.

362. MCU: *Oswald looks at her with a surprised, but admiring, expression.*

   SENKENBERG (*to Oswald from the background*): This is getting
      ridiculous. If I may point out, Frau Braun, you're now going beyond
      matters of translation.
   OSWALD: Please, Senkenberg.

363. *Reverse angle from 362. Oswald's torso is seen in foreground left. Maria
   and the American are seen in the doorway in* MLS.

   MARIA: Herr Senkenberg is right. I don't know a thing about business.
      But I do know something about the German woman and the difference
      between nylon and cotton. (*Pan to follow her across the room as the
      American watches her.*) I understand quite a lot about the future. You
      might say I'm a specialist in it. (*Pan to follow her in the opposite
      direction.*) And what can it hurt, if the deal's off anyway?

   Camera dollies back to take in all four men in FS *facing Maria, who
   is now out of the frame.*

   MARIA (*off-screen*): You can always say no at the last minute.
   OSWALD: That's the first constructive idea I've heard this whole
      wasted day.
   SENKENBERG: With all due respect, Herr Oswald . . .

364. CU: *Maria turns toward them.*

   SENKENBERG (*off-screen*): . . . Frau Braun really has no experience
      whatever in our field.
   OSWALD (*off-screen*): Then it's about time she got some.

   Maria smiles.

365. LS: *the dining room of Oswald's home, seen through the doorway from
   the adjacent drawing room where the conference was held.*[30] *A piano is
   in the drawing room in the foreground to the left of the doorway. Oswald,
   Maria, and Senkenberg are seated at the dinner table. A piano concerto
   is heard throughout the dinner sequence.*

OSWALD: Maria Braun, you have well served the good of the firm. (*He toasts with Maria.*) Come on Senkenberg, you too!

SENKENBERG: I'd drink to the good of the firm in five years—if it still exists then.

OSWALD: Senkenberg, you're such a bore. It's no fun being with you. You're the best accountant in the world and the smartest financial adviser, but you don't have a mark's worth of imagination—(*Oswald gets up from the dining table and comes forward to* FS *into the drawing room*) a Reichsmark.

MARIA (*to Senkenberg*): I don't take that as an insult.

366. MARIA (MCU, *profile, left of center frame*): In your profession, imagination would be a liability.

367. MCU: *Senkenberg's profile.*

MARIA (*off-screen*): Somebody has to keep an eye on the money, be responsible for financial planning and getting credit.

368. *As 366. Maria looks up to face the camera.*

369. *As 367. Senkenberg continues eating.*

370. MS: *Oswald lights a cigarette.*

MARIA (*to Oswald*): Herr Oswald, where would you and your firm be without your Senkenberg? At the racetrack.

As Maria talks, the camera tilts down from Oswald and pans left slightly to Maria at the table, seen through the doorway, with Oswald's torso in foreground right.

OSWALD (*laughs and goes into the dining room*): Well said, eh Senkenberg?

The camera dollies back in toward the doorway and pivots for a slightly different angle on the dining room scene in MLS.

SENKENBERG (*beaming*): I'd like to drink to Frau Braun. If it were up to her, we'd be playing the horses for sure, but without her, we'd probably be in the cemetery. (*He toasts Maria.*) Now I'm going to say good night. I'm very tired. It's been an exhausting day and, anyhow . . . (*He gets up from the table.*)

OSWALD: And anyhow . . . you want to go off and figure out when we're going to go bankrupt. But seriously, we two survived the war, and the three of us are going to survive the peace!

SENKENBERG: Excuse me, Herr Oswald, but the company had to get through the war and the years before it without you. (*Oswald looks affected by the remark. He turns away from them as Senkenberg comes forward into the drawing room and raises his voice.*) The only contact between you and your company was through your bank account. Not that I hold it against you (MS, *Senkenberg standing beside the piano in foreground left*), especially since subsequent political developments confirmed your feelings and made your cowardice seem like wise foresight and humanitarianism.

Senkenberg tensely plays with a spoon and finally throws it down on the piano. Maria, in FS, gets up from the table and turns to Senkenberg, then to Oswald, who is facing away in the background in LS. Senkenberg goes back into the dining room.

SENKENBERG (*to Oswald*): Anyway, I'm glad that the company can count on you again, Herr Oswald, like before '33. (*He turns toward Maria.*) And not least, Frau Braun, I'm glad to have found in you such a good and unorthodox opponent. (*He bows, she extends her hand, he kisses it, and leaves.*)

MARIA: Don't be angry. I think he really likes you.

OSWALD: I'm not angry at all. In a way, he's quite right. (*He finally turns around to Maria.*) Maybe not completely, but . . . he really does love the company—with all his heart. (*He walks into the drawing room.*) I did leave him alone for those "thousand years." (*He leaves the frame. Maria is still facing Oswald's original position, and away from the camera.*) I dreamed up my own world, where I could live a comfortable life—(*he reenters the frame and sits at the piano*) but now . . .[31]

371. OSWALD (MCU): Looking at the riskiness of this investment from a purely business standpoint, I couldn't agree with him more. But I'm more of a gambler than he is. (*He plays a measure of the same piece heard throughout this sequence. Each measure he plays is then echoed on the soundtrack.*) But, all things considered, I think we're going to have to wait for a miracle.

372. MARIA (MCU, *finally turns toward Oswald*): I'd rather make the miracles than wait for them.

373. OSWALD (*as 371*): You're really an extraordinary person.

374. *The camera is now just inside the entrance of a study that adjoins the drawing room. Oswald gets up from the piano and goes to Maria in the dining room deep in the background.*

    OSWALD: Shall we have another drink?
    MARIA: No. I'd like to sleep with you. Where's the bathroom?
    OSWALD (*pours a drink*): First door on the right.

    She goes off, right.[32]

375. CU, *low lighting: the camera pans to follow Oswald's hand caressing Maria's naked body.*[33]

    MARIA: I'd like you to go on calling me Frau Braun.
    OSWALD (*surprised*): Alright . . . if you wish . . . You know . . . I was really surprised, when you . . .
    MARIA: Didn't you want to?
    OSWALD: Yes, very much.
    MARIA: So did I, and I want my relationships to be clear cut.
    OSWALD: Do we have a relationship?
    MARIA: Yes, a clear-cut one.

376. MLS: *Maria's office. Her secretary is seen through a doorway on the right side of the frame. Maria is seen through a square opening in the wall on the left that separates her office from the secretary's. The daylight coming*

*in through the window in the background emphasizes the stark white walls
and casts a shadow of the window frame on the wall of Maria's office. The
incessant rhythm of the pneumatic drill is heard, low, throughout the
office sequence.*

MARIA: The taxi was from the apartment to the train station. You should
have the receipts. Senkenberg paid. Taxi back from the station to the
apartment, then the hotel—that's all.
SECRETARY: And breakfast—anything to deduct? (*There is a knock at
the door.*) Come in. Hello, Herr Oswald.
OSWALD (*enters from the left*): Hello, Frau Braun, Frau Ehmke. Am I
disturbing you?
MARIA (*turns toward him*): Not at all. Hello, Herr Oswald.
OSWALD: I just wanted to . . .
SECRETARY: I was just finishing here. (*She gets up from her desk.*)
OSWALD: We need to work on the conference a little more.
SECRETARY (*gathers her papers*): I'll be in Herr Senkenberg's office.
(*She leaves.*)
OSWALD (*slyly*): Ehmke and Senkenberg—the great conspirators. (*To the
secretary.*) Tell Herr Senkenberg he should come by my office at about
four.
SECRETARY (*off-screen*): Alright.
OSWALD (*low*): And you too, Frau Braun—(*tenderly*) you too, Maria.

*As Maria comes toward the doorway, he meets her there and starts to
embrace her. She walks past him to her desk in foreground left, at ¾s.*

MARIA (*formally*): At four, Herr Oswald?
OSWALD (*in the doorway*): I just dropped by . . . I wanted to see you,
privately.

377. MARIA (MCU, *from Oswald's point of view*): This is no place for private
talks. This is an office in your firm.
OSWALD (*off-screen*): Alright, fine.

378. OSWALD (MCU): The company's closed on the weekend. Will you come
with me to the country?
MARIA (*off-screen*): I'm sorry, but . . .

379. MARIA (*as 377*): I want to visit someone on Saturday.

380. OSWALD (MS, *in a two-shot with Maria*): You're . . .
    MARIA: I am how I am. (*She turns to work at her desk.*)

    Dolly in slightly to MS of Maria, facing the camera, in foreground left. Oswald goes into the secretary's office in background right.

    OSWALD: You were different last night.
    MARIA (*puts paper in the typewriter and starts typing*): Last night I was Maria Braun who wanted to sleep with you. Today I'm Maria Braun who'd like to do some work for you.
    OSWALD: Maybe you're afraid that people will think I'm having an affair with you.
    MARIA: I don't care what people think. I do care what you think. (*Oswald looks exasperated and confused and turns away.*) And I don't want you to think that "you're having an affair with me." The truth is, I'm having one with you.
    OSWALD: But . . .
    MARIA: It is true that I feel something for you, that you're my boss, and that I don't want to complicate matters for your sake. I want to know at all times exactly who I am dealing with—either with you or with my employer.
    OSWALD (*formally, in French*): Good, I can respect your point of view. (*He walks out of sight.*)
    MARIA: Now I'd like to talk about my salary.
    OSWALD (*off-screen*): How much were you thinking of?

381. *Reverse angle from 380. ¾ S: Maria goes into the secretary's office as he comes forward to meet her from a door in the background.*

    MARIA: I have to earn a lot of money in the next few years.
    OSWALD: Don't we all.
    MARIA: But I have a reason, Herr Oswald.
    OSWALD: Oh?
    MARIA: I think you should be able to estimate what my work is worth to you. And that's exactly what I want—nothing more.

OSWALD (*moves closer to her*): Then I'll have to decide how much you're worth to me.

382. MARIA (MCU, *over Oswald's shoulder*): Not me—my work.

383. OSWALD (MS, *reverse angle from 382, ironically*): Yes, of course—your work, Frau Braun. I'm an old man, and it takes a while for things to dawn on me, but I'll do my best, and then . . .
    MARIA (*interrupts him by putting her hand to his mouth*): Shhh. Don't say anything now. Please.
    OSWALD: Yes I will. (*He embraces and kisses her.*)[34] What about Saturday?
    MARIA: I'm afraid you're going to have to go to the country all by yourself. (*She goes off. Low background music begins.*)

384. LS: *Maria and Hermann sit at a table in a small room in the prison. An archway frames the shot. A guard stands in FS in foreground right. Low background music is heard throughout the prison sequence.*

385. *Reverse angle from 384.* MS: *Maria is seen from behind Hermann's back with a guard in FS in background right.*

    MARIA: Why shouldn't I tell him I've slept with another man? After all, he knows I love you.
    HERMANN (*somewhat upset*): That's not the same thing.
    MARIA: That's just it. Because it's not the same, it won't hurt him to hear it. And because it's not the same, I want you to know about it. If it were the same thing, then I wouldn't be here at all.

386. HERMANN (MCU, *at left of center frame, from Maria's point of view*): Is he handsome?
    MARIA (*off-screen*): He's handsome, . . .

387. MARIA (MCU, *from Hermann's point of view*): . . . he's kind, and he would never hurt me. And I want you to know that I wanted to sleep with him and that I wasn't forced to. And since he's my employer and I'm dependent on him, . . .

388. *Reverse angle from 387.* MS: *Hermann is seen from behind Maria's back.*

> MARIA: . . . I wanted to take the initiative, so I could be in control, at least in this.
> HERMANN: Is that how it is between people outside? So cold?

389. MARIA (*as 385*): I don't know how it is with other people. It's a bad time for emotions, believe me. But I like it better this way, so nothing can ever really hurt me.

The music ends.

390. MLS: *the two sit at the table at left.* MCU: *keys are being jangled in the guard's hands in foreground right.*[35]

391. ¾S: *Oswald, holding flowers and candy, stands in the hallway of Maria's apartment building, waiting for her to come home. As Maria comes into the hallway and starts upstairs, Oswald steps back behind a wall, then calls her. The lighting is low.*

> OSWALD: Maria. (*Pan to her on the stairs.*)
> MARIA (*seen between the banister rails*): I thought you were going to the country. (*Pan to follow her downstairs.*)
> OSWALD: The flowers are wilted and the chocolates melted.
> MARIA (*takes the gifts and throws them into the trash*): You have no claim on me.

She then looks at Oswald, smiles slightly, and hurries upstairs as he follows. Dissolve.

392. *Tilt down to follow Maria, in* MS, *dressed only in a sheet as she comes down a loft ladder in her apartment. Pan as she crosses to Oswald, who is wearing his leather coat as a bathrobe, at the kitchen table. The lighting is low.*

> OSWALD (*good-naturedly*): I'm acting like a schoolboy.
> MARIA: Because you are a schoolboy—a dear, dumb schoolboy.

*The camera pulls back slightly as Maria goes to Oswald in the
background. They are seen through a doorway in the foreground.*

OSWALD: Why didn't you want to come to the country with me?
MARIA: Because you would have proposed to me.
OSWALD: Right, and that's why . . .

393. OSWALD (MCU, *from behind, then he turns toward the camera and
Maria*): How did you know?

394. MARIA (*as end of 392*): Because that's what schoolboys do. (*He looks
away from her, sullenly.*) I'm sorry. You meant it seriously and I won't
make fun of you. I should have told you before that I'll never marry
you. (*Dolly in slowly through the doorway to* MCU *as Maria sits in
his lap and gives him a quick kiss.*) But I'll be your lover if you want.

*Oswald embraces and kisses her as the shot fades out and music comes in
and continues over the first few frames of the next shot.*

395. *Fade in on a makeshift, windowless conference room in the textile factory.*
LS, *high angle, of a cluttered conference table with many people standing
around and the clamor of many voices talking at the same time.*[36]

396. MS: *Willi is at left. Senkenberg is at center frame.*

SENKENBERG: Herr Klenze, I find these agitational tones your union is
leveling at us openly offensive.

They move into a back room.

WILLI: Well, you're just getting back what you've been dishing out. It's
no wonder, the way you play the lord of the manor.
SENKENBERG: Herr Klenze, our Minister of Finance himself said . . .

*They walk through the building as the camera tracks laterally along
with them. They are occasionally hidden behind a wall and behind other
people who are standing around talking in pairs and small groups.*

WILLI: Yeah, yeah, I know—we're all in the same boat. The only difference is, the boat belongs to you and we have to row it—your lovely boat. And it seems to make you mad to have to pay us decently to do it. (MCU *as Willi and Senkenberg and the camera movement stop.*)

MARIA (*appears over Willi's shoulder*): I think the meeting's been adjourned for the day. We can continue our argument next week.

WILLI (*still looking at Senkenberg*): I'm sure we will. Though there are some people who never seem to learn. Come on, let's go out for a drink, Maria.

397. *Reverse angle from 396.* MS: *the three are seen from the opposite side of a window and are framed, even as they move about, in the window panes.*

SENKENBERG (*surprised*): You . . . know each other personally?

MARIA: Very personally, in fact.

SENKENBERG: God knows, you could never guess it from the past three hours. (*He walks toward the window.*)

MARIA (*secretively; the shadow of the window frame crosses her face and Senkenberg's*): Because I'm a master of deception. A capitalist tool by day, and by night an agent of the proletarian masses. (*To Senkenberg in a tone of mock seductiveness.*) The Mata Hari of the economic miracle! (*She sighs.*) Ah, Senkenberg! Why are your ideas about people so much duller than you are. (*She turns to Willi.*) Let's go Willi.

Senkenberg looks after them as they go off. A reporter approaches him.

REPORTER: Do you mind if I ask you a few questions?

SENKENBERG (*nods toward Maria*): Ask Frau Braun.

REPORTER: Is she empowered to speak for the management?

SENKENBERG: Frau Braun is our spokesman.

REPORTER: I see. Thank you. (*He goes off.*)

A pan right takes in Willi and Maria talking in ¾s.

MARIA: I don't have much time, but I'll take you home.

WILLI: Great. Shall we have a drink first?

REPORTER (*appears and interrupts them*): Do you mind if I ask you a few questions?

MARIA: The demands of the union as presented here by Herr Klenze (*nods toward Willi*) can only be described as blackmail.

Senkenberg enters behind the reporter and giggles at Maria's remark.

MARIA (*to Willi*): I'm going to the bathroom. (*She goes off as Senkenberg comes forward.*)
REPORTER: Do you agree with these harsh words? (*Pan slightly to reframe the reporter and Senkenberg in* MCU *as Willi goes off after Maria.*)
SENKENBERG: Obviously. Do you have a different opinion?
REPORTER (*with a shy smile*): I don't have any opinion. I'm a journalist.

398. ¾S, *low angle: Maria joins Willi on a stairway landing in foreground right.*[37]

WILLI: You've really made it, kid.
MARIA: Funny, isn't it? Us sitting across from each other and tearing each other apart. (*Tilt and pan to follow them downstairs.*)
WILLI: It's better than this "all in the same boat" crap.
MARIA: How's Betti?

The camera now takes in Senkenberg, who is standing on the next landing down, watching unnoticed as they pass.

WILLI (*who is momentarily out of sight*): Why do you ask?
MARIA (*also momentarily out of sight*): Why? Why, is something wrong?

Tilt down further to include them again in MS, *high angle, on the third landing down. A beam cuts diagonally across the foreground. It divides the frame with Senkenberg at right and Willi and Maria at left, until the camera tilts to exclude Senkenberg. Their shadows are seen on the wall of the dim stairwell.*

WILLI: No, nothing is wrong. It's just that I need somebody I can talk to, and I've got somebody that cooks for me.
MARIA: She does what she learned how to do.

WILLI: Of course. She does what she's learned how to do. But she never learned what's important.

Maria faces the camera as it tilts to an even more acute high angle on them.

WILLI: She's very different from you. And she's not happy all the time, like you are.

MARIA (*embraces Willi*): I have to be happy for Hermann—so he has something he can be happy about and that he's proud of. After all, a man can't be happy about an unhappy wife. Or be proud of her either.

WILLI: You put it very nicely.

A phone rings. Maria looks upstairs, then sticks her tongue out and says, "Bahhh."

MARIA: That was nice too—what you said before. "You've really made it, kid."

The phone rings again. She looks up again, while Senkenberg's shadow moves down the wall.

MARIA: I've made it—I like that.

Willi and Maria leave as the phone continues to ring. Pan and tilt to Senkenberg on the stairwell above. The strong lines of the beam, the staircase, and the shadows of the steps appear to enclose him. He turns at the end of the shot as if he were looking at something that is off-screen.

399. LS, *high angle: Maria enters and talks to a man in a dark coat and hat—the lawyer—in the prison stairwell.*[38] *The composition of the shot is almost a mirror image of the end of 398. Their small figures are completely confined in a network of rigid lines. There is the sound of typing.*[39]

MARIA: It's no use, Dr. Klaus. He's so sad again today—(*there is the sound of a heavy gate swinging shut and slamming closed*)—so sad and so terribly hopeless. (*She puts her head on his shoulder and cries.*)[40]

LAWYER: Don't worry, Frau Braun. I told you before (*a guard comes through the door*), I can help your husband without seeing him. Please believe me.

Their voices echo.

MARIA: Money is no object. I have enough—no matter what.
LAWYER: In this situation, it's not primarily a matter of money. One has to proceed with utmost caution. (*He starts downstairs.*)

400. MLS, *high angle: the lawyer starts downstairs while talking to Maria, who is still on the landing above. The shot is nearly a reverse angle from 399, and is also very densely composed and confining.*

LAWYER: The right word to the right person at the right time can tip the scales of justice one way or the other. (*He is seen, with his oversized shadow, behind a wire mesh banister as he turns toward Maria.*)

401. MS: *Maria starts down the stairs.*

LAWYER (*now off-screen*): But it will require discretion and delicacy.

MARIA (*pan to follow her down the stairs*): I know that if anyone can help him, you can. (*Her shadow is also seen as she joins him on the landing below in* ¾s.)

LAWYER: But . . .

MARIA: Yes, it's true.

402. MCU, *slight low angle: Maria and the lawyer are seen through the meshwork banister.*

MARIA: You'll help him, and me. I know you will. But how much longer do we have to wait?

LAWYER: That depends entirely on the political situation—eight days . . . eight years.

Low music begins over the last few frames of this shot.

403. MS: *Maria lounges on her bed. She is wrapped only in a sheet and is wearing the same red hat she wore in the previous sequence. She is facing the camera at screen left. Oswald enters, out of focus, in LS on the right. Low music continues throughout this sequence in Maria's apartment. The lighting is low.*[41]

OSWALD: I don't want to know where you were today after the meeting, only why you don't want to tell me.

MARIA: I went to lunch with Willi Klenze.

404. OSWALD (MCU, *dressed in a robe*): Why didn't you just say so? (*He takes a pill.*)

MARIA (*off-screen*): Because it's a lie.

OSWALD: I despise you.

405. MARIA (MCU, *from Oswald's general direction*): I like you. Why don't you love me?

406. *Reverse angle from 403. Oswald is in the foreground. Maria, seen through the kitchen doorway, is on the bed, out of focus in the background.*

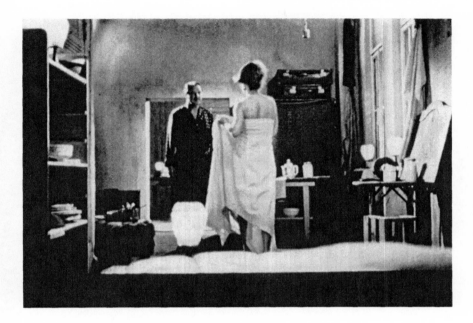

OSWALD: Because you lie to me.
MARIA: But this time I'm not lying.
OSWALD: You're making me lose my mind.

407. OSWALD (*as 404*): Alright, once more . . . I don't want to know where
you're going tomorrow. (*Dolly out as he comes toward her in* MCU.)

408. MARIA (*as 405*): Good. Thank you. (*She smiles seductively.*)

409. OSWALD (*as 406, he is now in the doorway at* MLS): Let me finish.
MARIA: Why should I? (*She gets up to meet him in the middle of the room.*)
OSWALD: What do you mean why?
MARIA: Why don't you want to know where I'm going tomorrow, really?
You don't care about me, I despise you.
OSWALD: I love you. Why don't you love me too?
MARIA (*drops the sheet and is wearing only her hat as he embraces and
kisses her, and the music ends*): I thought we were having dinner first.

OSWALD: A good businessman can always be recognized by his ability to adapt quickly to circumstances.

410. LS: *Maria comes out of her apartment building and gets into her car, a VW "beetle." Parked across the street is a large, black, expensive car. It is daytime. As a pan follows her car off left, Oswald is revealed in the foreground, watching, from the driver's seat of the black car. There is loud sinister music at Oswald's appearance.*[42]

411. *Betti is standing outside the door of her apartment. She is seen from below. A flight of stairs cuts across the left side of the shot.*[43] *She seems distressed as blaring music from 410 continues. She starts downstairs, looking around suspiciously, then stops and leans against the wall, looking down with apprehension. Footsteps are heard.*

BETTI (*calls*): Maria? (*A pan follows her glance down the stairwell to Maria.*)
MARIA (MCU, *high angle*): Betti.
BETTI: Did you come to see me?

412. FS, *low angle: Maria goes upstairs to meet Betti on the landing at* MLS.

MARIA: Why? Shouldn't I come over?
BETTI: Of course you can. But why didn't you call?
MARIA: Because I want to see you and touch you.
BETTI (*embraces Maria*): You're crying. Maria, what's the matter?

The sound of the pneumatic drill begins and continues throughout the sequence on the stairs.

413. MARIA (MCU, *from over Betti's shoulder*): I'm crying. What do you know, I'm crying. (*She smiles.*) And I don't have any idea why.

414. *Reverse angle from 413.* MCU: *Betti is seen over Maria's shoulder.*

MARIA: And now *you're* crying.
BETTI: I never cry—never. I never cry.

415. MARIA (*as 413, Betti puts her head on Maria's shoulder and cries*):
Come with me.
BETTI: Why?
MARIA: You'll see.⁴⁴

416. MLS: *the same small prison room in which Maria last visited Hermann,
but seen from a slightly different angle so that several cell doors can be
seen on the right. Oswald is waiting there with his back to the camera.
There is the sound of a door opening and closing.*

417. MCU: *at the sound Oswald suddenly turns toward the camera with an
anxious expression.*

418. LS: *Hermann is led into the room as seen from Oswald's point of view.*

419. *As 417. Oswald looks intently toward the camera.*

420. *As 418.* FS *as Hermann comes forward with a guard behind him.*

421. *As 417. Oswald still looking.*

422. *Hermann, with his back to the camera, stands facing Oswald. The guard's
torso is in foreground right as Oswald takes a few steps toward Hermann
from the background.*

OSWALD: My name is Karl Oswald.

423. MCU: *Hermann, slightly off center frame, from Oswald's point of view.*

424. MCU: *Oswald, slightly off center frame, from Hermann's point of view.*

425. HERMANN (*as 423, expressionless*): Hermann Braun.

426. OSWALD (*as 424*): I'm a friend of your wife.

427. HERMANN (MCU, *seen over Oswald's shoulder in foreground left, with a
guard in ³⁄₄s in background right*): I know, what do you want?

428. OSWALD (*as 424*): I wanted to meet the man . . .

429. *As 423.* MCU: *Hermann.*

OSWALD (*off-screen*): . . . she loves.

430. *Oswald, as 424.*[45]

431. MLS: *Maria and Betti are climbing the stairs of an old, bombed-out building.*[46] *They are seen through an opening where a window once was. The pneumatic drill sound is louder now, recalling the sound of the antiaircraft guns heard over the opening sequence.*

432. MLS: *the two women are seen through a doorway in the left third of the screen. The shabby interior wall beside the doorway masks off the rest of the frame. The pneumatic drill sound continues.*

MARIA: Do you remember?
BETTI: Why aren't they rebuilding around here anymore?
MARIA: At least they treat children better nowadays.

Tilt down slightly as the two women, dressed up in high heels and hats, sit down on a ledge and Maria puts her arm around Betti.

433. MARIA AND BETTI (MCU, *they sing*): "Don't cry for love. There's more than just one man in life. There's plenty of men to go around. And I love any one that pleases me."

434. LS: *Maria and Betti are seen from behind a partially destroyed wall. Pan left slightly along the broken top of a wall in the foreground as they continue to sing. Then a tilt up reveals that they are sitting in a large, open room with no roof. The pneumatic drill is heard again.*

435. *A room in Oswald's house as Oswald pours a drink in* MLS *and talks with Senkenberg, who is at* FS.

SENKENBERG: Did I understand you correctly? You want me to put that in writing?

OSWALD: Yes.

SENKENBERG: You can't be serious.

OSWALD: Yes I am, Senkenberg. Would I joke about something like this? (*A pan follows Oswald to the foreground as Senkenberg goes to get a drink.*)

SENKENBERG: You're crazy. The both of you.

436. *Reverse angle from 435.* MCU: *Oswald is seen from Senkenberg's direction. He takes his coat out of the closet. His shadow is seen behind him.*

OSWALD: No, we're both quite sane. (*Oswald puts on his coat.*) Because . . . I've got maybe two, three years left, Senkenberg. You know that very well. And I want to live in the time I've got left.

437. SENKENBERG (¾S, *seen from Oswald's direction*): An idea like this could only occur to a sick mind. (*He drinks.*) Your brain's in a lot worse shape . . .

438. ¾S: *Oswald is seen from Senkenberg's direction, including Oswald's oversized shadow.*

SENKENBERG (*off-screen*): . . . than your liver.

OSWALD: I'm sure you're right, Senkenberg (*pan and dolly back slightly as Oswald closes the closet door and opens up a wash basin*), but I've got life, adventure, the key to the universe.

439. SENKENBERG (MCU): Um hm. And a slight case of madness.

440. OSWALD (MS): No. But maybe I live in a place with that name— madness. (*Pan and tilt up to Senkenberg in* MCU *in the foreground. He is drinking from the bottle as Oswald leaves.*)

441. MCU: *Maria dials at a public phone.*

442. LS: *Oswald is seen, through the dining room doorway, in the drawing room. His head is down on his desk and his hand is on the phone receiver. The left side of the shot is masked off by the dining room wall,*

*and a second doorway into another room is seen in the background. The
moment the phone rings, he picks it up and answers, "Yes."*

443. MARIA (*as 441*): You didn't come yesterday—is anything wrong?

444. OSWALD (MS, *dressed in a coat and scarf, he is at left of center, with the
second doorway in the background at right*): No, nothing's wrong.
Everything is fine.

445. MARIA (*as 441*): Got a hangover?

446. OSWALD (*as 444*): Yes, a bit.

447. MARIA (*as 441*): You know today is my mother's birthday?

448. OSWALD (*as 444*): Yes, shall I pick you up?

449. MARIA (*as 441*): No. (*Said indifferently as she hangs up.*)[47]

450. *As 442. Oswald appears surprised. He hesitates a moment, then goes to the piano, plays a few notes, and sits down.*[48]

451. MLS: *Maria at the far end of a low-lit foyer at Mother's apartment. Coming forward, she leaves a huge fruit basket inside a door off the foyer. Then she returns down the long foyer as the camera dollies in a bit toward her. She looks into another door, then walks forward past the camera as it continues to dolly in.*

    MARIA: Mama!

    The camera movement stops as a second door from the end of the foyer opens. Mother comes out in MS in curlers and a towel.[49]

452. *Reverse angle from 451. FS: Maria is seen from over Mother's bare shoulders.*

    MOTHER: Maria! (*She goes to meet Maria. The camera dollies in slightly as they hug and spin one another around.*)
    MARIA: Happy Birthday!
    MOTHER (*sees the basket*): Ohhh! (*She goes off to look at it.*)

    The camera continues to dolly in from a MS to MCU of Maria, then turns with Maria, who is following Mother off the foyer into the parlor. The camera looks over Maria's shoulder as she stands in the doorway watching Mother fussing excitedly over the fruit basket. Maria suddenly turns around toward the camera.

453. MLS: *a man comes out into the foyer at the opposite end of the apartment in shorts and slippers. He is putting on a torn undershirt. He looks at Maria, seen from behind in FS, as she looks at him. Low ominous music begins and continues to the end of 460.*

454. MCU: *Maria, seen at right of center frame, looks him up and down without expression.*

455. ¾S: *Wetzel, seen at left of center frame, looks at her with an inquisitive expression. He is a little overweight and looks somewhat younger than Maria's mother.*

456. As 454. *Maria starts to smile.*

457. As 455. *Wetzel returns her look as he finishes putting on his undershirt; a smile starts to form on his face.*

458. As 454. *Maria is seen smiling at right of center frame.*

459. CU: *Wetzel is seen at left of center frame. He looks Maria up and down and breaks into a full, friendly smile.*

460. MOTHER (*as end of 452*): Just look at what's in that basket! (*She comes toward Maria, who is in the foreground.*)
    MARIA (MCU): Shall I dry your hair for you?
    MOTHER: No, no. You work enough as it is. You just go into the kitchen and make us some coffee and . . .

    Mother backs away from Maria into the foyer. The camera pivots and dollies out behind Maria, now in the foreground looking down the foyer at Mother and Wetzel, who is, unbeknownst to Mother, standing behind her at ¾S. A loud, sinister pounding on piano keys is heard while Mother backs down the foyer, unaware that Wetzel is standing there. The sound continues over the beginning of the next shot.

461. MCU: *Maria is seen at right of center frame. From a sly smile she breaks into a full one and laughs.*

462. MOTHER (*as she is cuddled and kissed by Wetzel*): This is Herr Wetzel, a good friend of mine—a very good friend.

    The piano music trails off into a pleasant melody and ends. Dolly past Maria to a closer shot of Mother and Wetzel at ¾S.

    WETZEL: Just call me Hans. (*He kisses Mother on the cheek.*)

463. MARIA (*seen from Mother and Wetzel's point of view*): Hello, Herr Hans. (*She seems slightly surprised and amused, then turns as Grandpa comes into the foyer behind her. She goes to him in* FS.) Grandpa Berger! How are you? (*They embrace and kiss.*)

464. MOTHER (MCU, *two-shot, whispers, annoyed, to Wetzel*): Did you have to come out now?
WETZEL: I have to take a piss.
MOTHER: Now, of all times.
WETZEL: You can't plan these things.
MOTHER: Well, then go.

He goes off as the camera dollies in to Mother. She is in CU *on the left side of the frame, looking after him with a suspicious expression.*

465. *As end of 463, from Mother's point of view. Wetzel goes toward the bathroom door. Maria comes forward, then turns to him and he takes a few steps toward her.*

MARIA: Anyway, my name's Maria.
WETZEL (*bows slightly*): Hello, Maria.
MARIA: Maria Braun.
WETZEL: Hello, Frau Braun. (*Grandpa slips into the bathroom behind him. Wetzel turns quickly but too late to keep Grandpa from locking the bathroom door.*) Hey, you sneaky old son-of-a-gun!

Wetzel bangs on the door, then restrains himself when he realizes Maria is present. He turns toward her, a bit embarrassed, making apologetic gestures, and smiling at her with a silly look on his face as she smiles back.

466. MCU: *Mother glares, then turns to go in the door Wetzel came out of, closing it into the camera. The sound effect of the door closing carries over into the first few frames of the next shot.*

467. MCU, *high angle: a table in the parlor is full of empty bottles and plates from the birthday celebration. Boom down and tilt up to Mother posing in a cheesecake pose reminiscent of American pinups from World War II*

in front of a mirror shaped like a painter's palette. The apartment is decorated like a typical middle-class home of the time and everyone is dressed much better than the last time they were all seen together. Wetzel, in ¾s, takes Mother's picture with a portable flash camera. He offers his hand to help her from a sideboard, then pats her on her derriere.

MOTHER: So, how was I?
WETZEL: Sweet.
MOTHER (MS, *coming forward to the table and excitedly surveying the food laid out there*): Oh, this is awful! I can't make up my mind what I want—something sweet or . . . Now let's take one with the whole family.

468. FS: *the whole family. Maria moves to the center of the room in* MS.

MARIA (*wearily, as if she's had enough of the birthday party*): I'll take it, Mama.

Mother comes over to her as Betti reaches for candy and Willi pours a drink.

MOTHER: Nonsense! No you don't. The whole family has to be in it. Herr Oswald . . .

469. MCU: *Oswald, seen from behind, is looking out a window.*

MOTHER (*off-screen*): . . . if you would be so kind.
OSWALD (*turns around*): Why not? But Maria knows that I'm not very good with technical things.

470. MCU: *Maria smiles in his direction. Betti is seen over Maria's shoulder, slightly out of focus, eating, in the background.*

471. LS: *Mother and Oswald, in the parlor, are seen through the doorway from the foyer. The camera then swings around to include the rest of the scene, but excluding Mother.*

MOTHER: Rubbish! Any idiot can take pictures with that.
OSWALD: If that's true, then nothing can go wrong.

Wetzel motions to Willi to lift up Grandpa, who is asleep in a chair.

WILLI: Yeah, Grandpa Berger has to be in it too.

The camera pivots to the other side of the room as they move Grandpa to where Mother is. The others cross to Mother's side of the room. The edge of the doorway now excludes Oswald from view at screen right.

WETZEL: Set it at four meters. The opening's okay.

All pose facing right. Wetzel holds Mother around her waist as she poses coquettishly.

BETTI: You can't wiggle or we'll come out blurry.
WETZEL: Yeah, we're blurry enough as it is. (*They all laugh. Wetzel puts his hand on Mother's breast.*)

472. OSWALD (MCU): Here goes.

473. FS: *all pose. They are seen from behind Oswald, who is at* MS.

BETTI: Shouldn't we wake Grandpa?
MOTHER: No, we want everybody to look natural. Grandpa Berger's always asleep.
WILLI: And free of sin.
MOTHER: Still, he's the only one who kept me warm in those cold days after the war.
WETZEL: Is that so?
MOTHER: Yes. He always brought us firewood. (*There is laughter, a flash, then they break up and scatter around the room.*) He never even woke up for Goebbels's speeches.
WETZEL: *He's* toned down a bit too. (*Wetzel turns on the record player.*)

Willi, with a drink in his hand, walks over to Oswald, puts his arm around him and they walk off left. Betti and Maria walk off right, leaving

Mother and Wetzel, who are dancing to the record player, and Grandpa, asleep in the background. The two dancers dip and glide to a corny, prewar song that continues, low, through most of the party sequence.

474. MCU, *two-shot: Betti and Maria watch them.*

MARIA: It never occurred to me before that my mother's a woman too. Then somebody comes along, and all of a sudden—she is one.
BETTI (*eating an hors d'oeuvre*): I still think it's indecent—at her age. It may be narrowminded and unfair, but that's how I feel about it.
MARIA: When somebody's unhappy, happy people always look a little indecent.
BETTI (*still eating*): When Willi and I are alone, I sometimes have the feeling we're already dead.

475. MS: *Mother and Wetzel dance holding each other closely as Willi and Oswald talk in the background at 3/4s.*

WILLI: You know, when you come down to it, it's all the same.

476. BETTI (*as 474, still eating*): What did I say? Dead? He just finds me boring, that's the worst part.
MARIA: Then do something about it.

Maria turns away from the dancers toward the window. The music comes up. Now the song is a popular 1950s ballad, "The Fishermen of Capri," with its refrain: "Bella, bella, bella Marie—don't ever forget me." The song continues to the end of the party sequence.

BETTI: What am I supposed to do when I don't know how to do anything—except maybe putting on weight? That I can do.
MARIA: We're all putting on weight.
BETTI: Then one day I'm going to find out I can't get a lover anymore.
MARIA: The lovers are getting fatter too.

477. *Begins as 475. Then pan with Willi as he crosses the room to Grandpa. The camera passes Wetzel kissing Mother on the earlobe as they dance.*

Willi drinks from a bottle as he passes the dancers and looks at them. The dancers are then seen in the palette-shaped mirror as Willi pulls the sleeping Grandpa out of his seat and starts to dance with him. He is still drinking and looks off-screen toward Betti.

478. BETTI (*as 474*): Does Oswald know—about Hermann?
     MARIA: No. When it first started between us, it didn't seem important. And when it started to matter, then I couldn't tell him anymore.
     BETTI: Tell him about it now.
     MARIA: He'd kill himself.

Maria crosses the room as the camera tracks and pans to follow her at ³/₄S. As she crosses the room, she takes single turns with Willi, Grandpa, Wetzel, and her mother. She finally reaches Oswald, who is still standing in the doorway where he was last seen talking to Willi.

MARIA (MS, *two-shot, to Oswald*): You look sad.
OSWALD (*smiles*): I am sad.
MARIA: Come on, let's dance—until we drop.
OSWALD: Until we drop.
MARIA (MCU: *pan slightly to the right, two-shot, to Oswald*): Tell me what's wrong.
OSWALD: I'll always love you—as long as I live.⁵⁰

The camera tracks right, taking in Mother and Wetzel, then Willi and Grandpa as they dance. Willi lifts the bottle to drink again as he looks over Grandpa's shoulder. Pan to Betti facing away from the party and brooding in profile in MCU. *The refrain of the song—"Bella, bella, bella Marie—don't ever forget me"—ends as the shot ends.*

479. MCU: *Maria is smiling and dressed in a coat with a fur collar and a stylish hat with a sheer veil. A prison guard stands, out of focus, in the background.*

HERMANN (*off-screen*): What's this?
MARIA (*her smile disappears*): I want everything to belong to you. So you can feel independent.

480. *As 416. The same prison room where Maria and Oswald last visited Hermann. A guard's long shadow extends across the floor. There is a bankbook on the table.*

> HERMANN (*gets up from the table, comes forward, and walks past the camera in the foreground*): It's your money and your life, Maria. I live my life and I won't let anybody give me theirs.
> MARIA (*still facing the place where he was sitting*): But it's your money. (*She gets up and starts toward him, then stops in the middle of the room as the camera dollies in to meet her at* MCU. *She looks distressed.*) But I've lived my life for you. For us![51]

481. *Reverse angle from 480.* FS: *Maria, in foreground right, faces Hermann. He is standing, in* LS, *in a doorway under the arched entrance of the visiting room. A guard is standing between them. Hermann's figure casts a long shadow.*

> HERMANN: Take me back please.

> *Hermann and the guard leave as Maria turns and comes forward to sit at the table in* MS. *She takes back the bankbook, which is wrapped as a gift, and puts it in her purse as a pounding rhythm blares up on the sound track. Fade out.*[52]

482. *Fade in,* MS: *the secretary, seen through a decorative wrought iron plant holder, answers the phone. Blaring music from the previous shot continues over the first few frames of this one. The sound of the pneumatic drill begins and continues to the end of the office sequence.*

> SECRETARY: It's for you, Frau Braun. A Dr. Klaus.

483. ³⁄₄S: *Maria is at her desk, seen from the secretary's point of view. The shadow pattern from the window frame is cast on the wall behind Maria.*

> MARIA: Braun. (*She listens, then lets the arm with the phone receiver fall into her lap, then picks it up again.*) When? On the twenty-third?

484. *As 482. The secretary leans forward and stares nosily from behind the wire partition.*

485. MARIA (*as 483*): Why that's next week! (*Maria looks up, presumably sees the secretary staring, and turns away.*) It's all so sudden. I . . . please excuse me, I . . . (*She taps a few keys on the adding machine.*)

486. *As 482. The secretary leans back again in her seat and puts something to eat in her mouth.*

487. MARIA (MCU): I have to . . . I'm so confused. (*She speaks low, distractedly, as the camera tilts down to a* CU *of the adding machine as her hand punches keys and she talks.*) I have so many things to take care of. (*Her hand punches some keys, hits the total bar, then repeats this four more times.*) So many . . . things . . .[53]

488. LS: *Maria is at the door of the large prison visiting room. She is seen through a network of bars and is very dressed up.*[54] *A guard comes in.*

    GUARD: Hello, Frau Braun.
    MARIA: Hello. I'm picking him up today—forever. I won't be coming anymore.
    GUARD: You're too late, Frau Braun. Your husband's gone already. (*She turns to face him for the first time.*) But he left a letter here for you.

489. MARIA (MCU): Who?
    GUARD (*off-screen*): Your husband.
    MARIA (*nods*): Oh, my husband. (*Her tone is tense, confused.*)

490. MS: *Maria, as the guard hands her a note. The two are now seen behind one set of bars.*

    GUARD: He left more than an hour ago—in a taxi.

    Maria turns to face the camera and is seen through the bars as she reads the note. A voice-over of Maria's voice reading the letter begins and continues after she drops the note and the rose she is carrying and walks out.

VOICE-OVER (*low, measured, unemotional*): Maria, I'm going away. To
Australia—or Canada. We'll live together when I've become a man,
and not until then. We'll have to wait 'til then. You'll hear from me with
a rose every month. Hermann.[55]

After she is gone, the guard comes in to pick up the rose she dropped.[56]

491. MCU, *low angle: dolly out from Oswald holding the phone receiver. He is
seen from behind as he listens to the phone ringing, with no answer. As
the camera reaches the doorway of an adjacent room, it stops. Oswald
lays the receiver down on the desk in his drawing room and it continues
to buzz and beep. Oswald, seen through the doorway, moves across the
room and out of the shot at left. The off-screen sound of Oswald pounding
out some chords on the piano is heard. Piano notes continue as Oswald
reappears—pacing around the room and flexing his fingers nervously. He
goes out of view again, then comes back into view as he returns to the
desk and picks up the phone. The camera now dollies in at desk level.
As he dials, the camera focusses on Oswald's other hand as it nervously
clenches and unclenches on the receiver. The piano notes become louder
and organ chords come in. This music continues to the end of this
sequence.*[57]

492. CU: *a ringing phone in a dark room. A door opens in the background and
a woman's figure emerges, illuminated by a shaft of light from the open
door. As she nears the phone, she can be identified as Maria's mother.*[58]

MOTHER (*only her torso visible*): Hello.

493. OSWALD (MCU, *seen at left of center frame, now facing the camera*):
It's Oswald. Is Maria there? . . . Sure, sure . . . (*He laughs,
embarrassed.*) I just thought . . .

494. CU, *low angle: Mother puts down the receiver. She has a pensive
expression.*

495. MLS: *Oswald bursts through the door of Maria's office at the far end of a
hallway at screen left. A wall, nearer the camera, fills the right half of the
frame.*

OSWALD: Maria!

The music reaches a climax and ends as he reaches the end of the hallway in foreground left and sees Maria, who is off-screen. Then pan right to Maria, working at her desk in the dim light of a desk lamp.

OSWALD (*off-screen*): Thank God!
MARIA (FS): I beg your pardon? (*Slight dolly out as she continues to work on an adding machine without looking up.*)

496. ¾S: *Oswald, standing in the doorway with the top half of his face in shadow, laughs, embarrassed. The sound of an adding machine is heard.*

MARIA (*off-screen, low*): Yes?
OSWALD: I don't know. . . . What are you doing here?
MARIA (*off-screen, calmly*): I'm working.
OSWALD: So late?

497. MARIA (MS, *from Oswald's point of view, without looking up*): Why not? I have some peace and quiet at night. I'm almost finished. Then you can take me home.

498. MCU: *Oswald, in the doorway, looks at her with an amused smile. There is a shaft of light across his eyes.*

499. *As 497.*

500. *As 498. As Oswald's smile disappears, the rhythmic music comes in again, low, over the last few frames. Fade out.*[59]

501. *Fade in,* LS: *Maria's large country house is seen through a wire mesh fence. The music from the previous shot continues over the first few frames, followed by the sound of birds. A mover carries in a large crate as a woman stands in the front doorway.*

502. *Maria stands in the foyer of her new house with her back to the camera, looking out the front door. As the mover approaches, the camera pivots and pans to follow him to the cellar door off the foyer.*

MOTHER (*coming up the cellar stairs*): Down there on the left.

The camera now precedes Mother in MS *as she comes through the doorway of the sitting room, which is off the foyer and opposite the cellar door. Mother is now tastefully and expensively dressed. She seems to enjoy being in charge of the moving operation. As she enters the sitting room, she looks around, as if taking in all the materialistic pleasures Maria's status now affords.*

MOTHER: Until now, no one in our family ever owned a house of his own. You're the first one, child.

A lateral track across the room with Mother stops when she stands before a mirror in MCU. *Mother's reflection is now also seen in* MS. *Maria is seen in the mirror entering the room through the same door.*

MARIA (*in the mirror, momentarily framed between the two images of her mother*): Somebody had to be first.

Mother turns toward Maria as the camera pivots to the windows on the opposite wall and dollies back into yet another doorway. Mother goes to Maria, who is standing by the windows in MLS. *Maria now wears her hair pulled back in a French twist and dresses in conservative business suits.*

MOTHER: If your father had lived, he would have built us a house too.
MARIA (*tired, sarcastically*): Unfortunately he didn't.

They exchange positions.

MOTHER: Child, child . . . how can you talk like that?

Mother follows Maria to the doorway in the foreground, where she stands looking after Maria, after Maria leaves the shot.

WETZEL (*off-screen*): Well, it's the truth.

503. *Reverse angle from 502. Wetzel comes from an adjacent room to meet Mother in the doorway at* FS. *He is now well dressed in a grey, double-breasted suit.*

WETZEL: You weren't always so sentimental.
MOTHER (*crying*): That's not it.

Wetzel makes an exasperated face. As he passes Mother in the doorway, the camera pivots and pans left to follow him into the sitting room.

MOTHER (*off-screen*): Maria, you've changed so much. You're like a stranger.

Wetzel goes out the sitting room door into the foyer. Maria is seen through the doorway from inside the sitting room as she follows Wetzel to the front door. Then Mother follows her.

504. MS: *Wetzel and Maria come out the front door onto the front steps, then Mother joins them.*

MARIA: And, anyway, cold. Right? Cold.
WETZEL: So? That's nothing so unusual these days.

Mother puts her arm around Wetzel in reconciliation as Maria goes back inside.

MARIA: Why don't you just say so?

Mother and Wetzel stand on the doorstep at left kissing and cuddling as Maria is seen through the open door starting upstairs from the foyer. The mover enters the foyer from the front steps.

MARIA (*from the stairs, to the mover*): You can put those boxes over there. (*There is the loud noise of a crate falling.*) I said put it down, not throw it down. (*Loud, angrily.*)
MOTHER (*turns toward Maria and yells*): Those crates are sturdy enough.

WETZEL: Just keep out of it.

MOTHER (*goes inside*): That's no way to treat people.

MARIA: Never mind. The man is being paid for his work. The least you can expect is that he does it properly.

WETZEL (*looking on from the front steps in the foreground*): Exactly right.

MOTHER: You should talk. When was the last time you put in a day's work?

As Wetzel goes inside, the camera tracks across the front exterior of the house and stops at the windows. Maria is seen behind the panes of one window at MS. *The mover is seen in the other window at* ³⁄₄S.

MOVER: I guess that's it.

MARIA (*looking out the window*): Good. . . . (*Impatiently.*) What's he still standing around for?

505. *As end of 503. The cellar door seen through the sitting room doorway.*

WETZEL (*off-screen at first*): He's probably waiting for a tip.

Wetzel passes the doorway as the camera pivots and pans to the mover, now in MCU *in the foreground, who shrugs his shoulders, laughs, and scratches his head.*

MARIA (*off-screen*): A tip!

506. MARIA (FS, *facing the mover as Wetzel reenters the sitting room through another door*): You usually get a tip. Why didn't you just say so? You have to demand what's due you. (*To Wetzel.*) Is this enough?

WETZEL: Give him another one. (*He exits at frame left.*)

MARIA (*hands the mover the tip*): So, now I don't have to say thank you. I'd rather pay than still have to thank somebody.

MOVER: Thank you. (*He exits, then the sound of a door opening and closing is heard.*)

MARIA (*slight pan to take in a door which masks off the left side of the frame as Maria opens the suitcase*): What's this? There's one missing!

507. ¾S: *Wetzel looks out the window at screen left, with his reflection in a full length mirror on the right side of the frame. Mother turns toward Maria (off-screen) in* MS.

MARIA (*off-screen*): There were four shirts in here.

Mother turns to Wetzel.

WETZEL (*turns around, looks at Mother, then toward Maria*): She gave me one. (*He leaves the frame.*)
MOTHER (*smiles tensely*): Yes.

508. *Reverse angle from 507. Wetzel reenters and stands beside Mother. Both are seen from the rear in* ¾S *facing Maria at* FS.

MARIA: Well, why didn't she say so?
MOTHER: He hasn't worn it yet.
MARIA (*approaches Mother as Wetzel moves toward the background*): So, you figured that Hermann wouldn't need it anymore since Hermann's never coming back.
WETZEL (MLS): But I can really use it.
MARIA (*goes to the suitcase and throws in the shirts*): Oh, that's not the point. (*She raises her voice, angrily.*) I don't like her lying to me all the time, damn it!

Wetzel, now in the middle of the room between Maria at background right and Mother at foreground left, looks at Mother then back to Maria.

MARIA: I live the best I can.

509. MOTHER (MCU): You don't live at all.

510. MARIA (CU, *turns toward her, speaking low, angrily*): What?

511. MOTHER (*as 509*): It's true.

512. WETZEL (*as 508*): She probably wants you to ask her to move in here with you.

MARIA (*approaches Mother*): You know very well that I bought this house so I could be alone. (*Pivot and track to follow Maria following Mother, as she tries to avoid Maria.*) You know very well what I want.

MOTHER (*finally turns to confront Maria at* ¾s): Yes . . . to live . . . like in a prison!

MARIA (*coldly*): Not bad . . . for you to come up with—I have a sentence to serve. (*Pivot and track in the reverse direction to include Wetzel in the shot again. To Wetzel.*) Or was that your idea?

WETZEL (¾s, *in the doorway facing Maria*): My idea? Of course not. No . . . no.

MOTHER (*off-screen, yelling*): You and your roses (*she reenters the frame*) and your position and your money. Every month she gets a rose and that's all she hears from him. It's like dying a little every month. (*She goes to a vase of roses as Wetzel comes to calm her down and Maria leaves the frame.*) Aren't I right?

WETZEL (*holding and humoring Mother as if she were a child*): Oh, yes.[60]

513. FS: *Maria is leaning against her desk dictating, seen in a narrow central panel of the shot, which is masked on either side by the doorway.*[61] *The sound of a pneumatic drill is heard throughout the office sequence.*

MARIA (*officiously*): We can only express our surprise that you are not meeting the stipulated quality standards agreed upon in our contract.

As Maria starts to walk around, the camera pivots and pans to include the secretary, who is taking dictation at her desk. Maria is now seen from the secretary's office through the leaves of plants which hang in the opening between the secretary's desk and Maria's office.

MARIA: We sincerely hope that you will reconsider your position immediately and bring it into line with our agreement. Otherwise we shall find ourselves . . . and so forth.

SECRETARY: . . . obliged to turn the matter over to our legal department?

MARIA (*turns and takes a few steps toward her in* ¾s): My dear Frau Ehmke, you are driving me crazy. (*The camera pivots and returns to its original position outside the door of Maria's office as Maria returns to her desk in* MLS.) We've used this sentence at least a hundred times, so when I leave it out, you don't have to say it.

514. SECRETARY (MS, *at left of center frame*): But I've always done that . . . I always . . .

515. LS: *Maria is seen over the secretary's shoulder through the opening. Maria is almost obscured by all the clutter around the secretary's desk— hanging plants, the wire mesh planter, hanging toys, snapshots. Maria's office is sparsely decorated, with bare white walls, except for a picture of the factory and an institutional quality art reproduction.*

MARIA: You've said this stupid sentence through to the end ninety-nine times when I choose to leave it out. And that's too often and *I'm sick of it*! (*Her voice is loud and angry, then low and apologetic.*) I'm sorry.

SECRETARY (*comes into focus in* CU *as she turns into profile, away from Maria, who is now out of focus in the background in* MLS): That's all right. We all lose our temper sometimes. And it's no wonder, with all the work you do. (*The secretary turns toward Maria, who now comes into focus again.*) Shall I make you a nice coffee with cognac? You don't look very well. (*The phone rings.*)

MARIA: And please keep out of my personal affairs. How I look or don't look is my own business. (*Louder, agitated.*) Now will you get that? But I'm not here. (*The phone rings again.*)

SECRETARY (*out of focus in the foreground*): Frau Braun's office, Frau Ehmke speaking. Hello, Herr Oswald.

516. SECRETARY (*as 514, holds her hand over the receiver*): He wants to talk to you.

517. MARIA (MCU, *tight-lipped*): I already said, I'm not here.

The off-screen drilling sound is loud, to the end of the sequence.

518. SECRETARY (MS, *from Maria's point of view*): I'm sorry, Herr Oswald, Frau Braun isn't here right now.

MARIA (*off-screen*): And I don't want to go to lunch with him either.

SECRETARY: And she doesn't want to go to lunch with you either . . .
Oh, God, please excuse me . . . Hello? Herr Oswald? (*She puts down
the receiver, puts her head on the desk and cries.*)

519. MARIA (*sitting at her desk, seen through the doorway, but closer than
the end of 513, in ¾s, throws back her head and laughs loudly*): My
God, that was funny! (*She gets up and goes toward the secretary in
MS.*) That's the funniest thing I've seen around here in a long time.
(*Pan and pivot to include the secretary with her head down as Maria
leans over into the opening.*) Stop crying, Ehmmie, and call Herr
Oswald back. Tell him Maria Braun is possessed by the devil. (*The
secretary looks up, sobbing.*) . . . Yes, yes. And if he wants to have
lunch with the devil, then he should meet me at one at the Bastion.
(*She leaves the frame.*)
SECRETARY (*picks up the phone, sobbing*): Herr Oswald . . .

520. MLS: *Oswald comes down the stairs to the Bastion restaurant. He is
seen behind a very dense, confusing foreground composition of etched
glass doors, stone pillars, and reflections of gothic window frames on
the doors. As he moves through the entranceway, his figure is always
narrowly confined by the vertical lines of a door frame or pillar. Then the
camera pivots and tracks ahead of Oswald into the dining room, where
Maria is sitting at a table in the center of the frame. It is a very elegant
restaurant with a vaulted ceiling, apparently occupying a remodeled
castle or fort. Half-a-dozen waiters are standing at attention around the
room, awaiting the bidding of the diners. The camera now tracks with
a waiter who crosses the room in the opposite direction, now taking
in Oswald, who is standing in the entranceway at MS. He hesitates
a moment as if to leave, before entering. Chamber music is heard
throughout the luncheon sequence.*

521. MLS, *reverse angle from the beginning of 520: Maria at the table eating,
at right of center frame, with a gothic, arched window in background left
and three waiters stationed around her. Oswald appears, standing under
the arched entrance in the background. Waiters surround him to take his
coat and hat. Oswald joins Maria at the table as waiters and maitre d'
move in and out of the shot.*

MARIA: You're late.

522. OSWALD (MS, *reading the menu, from over Maria's shoulder*): Sorry.
    I'm almost afraid to breathe. I have to remind myself over and over that
    I enjoy life.

523. MARIA (*reverse angle from 522, MCU, seen over Oswald's shoulder*):
    That's life . . . it's not as if we've signed a contract to enjoy life.

524. MCU: *Oswald at right of center frame.*

    MARIA (*off-screen*): And when we go out for a good dinner, we talk
      about what a good dinner it is.
    OSWALD: You're cynical.
    MARIA (*off-screen*): Maybe I am cynical.
    OSWALD: You're bored with me.

525. MARIA (MCU, *left of center frame*): Maybe I am bored with you. (*She
      smiles.*)
    OSWALD (*off-screen*): Why don't we just go?
    MARIA (*low*): Because you were well brought up and I'm pretending
      I was, and there's something between us I can't put into words.

526. *Oswald, MS, as 522.*

527. MLS: *Maria and Oswald at the table are barely seen in the background.
    Two women diners dominate the foreground in FS. Stone pillars close off
    the space on either side of the frame. The camera now swings around one
    of the pillars in a 180° arc that ends in a MLS, from behind Maria, of
    Oswald and Maria at the table. Oswald is the pivot point of the camera
    movement and is periodically obscured as the camera passes the two
    women and other diners in the foreground.*

    MARIA: And then . . .

528. MARIA (MS, *over Oswald's shoulder*): . . . I like the way we live. (*She
      smiles and cuts her food.*) I have no other choice. Oh . . . (*she looks at*

him with a serious expression) . . . it may not sound like much, but it's everything, because it's the truth. I can think of a lot of things I don't have. That nobody has—not even you. You and I have each other. (*She smiles.*)

OSWALD: Do you want to leave me?

MARIA (*dolly in slowly past Oswald to her*): Why should I? Then we'd be even more unhappy and that would be stupid. After all, only when you're unhappy can you have hope.

The camera now pivots to Oswald, in profile at MCU, *with the restaurant interior filling the left two-thirds of the frame. The shot is framed on either side by two pillars.*

OSWALD: I'm not bored with you.[62]

529. *The stairway of a ruined building extends across the left side of the shot. The scene is strewn with rubble. Low music from a radio is heard over the sequence.*[63]

WILLI (*off-screen*): And you know . . .

The camera pivots and tilts up as Willi and Maria come upstairs into the shot.

WILLI: . . . the worst part of it is, she thinks we broke up because she was getting fat.

As they pass through the shot, the stairwell is now seen across the right side of the shot, with a doorway in the background. The pop song, "I Love Paris," continues to the end of this sequence in the building.

MARIA (*off-screen*): She still thinks that.
WILLI (*off-screen*): But that's not true.

530. WILLI (FS, *high angle from the next landing above*): Actually, she was even losing weight.

FS, *low angle, tilt up from Willi to Maria, who is two landings above.*

MARIA: Don't talk like that, Willi. Betti was your wife, after all. . . .
(*She laughs.*) And she's my friend—the only person I can talk to about
anything.

*Maria, in high heels, a black dress and pearls, an expensive coat with a
leopard fur collar and cuffs, picks her way down the stairs. Pivot and pan
to follow her, carefully making her way to Willi.*

WILLI: Because she doesn't listen.
MARIA: Could be. The same way you need somebody who listens to you,
maybe I need somebody who doesn't. (*He helps her down to him in a
MS two-shot.*) And she's done very well with her boutique.
WILLI: *Her* boutique! Don't make me laugh. You mean, your boutique.
If it wasn't for you, she'd still be sitting around on her fat fanny.
MARIA (*walks into the background toward the doorway*): Aha, so she
was fat. (*She comes forward again.*) You still haven't gotten over her.
Otherwise you wouldn't criticize her so much.

*As Maria passes by the camera, the doorway at the end of a hall is seen
again in MLS on the left. Willi leans against a wall at MS on the right,
facing her.*

MARIA (*off-screen*): This was once our classroom.

531. MLS: *Maria, with her back to the camera, from Willi's point of view. She
is framed on either side by a doorway, and rows of benches can be seen
in the background.*

MARIA: Betti and I used to sit together, and Betti always used to copy
from me. (*She goes into her old schoolroom.*) And what about
Anneliese?

532. MARIA (MLS, *low angle, seen through the bare floor beams of the
schoolroom which cut diagonally across the frame*): What's she like?

WILLI (*comes into view behind Maria*): What's she like? It's hard to say. She's just what a woman should be for a man—his equal. She can talk, think—like a woman should—equal.

MARIA: Oh, so that's how it should be—the women should be equal with the men.

The camera zooms in slowly during the discussion.

WILLI: Of course. But most men haven't developed the right consciousness. People's consciousnesses always lag behind real developments.

The zoom stops at MS, *low angle, of the two, who are looking down between two floor beams that cut diagonally across the frame.*

MARIA: Is that what Anneliese says?
WILLI: Why?

533. *As 531, except that both are now seen through the schoolroom doorway. They come back out the schoolroom door.*

MARIA: Oh, Willi. One day you'll wish you had your fat Betti back. Or maybe you already do sometimes. At night, especially. Secretly—in your sleep.

WILLI: Forget it. I don't understand why you, of all people, would say something like that.[64]

MARIA (*pan to follow her as she starts down the stairs behind a brick wall that fills the left half of the frame*): Because with me it's just the opposite. With me, real developments lag behind my consciousness. (*She disappears behind the wall. The sound of Maria singing, low, from 534, is heard over the last few frames.*)

534. MCU: *Maria, in profile, is seen in the right half of the frame, in the same outfit as in the previous sequence. The camera tracks along with her as she continues to sing to herself. A green lawn and trees are seen in the background. Then the camera stops and pivots as she passes. Pan and tilt up as she goes up the front steps of her house in* MLS. *The camera*

*movement stops when she notices something ahead on the top step and
she stops.*

535. CU: *there is a rose on the top step, from her point of view.*

536. ¾S: *pan as she goes upstairs, picks up the rose, and goes in the door.*

537. MLS: *Maria is seen passing the sitting room doorway as she walks
through the foyer to the right. The camera, inside the sitting room, tracks
right across the room to the flower vase. Maria comes back into the shot
from the right at MS and puts her clutch purse into the flower vase. Dolly
in a bit on the vase of roses, which are in various stages of decay. As she
goes off right again, the viewer sees that the original MLS, showing the
interior of the room adjoining the sitting room, was a reflection in the
sitting room mirror.*

538. MCU: *Maria is seen from behind as she walks away from the vase, stops
in her tracks, and turns toward the vase, which is now off-screen.*

539. CU: *the purse sits among the roses in the vase.*

540. MARIA (*as 538, laughs, holding the rose*): Maria Braun, you better
watch out—you're getting a little strange.

541. *Reverse angle from 540.* MS *to* ¾S *as she goes through a draped
entrance to the vase, puts the rose in and removes her purse. She takes
out a cigarette, but has no match. She comes toward the camera in* MCU,
*looking around for a match. Low, whimsical background music comes in
and continues through 544.*

542. *As 538, reverse angle from 541. She continues on through the kitchen
doorway at* MLS *and lights her cigarette from the gas stove. Her figure is
masked on either side by the doorway.*

543. MCU: *she lights her cigarette at the gas burner. Maria lifts her head out
of the frame and the camera holds on the flame and Maria's hand turning
the gas knob off.*

544. *As end of 542. She comes back toward the camera, which shifts to a* CU *of the phone as Maria's hand reaches for it. The background music ends.*

> MARIA (*off*): Herr Oswald. This is Maria Braun. I need somebody to sleep with. (*She hangs up and her hand leaves the frame.*)[65]

545. MLS: *Maria is seen through the doorway at her desk. A man's hand closes the door, which had filled the left foreground. A man's torso is now seen at screen left and the secretary comes into view at her desk at midground. The sound of typing and the pneumatic drill are heard. The drill continues to the end of the office sequence.*

> SECRETARY (*stops typing and looks up a moment*): Hello.
> SENKENBERG (*off, and as yet unidentified, in a serious tone*): Frau Braun. (*Both women look up.*)

546. MCU: *Senkenberg is in the left third of the shot.*

547. ¾S: *Maria is at her desk with a vase of dried-out roses on the desk.*

> MARIA: Well, my little Senkenberg, what's wrong? (*Then, a bit annoyed.*) Why are you staring at me like that?

548. MLS: *Senkenberg in the doorway at left, separated from the secretary, who is partially seen behind a wall at center frame.*

> SENKENBERG (*facing Maria*): Herr Oswald is dead.

A gasp is heard from the secretary, who now comes up behind Senkenberg and leans on him. Dolly in.

> SENKENBERG: His housekeeper found him. (*He turns his face from Maria.*) Heart attack. (*He starts to cry.*) He died in his sleep, quite peacefully.

As it dollies in, the camera revolves so that Senkenberg and the secretary are now seen embracing in MS *through the opening and the clutter of things that obscure it.*

SENKENBERG: She said he had a smile on his face, just like a baby.

The sound of the drill comes up.[66]

549. LS: *Maria sits at her table at the Bastion. Five waiters are stationed around her. She is facing away, barely seen, almost nestled next to a wall and enclosed by the walls on each side of a doorway in the foreground.*

RADIO: . . . In opposition, CDU chairman, Chancellor Dr. Konrad Adenauer explained: "My friends . . ." (*Maria puts down her fork with a clang, gets up from the table, and comes forward.*) ". . . We have the right to rearm—as much as we can, as much as we want."

Maria leans against the wall at FS *and vomits as the waiters rush over to support her and scurry around her feet cleaning up.*

RADIO: And now the sports. There is barely . . .

The camera tracks laterally and slightly to the left to take in a couple behind a glass door in foreground left at MS. *The man is kissing the woman's shoulder while he caresses her exposed breasts. She leans her head back on his chest.*

RADIO: . . . twenty-four hours to the opening whistle of the final game of the soccer world championship in Bern's Wankdorf Stadium where Germany faces off against the Hungarian team. From the beginning, Hungary has been the undisputed favorite of this finale.

Maria tips the maitre d' and goes off right as the men look after her.

RADIO: And with the news, Bavarian Radio now ends its day at 11:00 P.M.[67]

550. MS: *Maria is sitting with her head down at her kitchen table. She is still dressed in the hat she wore in the previous sequence. There are several empty bottles and glasses on the table. She stirs a bit at the sound of a ring.*

551. FS: *Maria sits with her head down on the table. She is seen through the kitchen door from the adjacent room. The room interior on either side of the doorway masks her figure in the background. There is another ring, then one more.*

552. *As 550. As the bell continues to ring, Maria lifts her head as if she were awakened by it.*

553. *As 551. Maria gets up from the table, with difficulty, and goes off left. As she goes through the foyer to the front door, the camera tracks parallel with her but goes, instead, through the sitting room. She is seen passing the sitting room doorway on her way to answer the front door.*

554. MCU: *the front door is seen from outside. It opens slowly to reveal Maria. Her lipstick is smeared and she looks as if she were in a daze. Then her eyes open wider as the camera dollies back to take in Hermann's head and shoulders, and then both of them in MS. She continues to stare as Hermann grabs her to him, then she pushes the front door closed into the camera.*[68]

555. M L S, *high angle: Hermann is seen from behind, sitting with a drink.*

    R A D I O (*spirited*): . . . Cut off . . .
    M A R I A (*off-screen*): Are you hungry?
    H E R M A N N: Yes.

556. M L S, *low angle: Maria rushes down the stairs, seen through the sitting room doorway. She is dressed in a seductive black undergarment and black stockings.*[69]

    R A D I O: . . . precise shot with the right foot . . .
    M A R I A (*leans over the banister*): You're so mean. (*Maria is then momentarily out of sight, then comes into the sitting room and kisses Hermann in* M S *as the camera dollies out a bit.*) How can you think of food at a time like this? Oh, you.

The camera pivots and pans to follow Maria as she goes through the other doorway to the kitchen in ³⁄₄S. *The camera stops momentarily when she comes back and stands at one end of the sitting room, which now has a bed in it. The bedroom area of the room is set off by sheer curtains that are partially tied back. The radio commentary on the soccer match continues throughout this final sequence. The reporter's voice is very excited. It is sometimes drowned out when dialogue is spoken, and other times comes up on the soundtrack.*

MARIA (*standing under the curtained entrance*): Or do you want to take a bath? I'll pour your tub.
RADIO: . . . in the final game of the World Championship between Germany and Hungary . . .

Maria runs out through the kitchen as the camera pivots back to Hermann in his chair in MCU. *Maria now rushes past the sitting room doorway and starts upstairs in* FS *in the background. Hermann is dressed in his hat, shirt, and tie. He behaves rather indifferently.*

MARIA (*from the stairs*): Hot or not so hot?
RADIO: . . . corner kick for Germany from the left . . .
HERMANN (*the camera dollies in slightly*): Medium.
MARIA (*off-screen*): I'm getting it . . . be right there . . .
RADIO: . . . and if you can't . . . if you can't take this and have to switch off, then switch off. (*The reporter raises his voice.*) A corner kick for Germany. . . . but misses . . .

Dolly out slightly again and pivot back to the curtained entrance at MLS. *During this camera movement, Maria is seen rushing past the sitting room doorway, then she reappears between the curtains.*

MARIA: Here, catch! (*She throws him something in a can.*)

Hermann gets up from his chair. Maria is now seen from behind Hermann's torso, which is in the foreground. She stands facing him in a provocative pose at FS. *She has added pearls and high heels to her attire.*

557. MCU: *Hermann, seen at left of center, looks down at the can as his hat brim shades his eyes.*

558. MARIA (MS): Don't look at me like that—not until I'm finished.

Dolly out slightly to include Hermann's head and shoulders in MS, *seen from behind.*

MARIA (*now at ¾S*): You have a beautiful wife, you know. The opener's in the kitchen. You don't even know where the kitchen is.

Maria goes off left into the kitchen as Hermann follows her.

RADIO: . . . Droske had to shoot. Out of bounds. Off the head of Liebrich.

Maria comes back into the shot to the armoire in the bedroom area. She tosses some shirts to Hermann, who is now off-screen in the kitchen.

RADIO: It's Liebrich, again and again!
MARIA: You can put one of these on after your bath. There's one missing.

*Pan as she leaves the frame again through the kitchen. Hermann,
meanwhile, reappears in* MCU *in the foreground looking at a shirt.*

MARIA (*now off-screen*): Hans has it.
RADIO: . . . has put the ball into the air . . .

Track parallel with Hermann in profile at MCU, *holding the can of
sardines and examining the shirts, as he starts to circle the sitting room.*

MARIA (*off-screen*): Don't you want to know who Hans is?
HERMANN (*tosses the shirt down, unemotionally*): No. (*Pivot and track
    with Hermann as he continues circling the sitting room.*)
MARIA (*off-screen*): I'm not going to tell you anyway. Are there beautiful
    women in Canada?
HERMANN: Yeah. (*The camera pans and tracks as it continues to follow
    Hermann, from* MCU *to* MS *to* MCU, *as he circles around the room
    while eating out of the sardine can.*)
MARIA (*off-screen*): As beautiful as me?
HERMANN: Yeah.
MARIA (*off-screen*): You're lying.
HERMANN: Yeah.

*The panning/tracking shot continues to accompany Hermann around the
circumference of the sitting room to the doorway to the foyer and stairs.
It stops moving as he looks out the door, seen from behind in* MCU, *at
Maria coming downstairs. She is seen over his shoulder at* MS.

HERMANN: Why did you get dressed?
MARIA (*dressed in a sexy dark blue evening gown*): I did get dressed,
    didn't I? I have to get to know you first, Hermann Braun. (*She starts
    back up the stairs, then leans over the banister at* FS.) And if you
    remind me of someone I love very much, then I won't need this dress
    anymore. (*She turns, still seen over Hermann's shoulder, to put on her
    hat in the mirror that is over the stairway.*)
HERMANN: We haven't even kissed yet.
RADIO: Seven minutes remaining . . . seven minutes, it's been
    announced . . .

MARIA (*leaning against the banister, almost to herself*): Patience,
patience. (*As she turns to face him, the camera dollies in slightly
to Maria at* MS *and excludes Hermann.*) We were only married for
two days . . .
RADIO (*excited*): Time called! [literally, "an extension"]
MARIA: . . . and the days we have left are long.

*Maria is breathing in quick, short breaths. She comes quickly downstairs,
pushes past Hermann toward the camera in* MCU *as it dollies out to
precede her.*

HERMANN: Are you afraid?[70]
MARIA: Yes.
HERMANN: Me too.
MARIA (*from the bedroom, off-screen*): Let's take a trip—somewhere in
the country.

Pivot and pan past Hermann toward the curtained entrance.

MARIA (*off-screen*): . . . A honeymoon . . . to find out what I love
about you.[71]

The camera finds Maria looking out the window in the bedroom area at
MS. *Her figure is seen through the sheer curtain in the foreground.*

HERMANN (*off-screen*): Why don't we go?
MARIA (*turns toward Hermann and the camera, then rushes off toward
the kitchen; from off-screen, laughs*): Because you can't always just get
up and leave.

*Pan from the curtained entrance back again to Hermann as he continues
to eat in* MCU.

RADIO: . . . but Thöni has taken the ball and . . .

*The camera movement in this full two-minute shot has been a series of
erratic epicycles.*

559. MARIA (FS, *in the kitchen as seen from the adjacent bedroom area*): I still have certain obligations. (*She goes to the stove with a cigarette.*)

560. MARIA (*as 543, CU, she lights her cigarette from the burner*): I have to take care of them first. It'll take a few days. (*She blows out the flame and leaves the knob on "open." The sound of gas escaping is heard. Her torso passes out of the frame; her voice is heard from off-screen.*) Short days, Hermann, not long ones.
    HERMANN (*off-screen, as the camera remains on the hissing burner*): Maybe I'd better take my bath now.
    RADIO: . . . six more minutes . . .

    Maria's torso, with the agitated movement typical of her behavior in this sequence, passes in and out of the shot again as the camera remains fixed on the stove.

561. MLS: *Maria is standing behind the curtained entrance to the bedroom area. Hermann is eating his sardines in FS at foreground left.*

    MARIA: Maybe you'd better give your wife a kiss first.
    HERMANN: Let me finish eating first.
    MARIA (*approaches Hermann and takes the can*): So tell me about it.
    RADIO: . . . you only get to see a soccer world championship once every four years, then when you have Germany in a finale, it is so . . .

    Pivot slightly to center on Maria as she goes to the windows in LS and Hermann sits on the bed.

    HERMANN: I did it for us. For you. Because I'm only able to love you as your husband—not as somebody you have to give back his life to.

    The two face away from the camera and also from each other as they talk.

    MARIA: I didn't give you your life, Hermann. It was a checkbook!
    RADIO: . . . on the free kick [literally, "the choice"] . . . He's got the ball—he loses it this time. Now against Schäffer . . . Schäffer . . . head shot . . .

HERMANN: It was a checkbook. And I wanted to be somebody for you, so you could love me. Do you know what I mean?[72]

MARIA (*at the window*): No, but I love you.

RADIO: . . . from the backfield, Rahn shoots . . . Rahn shoots . . . (*The reporter screams.*) Goal! Goal! Goal! Goal! (*Cheering.*)

MARIA (*heard under the sound of the radio*): No, but I love you. Come here and undress me.

A subtle camera movement now includes the coffee table at which Hermann was sitting at the beginning of this long reunion sequence. On it is a bottle and his empty glass in MCU *in the foreground at center frame.*

MARIA: I want to be your wife. Listen, I have an idea. (*He takes off his jacket.*) We'll sign a contract that says that everything I own belongs to you.

HERMANN (MS, *he faces the camera while Maria, undressing, continues to look away*): Even your heart? (*He takes his shoes off.*)

MARIA: It always has been yours . . . or else it belongs only to me . . . which is maybe the same thing.

They undress.

RADIO: . . . goal for Germany—five minutes before the end of the game.

562. MARIA (MCU, *at left of center frame, turns toward Hermann*): You know, I'm serious about that contract.

RADIO: . . . you may think I'm crazy . . .

563. HERMANN (MCU): Offer refused. Because instead we'll make another contract and I'll give you everything I have.

RADIO: . . . you may think I'm nuts . . .

564. MARIA (FS, *her figure is masked on either side as if through a doorway, as in other shots*): Do you mean that?

RADIO: . . . My heart is pounding . . . the excitement . . .

The camera pans when Maria walks off. Her image is revealed to have been her reflection in a mirror. The pan settles on Hermann's profile in MCU *as he turns to her.*

HERMANN (*smiles*): I mean it.

565. *A longer shot of Hermann situates him in the room.*

566. MLS *of the bedroom area from the sitting room, as 561, but Hermann is now at foreground right in* FS *with his back to the camera.*

MARIA (*flings herself onto the bed*): Was it so important to you?
HERMANN: And now I have it.

Maria lies seductively across the bed with her head hanging over the side and looks up at Hermann undressing.

MARIA: Fine. But I'm rich. And I'm almost sure to inherit much more.

567. HERMANN (CU, *wearing his hat; he is seen upside down from Maria's point of view*): Anybody can inherit money.

568. MARIA (MS, *her face is also upside down over the side of the bed*): Anybody? Could be. But why do you want to give everything to me?

569. HERMANN (*as 567*): Because I became your husband today and don't need anything anymore.

570. *As 566. Hermann, dressed in his underwear and hat, sits down on the bed beside Maria. Just as they kiss, the doorbell rings.*

RADIO (*excited*): . . . Ball out of bounds . . .
HERMANN: Who can that be?
RADIO (*excited*): No . . . no goal! No goal! No goal!
MARIA: What time is it?
HERMANN: About a quarter past six.
MARIA: What day?

HERMANN: The fourth.

MARIA: Then it's Senkenberg with a ticket for Lyon. (*She jumps up and goes off right. Hermann sits on the edge of the bed.*) Can you imagine—Oswald filed his will in Lyon. (*She reenters the shot and hands Hermann a robe. She comes through the curtains and passes the camera.*) Funny—I almost forgot the date.

Hermann puts on the robe and sits on a stool beside the bed facing the rear wall.

RADIO: . . . great job of setting up the play by Kopfnagel . . .

571. MS: *Senkenberg and Madame Devoald come in the front door.*[73]

SENKENBERG: Excuse me, Frau Braun, I thought we . . .

RADIO: . . . which his teammates continued . . .

MARIA (*enters the shot, now a* MCU): Herr Senkenberg, I thought we agreed that . . .

SENKENBERG (*tips his hat and smiles on seeing her in her black underwear*): . . . people can be unpredictable.

MARIA: Very.

SENKENBERG (*seen between the two women in a three-shot*): May I introduce you to Mademoiselle Devoald?

DEVOALD (*shakes hands with Maria*): Bon jour, Madame.

MARIA: How do you do. Just go right inside. I'll just go change. (*Tilt past them to follow Maria upstairs. Then she leans over the banister in* FS.) Just go ahead and start.

572. MCU, *high angle: Senkenberg and Devoald look up at Maria, from Maria's point of view.*

SENKENBERG: But . . .

573. *As end of 571.*

MARIA (*on the stairs*): No ifs, ands, or buts about it, Senkenberg.

Maria goes upstairs as the camera tilts back down to Mademoiselle Devoald in MCU. *She is fashionably dressed and attractive, but acts rather aloof and affected. Dolly out to precede her and Senkenberg into the sitting room as Mademoiselle Devoald looks around.*

SENKENBERG: Excuse me, Mademoiselle, but we . . .
DEVOALD: You're not supposed to say "but" anymore. (*She looks off at Hermann and says, low.*) Hello.
RADIO: . . . Out, out. . . . The player in the white jersey . . .

574. HERMANN (MS, *wearing a robe and his hat, turns around to her*): Hello.
RADIO: . . . the German men quickly defend . . .

575. MCU: *Senkenberg turns toward the camera and Hermann.*

RADIO: . . . their own penalty kick . . .

576. HERMANN (*as 574*): I'm Hermann Braun.
RADIO: . . . and kick the ball away . . .

577. *As 575. Dolly in on Senkenberg, at left of center frame, to* CU.

RADIO: . . . passing with the hands to his comrades . . . as if he was saying . . .

578. ¾S: *Maria is in the bathroom, putting on a white evening dress. She is seen on the right side of the frame and a white tiled wall fills the left side. When one arm juts out from behind the wall, her image is revealed to be a mirror reflection. She goes off, as seen in the mirror, and the camera lingers there for a moment afterwards. The sportscaster's voice continues excitedly.*

579. ¾S, *low angle: Maria comes downstairs, seen from inside the sitting room.*

DEVOALD (*off-screen, reads, with a French accent*): "Regarding my estate, my instructions are as follows."

Tilt down and dolly out slowly to include more of the sitting room in the foreground as Maria reaches the bottom of the stairs.

DEVOALD (*off-screen*): "Ownership of all of the movable and immovable assets belonging to the firm, together with their use, . . ."

RADIO: . . . Three minutes to go in Wankdorf Stadium . . .

The camera continues to dolly out to a MCU of Senkenberg as Maria comes in and stands behind him. Her hair is pulled to one side, as when she first introduced herself to Oswald.

DEVOALD (*off-screen*): ". . . but excluding the above mentioned restrictions, as well as my entire private property, . . ."

580. MS: *Devoald faces the camera at foreground right. Hermann faces the wall as he sits by the bed in background left.*

DEVOALD: ". . . excluding the above mentioned restrictions, shall go, half to Frau Maria Braun (*Devoald reads this in a particularly dry, sarcastic tone*) who has given me more happiness than any other person in this world."

RADIO: . . . a goal kick for Hungary . . .

DEVOALD: "The other half of this estate, as per our contract, signed at Kreuzhof Prison on the fourteenth day of June, Nineteen Hundred and Fifty-One . . ."

RADIO: . . . Three to two, Germany's favor . . .

DEVOALD: ". . . shall go to Herr Hermann Braun, who was . . ."

581. MS: *the rear wall of the bedroom area. Hermann's face, mostly in shadow, is seen in a mirror on the wall as he looks up, as if trying to observe Maria in it.*

DEVOALD (*off-screen*): ". . . a friend to me, even though he loved the same woman I did."

582. MS: *Senkenberg and Maria. She stares, expressionless, in Hermann's direction.*

DEVOALD (*off-screen*): "Hermann Braun, for the sake of a love other than his own . . ."

MARIA (*turns around, moves to Senkenberg's other side, and faces off left*): You knew about the contract.

SENKENBERG (*facing the camera*): Herr Oswald was very sick.

DEVOALD (*off-screen*): ". . . sacrificed more, evinced more respect and more humility than is common, or possible, in most people."

Maria turns back in Hermann's direction and smiles mechanically.

583. *As 581. Hermann lowers his eyes.*

DEVOALD (*off-screen*): "Only one who is capable of great love . . ."

584. *As end of 582.* MS: *Maria leaves the room as Senkenberg turns to look after her.*

DEVOALD (*off-screen*): ". . . is also capable of appreciating great love in others."

585. MCU: *Senkenberg, from a different angle than 584 that takes in Maria going through a door beneath the stairway at* FS.

DEVOALD (*off-screen*): "And only one who can serve, may lead others."

MARIA (*turns back toward Senkenberg*): I have a headache. (*She exits and shuts the door behind her.*)

DEVOALD (*off-screen, without expression*): "Hermann Braun has earned the right to be a leader as few have." [74]

586. *As 581. Even heavier shadows almost totally obscure Hermann's face.*

RADIO: . . . With two minutes left to play, Hungary forwards the ball . . .

587. MCU: *Maria is seen from behind, holding her wrist under the tap as the sound of the dripping water is heard.*

HERMANN (*off-screen*): Maria! The reading of the will is over. Senkenberg and Mademoiselle Devoald want to go.

MARIA: Excuse me, please. (*Tilt down slightly on the basin.*)

588. ¾S: *Hermann closes the front door.*[75] *The camera pivots and now precedes Hermann at* MCU *as he comes into the sitting room.*

RADIO: . . . But he shoots somewhere else. Kicked away from Hungary's goal . . .

Now Maria enters from the background at ¾S *and looks around the room. Pivot and pan with Maria as she goes to the table with the vase of roses and picks up a pack of cigarettes.*

RADIO: . . . now in overtime due to the one or two violations that have taken place . . .
HERMANN (*sitting on the low stool by the bed in* LS): Don't you feel good?
MARIA: It's just a headache. (*She looks down at her cigarette.*)
HERMANN (*turning toward her*): Please don't forget, I gave you everything—all the money. I don't care about it.
MARIA: I gave you everything too. My whole life. (*She turns around to face him and says, louder.*) Do you have a match?

Maria goes through the bedroom area into the kitchen.

RADIO (*loud, hysterically*): . . . Hungary still has a chance! Csibor plays it off the right wing! Csibor has a chance! Stopped by Thöni! Stopped! And the great soccer player from Budapest . . .
HERMANN (*turns to look into the kitchen, yells*): No! Noooo! (*He jumps up from his seat and covers his face.*)

589. MLS: *Senkenberg and Devoald walk toward the front gate as the sound of an explosion is heard.*

Superimposed title fades in: The Marriage of Maria Braun.

Senkenberg and Devoald stop and turn around.

590. LS, *from Senkenberg's and Devoald's point of view: fire is coming from the second floor windows of the house.*

Superimposed title: Organization: Michael Fengler, Robert Busch, Thomas Wommer, Harry Zöttl, Dieter Dubine, Christine Fall, Jochen Losse.

591. *As 589. Senkenberg runs toward the house as Devoald screams.*

Superimposed title: Set design: Nobert Scherer, Helga Ballhaus, Claus Hollmann, Georg Bergel.

592. CU: *Senkenberg is inside the house. Devoald's scream continues over the first few frames of this shot.*

SENKENBERG: Frau Braun! Frau Braun! (*He puts a handkerchief over his mouth for protection from the smoke.*)

Superimposed title fades in: Costumes: Barbara Baum, Susi Reichel, Georg Hahn, Ingeberg Pröller. Sets: Andreas Willin, Arno Mathes, Hans Sandmeier. Technicians: Hans-Jürgen Höpflinger, Raimund Wirner.

SENKENBERG (MS, *enters the burning room*): Frau Braun!

As Senkenberg searches the burning room a second explosion is heard. He mutters something.

593. MLS: *the bedroom area is seen through the curtained entrance. Everything is destroyed. The phone is lying on the floor. The sound of the second explosion continues over the beginning of this shot.*

Superimposed title: Musical Assistance: David Ambach, Kurt Maas. Assistant Cameraman: Horst Knechtl. Assistant Editor: Christine Kolenc. Assistant Sound Technician: John Salter. Assistant Director: Rolf Bührmann. Script Girl: Helga Beyer.

RADIO (*comes in as the sound of the explosion ends, screamed hysterically*): Time's up! Time's up! Time's up! Time's up! Time's up! Time's up! Time's up! (*Beep.*) Time's up! (*Beep.*)

Superimposed title fades in: Fuji Film, Geyer Prints.

RADIO: Germany is World Champion!

The image fades to white.

RADIO: Beating Hungary three to two in the final game in Bern.

594. *A portrait of Konrad Adenauer in negative fades in from white. Ambient sounds of horns and cheering from the Bern stadium are heard, along with an electronic beeping sound, and continue to the end of the film.*

Superimposed subtitle: Dr. Konrad Adenauer, Chancellor 1949–1962.

Dissolve to . . .

595. *A portrait of Ludwig Ehrhardt in negative.*

Superimposed subtitle: Dr. Ludwig Ehrhardt, Chancellor 1963–1965.

Dissolve to . . .

596. *A portrait of Kurt Georg Kiesinger in negative.*

Superimposed subtitle: Kurt Georg Kiesinger, Chancellor 1966–1969.

Dissolve to . . .

597. *A portrait of Helmut Schmidt in negative, which dissolves to positive.*

Superimposed subtitle: Helmut Schmidt, Chancellor, 1974–present.

RADIO (*low, indistinct*): . . . after these last thirty seconds . . . This is the reporter for . . . You just can't imagine what's going on here. We'll try to . . .

Schmidt's image fades out along with the radio commentary, except for two last beeps over a dark screen.

Notes on the
Shooting Script

The Marriage of Maria Braun originated as an idea of Fassbinder's to make a film about "the marriages of our parents." Influenced by the grandiose scale of *Berlin Alexanderplatz*, which he was working on at the time, he dictated a story that would have filled eight hours of screen time. Because of the pressure of time, Fassbinder gave this rough draft to Peter Märthesheimer, a German film and television producer with whom he had worked, and Pea Fröhlich, a psychologist by profession, with the charge to reduce it to manageable proportions for a feature film. Fassbinder was pleased with the results. Nevertheless, throughout the filming, he made changes, shortening or replacing scenes and writing new dialogue.

From script to screen, the only major change in the plot involved the ending: the script concludes with Maria's suicide when she drives the car in which she and Hermann are riding over an embankment, while the film presents a more ambiguous ending in which both are killed when Maria sets off a gas stove explosion. The postscript sequence, consisting of portraits of the chancellors of the Bundesrepublik, was an addition to the script. Throughout the film, the rich complementary text of the soundtrack, with its historical evocations and its ironies, was Fassbinder's invention.

The most significant change in characterization made by Fassbinder was in the relationship between Maria and Oswald. The script devotes more attention to this than the film does, is more sentimental in tone, and is explicit in evoking psychological ties appropriate to a father/daughter relationship. In the film Fassbinder has also modified the script to convey the sense of a perverse sadomasochistic game between Maria and Oswald.

The following notes are based on a comparison of the continuity of the film as released with the script for the film submitted by Märthesheimer and Fröhlich. The notes describe any significant changes Fassbinder made in reworking the script during the shooting of the film. Very few camera directions or indications of mise-en-scène occur in the script.

The notes themselves are keyed to superscript numbers in the continuity. References to pertinent shots are given in parentheses.

1. In the shooting script (hereafter ss), Betti, Willi, and Maria's mother are present at the marriage (shots 1–15). There is a portrait of Hitler on the wall of the registrar's office.

2. In ss, two scenes intervene between the marriage scene which opens the film and the film's second scene (17–26). The first of these two scenes, which involves a man taking slats from a fence for firewood and being harassed by two boys, occurs later in the film (58–73). The second, not in the film, is as follows:

   PRISON BARRACK, INTERIOR/NIGHT
   We dissolve to Hermann's face. The camera dollies out and we recognize the interior of a barrack. It is a Russian prisoner of war camp. The prisoners lay sleeping on two-tiered bunks. The camera dollies back in on Hermann. He is lying on a lower bunk. Close-up of Hermann's face. He is staring at the ceiling. DISSOLVE.

   A transition to the scene in Mother's kitchen is indicated in a dissolve of Hermann's face in the barrack to his photo on the kitchen counter.

3. In the scene in the waiting room at the train station, Maria's line (43), "The ocean used to be where the mountains are now—before the last ice age," does not appear in ss. Maria's answer (46) to the nurse's question about why she is so sure Hermann is not dead, "Because I want him to come back," appears in the script as "Because I want to know it."

4. The business of going in and out the hole in the wall during the scene in Mother's apartment (52–57) is not indicated in ss.

5. In ss, instead of walking past the other women, Maria and Betti are themselves working as *Trümmerfrauen* (74–76). The dialogue in the scene is as follows:

> BETTI
> He's just a poor bastard.
> MARIA
> (firmly)
> That's just it. These aren't men, and we're not women. They all make me sick. It's no good.

6. The song Maria and Betti sing as Maria has her hair done (77) is not in ss. There the scene ends with the two crying over nothing in particular.

7. Here ss includes a brief scene that is not in the film:

> PRISON BARRACK, INTERIOR/EVENING
> Hermann is sitting on his bunk with a book. The camera dollies in on the book and we see that Hermann is secretly looking at a picture of Maria that is stuck between the pages. The man in the bunk above Hermann bends over and looks at the photo. Hermann swings at him angrily.

8. The business and dialogue about the concertina in the black market scene is not in ss.

9. Fassbinder added the references to Kleist and to burning books for fuel.

10. The following lines from ss were deleted from the end of 99:

> MARIA
> (gets down from the stool and puts her arms around Mother)
> You're always the grown-up, and always will be.
> MOTHER
> (takes a swig)
> That's how it should be. We women have to stick together.

11. In ss, Maria does not play on the parallel bars just before her meeting with Bronski (100–106). Instead, the script has a brief scene in which Maria inquires after Bronski of a woman who is sweeping in front of the gym.

12. In ss, there is a very brief scene in the doctor's waiting room just before the scene in his office. A woman who, along with Maria, is among those waiting to see the doctor, tells a racist "dirty joke" about a white woman and a black man. All the women laugh except Maria.

13. The doctor's self-administered drug injection (125–133) is not in ss.

14. The fight over a stolen glove that continues in the background or off-screen throughout the scene (134–146) is not in ss.

15. The following scene comes immediately after the train station scene in ss and is not in the film.

> STREET IN FRONT OF THE TRAIN STATION, EXTERIOR/DAY
> Maria comes out of the train station, goes to an old bicycle and unlocks the chain. There is a war cripple sitting nearby against the wall of the building. He has rings, pins, necklaces, etc. made from aluminum spread out in an old suitcase in front of him.
>
> CRIPPLE
> (to passersby)
> Rings, pins, necklaces . . . real American airplane aluminum. . . . (He looks over at Maria, pointing to the bicycle.) I kept an eye on it.
> MARIA
> Thanks. How much is a ring?
> CRIPPLE
> I'd rather have sugar stamps. Shall we say 50 grams worth?
> MARIA
> (looks at the display)
> Give me the ugliest one.
> CRIPPLE
> They're all ugly. Just the plane was beautiful, as long as it was still up there.

MARIA

How come you're not telling me you shot the plane down yourself?

CRIPPLE

What would it get me? You'll buy or you won't buy.

Maria takes a ring and puts it on over her wedding ring. She looks for the stamps.

CRIPPLE

Do you have something to forget, young lady?

MARIA

(laughs)

Forget? No, I want to protect something.

CRIPPLE

(takes the stamps)

God be thanked!

Maria, already on her way, hesitates a moment and takes a step toward him.

MARIA

What you just said! . . .

CRIPPLE

It's just an old saying.

MARIA

Tell me . . . are you good in bed?

CRIPPLE

Not too successful in my opinion.

MARIA

(chews on her lip)

Yeah, it looks that way.

CRIPPLE

But I can keep my fingers crossed for you.

MARIA

Oh, please, do that. Maybe that's better anyway for what I have in mind.

Immediately after this scene, ss includes a brief scene in the prison barrack, as follows:

INTERIOR/DAY
Music. Hermann stands in a line with others. A Russian guard sits at a table distributing rations of bread.

16. The brief dialogue with Bronski in the bar (147–152) is not in ss.

17. There is additional dialogue in ss in the scene between Maria and Bill on the wooded slope (163–168). This ss scene also includes "an older couple" who watch Bill and Maria disapprovingly from a park bench. The older couple make a demonstrative exit as the woman calls Maria "Ami-lover" and "Nigger's whore" under her breath. The rest of the dialogue is as follows:

BILL
What did she say?
MARIA
She not like when I (makes a hugging gesture) with you.
BILL
(laughs)
When I am your lover and you are my mistress.
MARIA
(also laughs)
When you are my lover and I am your mistress.

Both stop laughing and look a little self-conscious. Finally, Bill takes out a PX bag from beside him and pours the contents into Maria's lap and continues the English lesson.

BILL
Chocolate.
MARIA
(excited)
Chocolate.
BILL
Coffee.
MARIA
(excited)
Coffee.

BILL
(hesitating)
Nylons.
MARIA
(firmly, pushes the nylons away)
No. You are not my lover and I am not your mistress. You are my friend, my . . . *Bruder*?
BILL
Brother?
MARIA
Yes, you are my brother.

Bill puts her chocolate and coffee in the bag, then adds the nylons. He hands her the bag. Maria smiles at him, gives him a kiss on the forehead, then gets up quickly.

18. The gesture of Maria putting her hand under the tap (175–179) is not indicated in ss.

19. In ss, Maria says, "My . . . man . . . is . . . dead. Stay with me tonight." Then ss continues, "Bill leads the lifeless Maria outside past the curiously staring dancers." The elaborately choreographed gesture that appears in the film is not indicated here.

20. In ss, the love scene between Maria and Bill (183–188) follows the scene at the bar (180–181) and precedes the picnic scene (182). It is less explicit and refers more directly than the scene in the film to Bill as a father figure:

   Maria puts on a long flannel nightgown. Bill lies down in bed—then Maria. Bill turns out the lamp on the night table. Maria lays her head on Bill's shoulder. She falls asleep immediately, her thumb half in her mouth. Bill's eyes are open as he carefully strokes her hair.

21. The dialogue added by Fassbinder to the scene in the doctor's office (189–195), as well as the visual treatment, creates grimmer overtones than ss suggests.

22. Hermann's rush for the cigarettes after discovering Bill and Maria is not indicated in ss.

23. In the scene at the inquiry into Bill's death (220–239), the interpreter is not mentioned in ss and Bronski's entrance on the elevator is omitted.

24. The scene in which the doctor sees Maria off at the train station and they refer to the death of Maria's child (264–269) is not in ss.

25. In ss, Maria's first encounter with Oswald on the train is somewhat less calculated than in the film (283–295). He notices her first when, exhausted after pushing her way through the crowded second-class car, she happens to lean against his compartment door. He starts to rise to help her, but she has already moved on and does not notice him until she returns and takes a seat in his compartment.

26. The dialogue between Maria, Oswald, and Senkenberg in the automobile is set in the train's dining car in ss. Although the scene there does not include Senkenberg, the dialogue remains basically the same.

27. In ss, this is the first mention that the child is dead.

28. In ss, Maria's line here is "Because you haven't asked who will look after me."

29. In ss, the setting of the business meeting with the Americans is the conference room of a hotel in a converted palace.

30. In ss, the setting of this scene is the restaurant of the hotel.

31. Senkenberg's reproach to Oswald about his absence after 1933 and Oswald's comments on this to Maria (370) are not in ss.

32. In ss, the scene ends slightly differently, as follows:

MARIA
I want to sleep with you.
OSWALD
(is surprised, regains his composure, and waves to the waiter)
Waiter, please bring two bottles of champagne to Room 216.

The waiter takes down the order.

MARIA
Room 214. And make it in an hour.

Maria gets up and leaves. The waiter looks inquisitively at Oswald, who nods to him and follows Maria out.

33. The film changes the setting of the love scene from a hotel room to Oswald's apartment. In ss, Maria has Oswald sit on the bed while she undresses slowly in front of him. ss also includes a brief exchange between Maria and Oswald when the champagne is delivered. He wants to know why she asked for it to be brought in an hour. When she explains that, this way, it would be cold when they were ready for it, he tells her it would have been brought on ice and therefore would stay cold. She responds, "I didn't know that. See—it's just like you say, it's time I got some experience."

34. The moment when Oswald refers to his age and Maria puts her hand over his mouth to quiet him, after which they kiss, is not in ss.

35. The following dialogue at the end of Maria's visit to the prison is deleted in the film:

MARIA
Hermann—I love you, with all that's in me. And waiting for you is my life.
HERMANN
We'll be together again sometime. And then I'll take care of you. Until then, I trust you.

36. ss does not indicate that the setting of the labor-management meeting (395–397) is Oswald's factory.

37. In ss, the dialogue between Maria and Willi following the meeting takes place in her car as she drives him home.

38. A brief scene in which Maria drives up to the lawyer's office after dropping Willi off is not in the film.

39. In ss, this scene takes place in the lawyer's office.

40. Maria's reference to Hermann's state of mind is not in ss.

41. The scene in ss between Maria and Oswald in Maria's apartment (403–409) includes the camera direction, "We see both of them through the open door of the kitchen as in a frame."

42. In ss, Oswald watches Maria as she leaves the prison, rather than as she leaves her apartment.

43. In ss, Maria parks in front of Betti's apartment building and honks for her to come down. The scene in the hallway and stairwell, with its dialogue, is not in ss.

44. A brief scene in which Oswald waits nervously in the prison visiting room for Hermann to be brought in follows in ss immediately after Maria picks Betti up. The ss then presents a brief scene in a butcher shop, as follows:

    Maria and Betti are waiting in line for their turn. The store is full.

    BETTI
    Maybe it's this American-style pace. I can understand how it could make him nervous. (She glances at the display case.) The pig's knuckles look good.

    An old man in front of them is served.

    SALESWOMAN
    Okay if it's a little over?
    MAN
    (displeased)
    In the old days, you'd almost rather cut off your finger than give up a gram.
    SALESWOMAN
    The old days are over.

45. In ss, the dialogue that follows is a continuation of the prison scene referred to in note 44:

Oswald paces, agitated, back and forth while Hermann sits very quietly at a table.

OSWALD

Me, upset? I'm not upset at all! Of course I'm upset! You sit in here and you know everything; I'm outside and I don't know anything . . .

Oswald breaks down. He starts to cry softly. After a while, Hermann gets up and puts his arm around Oswald's shoulder. It almost looks like an embrace.

HERMANN

All that's not important. You'll soon understand. The only thing that's important is that we love the same woman.

OSWALD

She's your wife. And she loves you.

HERMANN

Yes, but she lives with you.

ss then includes a scene in which Maria comes home to find Oswald drunk and apparently asleep on her couch. He pretends to be asleep as she tenderly covers him up, talks to him as if he were her sleeping child, and kisses him on the forehead.

46. Fassbinder substitutes this different and more elaborate scene with Maria and Betti (431–434) for the butcher shop scene referred to in note 44.

47. Maria's phone call to Oswald (441–449) is a condensation of a longer scene that comes in ss after Maria's discovery of the drunken Oswald. Maria wakes the next morning, finds Oswald gone, and reads a romantic note from him. When she calls him on the telephone, there is a tender exchange that precedes the dialogue about his hangover included in the film. ss also includes some pleasant conversation about Mother's birthday party. In general, the ss scene does not convey the curtness on Maria's part that the film does.

48. In ss, after confessing to Maria on the phone, "I need you so. I don't want to live without you," Oswald stares, still holding the receiver, with tears

rolling down his face. In the film, his reaction to Maria's display of indifference is less explicit.

49. ss calls for Maria to discover her mother and Wetzel in bed together when she arrives for the birthday party and unsuspectingly opens the bedroom door. The business between Maria, Wetzel, and Grandpa, and the hint of Mother's jealousy (453–466) is not in ss.

50. According to ss, Oswald's comment as he dances with Maria at the end of the birthday party scene ("I'll always love you—as long as I live.") is said "solemnly, almost like an oath." Then, "Maria leans her head on Oswald's shoulder to hide her tears. They begin to dance slowly and tenderly. Oswald now has a happy and determined look on his face."

51. ss includes additional dialogue, as follows:

    Hermann methodically tears the checkbook into many tiny pieces and presses them into Maria's hand.

    HERMANN
    I don't want to be taken care of—especially not by you. That isn't good for us. You should understand that, since you're just like I am. Now, leave me alone.

52. The next scene in ss is not in the film: in it, Maria emerges from the prison and walks to her car "like a sleepwalker." There, she lets the pieces of paper fall out of her hand. "Her face is wet from tears."

53. The scene in which Maria is informed of Hermann's imminent release takes place in the lawyer's office in ss. She gratefully embraces the lawyer before rushing excitedly out of his office.

54. In ss, five scenes intervene between the end of the scene in which Maria learns that Hermann will be leaving prison (487) and the beginning of this one [her visit to the prison]:

    a) Maria goes shopping in a men's furnishings store to buy things for Hermann.

b) Oswald tells Senkenberg about the pact, an episode placed earlier in the film (435–440).

c) Maria and Oswald are lying in bed in her apartment after making love. She tells him it is the last time and confesses to him that she loves her husband. Oswald tells her that he knows and cries as he holds her. He dresses, says he is going somewhere to wait for her, then says goodbye. "Oswald's last words sound especially profound— almost like a warning. In any case, that is how Maria takes them. Oswald leaves. Dissolve on Maria's face."

d) Hermann is seen leaving the prison in a taxi. Then he is seen inside the taxi, saying to the driver "to Canada" but "first to the train station."

e) Maria rushes around her apartment, half-dressed, doing things like rearranging furniture and the clothing in the closet, then undoing what she has done in excited anticipation of Hermann's return. When calling her secretary to say that she will not be coming to the office, she asks where Oswald is.

55. In ss, this scene takes place at the prison entrance. Hermann's note is worded differently: "Because I love you, I need to have a life of my own. When I have it, I'll come back and ask if you want to be my wife."

56. Here ss includes a scene in which Maria is at home again. After just sitting for a while, she starts mechanically putting everything back the way it was before she rearranged things for Hermann's homecoming. She puts Hermann's clothes into a suitcase and replaces her own in the closet and drawers, puts the suitcase under the bed, then falls across the bed and starts to cry.

57. The use of the piano here is not indicated in ss.

58. In ss, Oswald goes to Maria's empty apartment, finds and reads the note from Hermann, and calls the office. Maria answers, but when Oswald speaks, she hangs up.

59. In ss, Maria collapses as she gets up from her desk to leave with Oswald. He picks her up and puts her on the couch. She opens her eyes and says to

him, "Take me home with you. Like a brother. I'm so alone in the world. I'm afraid."

60. In SS, Wetzel is not included in the scene at the new house (501–512). In the film, the same dialogue for Maria, Mother, and the mover has been adapted to include Wetzel.

61. In SS, Maria has moved into a larger and more luxurious office for the scene with the secretary (513–519). Maria also comforts the secretary after their argument.

62. The dialogue in the luncheon scene at the Bastion (520–528) is slightly altered and condensed in the film. In SS, the scene ends with Maria and Oswald laughing together.

63. In SS, Willi's talk with Maria takes place in a rowboat on a small lake.

64. There is additional dialogue in SS as Willi asks if Maria is still receiving a rose from Hermann every month. When Willi asks about Oswald, she replies that he is "still my lover too—every month."

65. In SS, Maria cries when she comes inside and simply forgets to take her purse off of her arm. After calling Oswald, she sets up a table beside the couch with an ashtray, a bottle, and a glass, and then she carefully arranges the lighting. SS continues with a scene not in the film presenting Maria's rendevous with Oswald. Directions call for the mise-en-scène to remind the viewer of their first night together in the hotel (note 33). After Oswald arrives, Maria undresses before him under the lamp she had carefully placed for this purpose. The scene fades out, then fades in to find them lying on the floor after making love. Oswald says that he is reminded of their first night together. Maria says that she wanted him to recall it and wanted to evoke it for herself as well. The subsequent dialogue is as follows:

OSWALD
You said then that you wanted it to be that *you* were sleeping with *me*. Does that go for today too?

MARIA
No. I think it wasn't true then either—or only half-true. I think it somehow seems to me that I'm like a whore and that I can only overcome that
if I act like one—or, at least, how I think a whore acts when she seduces
a man.

OSWALD
And was that how it was today?

MARIA
Yes. No. I don't know. Maybe.

OSWALD
And if it was something else?

MARIA
Yes?

OSWALD
What if it was then, and now too, that you just wanted to deceive your
husband? So you secretly made up this difference between loving and
sleeping together—so you wouldn't be ashamed, because you didn't want
to have to be ashamed.

MARIA
I don't know. And if it were that way?

OSWALD
So you arranged the lamp this way and left these roses out, for the same
reason you like to undress in front of another man.

MARIA
I don't know. What if it was?

OSWALD
I love you, Maria. I always wished that you'd say that to me once too. It
took me a long time to accept the idea that you would never love me, but
I was always happy with you. I *am* happy with you.

Oswald nestles up to Maria and closes his eyes. Maria kisses him tenderly, covers him lovingly, and cradles him in her arm.

MARIA
Thanks.

Oswald opens his eyes and looks at Maria for a long time.

OSWALD
I'm going now.
MARIA
Stay with me tonight.
OSWALD
No, I want to be alone. I'm very tired—and very happy.

66. In ss, Maria, arriving in a good mood, hears the news of Oswald's death from Senkenberg in the lobby of the firm.

67. In ss, two brief scenes follow. In the first, Maria is seen in the bathtub tearing Oswald's obituary notices out of the newspapers. She reads them all carefully, then rips them up and scatters them into the bath as tears run down her face. In the second, the setting is the cemetery where Oswald is being buried. Maria is the only one of those in the party who is not crying. She throws the first shovel of dirt on the grave.

68. In ss, when Hermann arrives at Maria's new house, she is discovered inside, sleeping on the couch "with her thumb in her mouth" and with empty bottles on the floor beside her. When the doorbell rings, she yells, "I'm sleeping. I'm sad. I want to die."

69. ss provides directions for Maria's frantic behavior as she tries to do several things at one time throughout the reunion sequence. The ironic commentary provided by the broadcast of the soccer World Championship throughout this sequence is Fassbinder's contribution.

70. When Hermann asks Maria if she is afraid, Maria answers in ss, "No. I trust in us—very much." Hermann replies, "Me too."

71. ss ends the scene with Maria and Hermann packed for the honeymoon trip she has suggested. She calls Senkenberg to tell him that she will not be in to work. She is reminded by him about the reading of the will and she says that she will be back in time. ss then calls for a cross-cut to Senkenberg at the other end of the line—"He looks sad." Maria hangs up and she and Hermann pick up their bags to leave, then drop them as Hermann passionately kisses Maria. The next scene in ss is also not included in the film.

Maria and Hermann are in her car on the way to the country. Hermann says he has never been in a car driven by a woman before, then asks if Maria remembers when she gave him the checkbook.

72. In ss, this dialogue takes place in a hotel room. After Maria explains that her gift was "just a simple checkbook," Hermann responds, "I felt dependent on you. I felt small beside you—like in a borrowed suit." It gets dark and they prepare to make love. There is a fade-out. Two brief scenes not in the film follow. In the first, Hermann and Maria are in bed after making love. Hermann embraces her in his sleep and Maria is crying softly. In the second, Hermann and Maria play table tennis at the hotel. They look happy. They don't play well, but they compete against one another in a friendly way, while bantering back and forth. Maria proposes her plan for a contract between them, a proposal placed elsewhere in the film (561). Hermann wins the table tennis match.

73. In ss, the reading of Oswald's will takes place in a notary's office. Maria, Hermann, and Senkenberg are present as the notary reads the will, which includes a ten percent share of the firm's future profits for Senkenberg. There are directions in ss for Senkenberg to glance nervously at Maria, and for Hermann to avert his eyes from hers while the will is being read.

74. In ss, Oswald's will states, "I gave him [Hermann] the chance for independence. He gave me the chance for happiness." The rest of Oswald's statement does not appear in ss. After the pact is disclosed, "Maria breathes deeply and closes her eyes" and ss scene fades out.

75. The last scene of the film, in ss, is as follows:

AUTOMOBILE RIDE, EXTERIOR/DAY
Maria drives, Hermann sits next to her. They are just leaving the suburbs and coming to open country.

HERMANN
Please don't forget that I'm giving you everything. All the money. It doesn't interest me anymore.
MARIA
I have given you everything. My whole life.

They are now on an open highway. Maria speeds up. There is a sharp curve in the highway up ahead.

HERMANN
(lovingly)
Where are you driving us?
MARIA
To the country.

We see the car approach the curve. Maria continues to drive straight ahead. The car races over the embankment and disappears. A moment of silence. Then we hear an explosion from behind the embankment and see a cloud of smoke rise up.

THE END

Contexts

Contexts

The section that follows includes some materials that provide background information on the preparation and production of *The Marriage of Maria Braun*.

The first piece, "Strong Emotions," is an interview with Peter Märthesheimer, producer of most of Fassbinder's works for television, who, in collaboration with the psychologist Pea Fröhlich, wrote the script of *Maria Braun*. The second is a letter from Märthesheimer to the editor of this volume.

The third piece is Hans-Jürgen Jagau's interview with Fassbinder, first published in 1979, and the fourth an interview by Ernst Burkel, also published in 1979, with both Fassbinder and Douglas Sirk. Fassbinder had worked under Sirk in 1978 on *Bourbon Street Blues*, a small production of the Munich Film and Television Academy, very much as if he had been a student enrolled in one of the classes Sirk was teaching.

The last piece, "Six Films by Douglas Sirk," was written by Fassbinder and first published in 1971.

Strong Emotions: An Interview with Scriptwriter Peter Märthesheimer

Int.: How did you come to work on this project?

Märthesheimer: It all started when Fassbinder told me the plot of this story and wanted to know if I found it interesting. He then handed me a rough draft for a crude tearjerker that somebody from Hamburg had already written down.

Int.: Why did Fassbinder come to you in this situation? Was it because of your experiences working together?

Märthesheimer: Rainer is surrounded by people who are dependent on him and whose relationship to him is to be completely uncritical. And when someone new comes on the scene, he sees to it that the newcomer soon loses his critical capacities, otherwise he feels crushed and punished. He tried that with me too, but I'm not dependent on him. And that's the reason he knows that my judgements about proposals, scripts, etc., are not judgements about him personally.

Int.: What interested you about the project?

Märthesheimer: My interest started out as a sporting one, since Fassbinder had said, "Do you think you can do anything with this disastrous structure?" And it pleased me to do the great Fassbinder this personal favor.

Int.: What difficulties did you have in working on the script?

Märthesheimer: None.

Int.: How did the character of Maria change from the original proposal to the script?

Märthesheimer: I had fun working on the character of Maria. When I think about it in retrospect, it always bothers me to think that I was being paid for work that was so much fun. Where else does anybody have this in his work! Maria is certainly not a realistic character, but something that is usually called a "film figure." By that I mean, a figure that embodies in a very condensed form the wishes, characteristics, and desires of the viewers. You could say that she's got guts, she's ambitious, and she's the type of person who relies entirely on her

From the press materials for *The Marriage of Maria Braun*. Translated by Joyce Rheuban.

emotions. She is therefore no mere pawn, but a highly capable, clever, skillful and practical person, who—as is generally not the case—in spite of all that, relies on her emotions.

Int.: Maria does indeed have a capacity for strong emotion—which she attaches to her husband. But yet she starts this affair with the businessman, Oswald. Is that so admirable?

Märthesheimer: First of all, she makes it quite clear to Oswald that she's not sleeping with him because he's the boss, but because she wants someone to sleep with. Maybe she's also sleeping with him not so much out of a sexual need, as out of the much stronger need of a little girl who sometimes needs a father figure whose shoulder she can lean on.

Int.: Maria definitely has a deficit in her emotions that must be satisfied. But the time she lives in presents an obstacle to that fulfillment. The early fifties was a time in which people were judged by their productiveness.

Märthesheimer: I think such a contradiction has to remain unresolved. Maybe the ending can serve to clarify what I mean by this. At the end, this film character comes back down to earth, so to speak. And she realizes that there aren't just little fleecy clouds up there in the sky, but that maybe the sun looms dimly over us, and that the world is really rather crooked and deformed. Then she says to herself: if that's the way it is, then I'm going to make an end of living in this world.

Int.: That's pathetic.

Märthesheimer: She says it very pathetically. What other alternatives does she have, as high-strung as she is? In the script, she purposely causes an actual automobile accident—in the film, it's an accidental gas explosion. The pathos that Maria has lived with for ninety minutes is, in this moment, juxtaposed against the actual circumstances of her life. Now I think it's important that this character, Maria, despite everything, is right; and that she is also right when she takes leave of the world in this way. But she is also right in the way she has led her life. She refused to live an easy life—she doesn't marry the eligible Oswald, who could offer her so much; she doesn't just give up on Hermann either.

Int.: Here she slaves away year after year, and yet all she gets out of this marriage is half a day and this one night.

Märthesheimer: I actually think that the script came forth out of my consciousness, shaped by my own experiences and observations. There is a sad part to this, as I see it. And that is the poverty that governs the way people deal with each other—the way they just don't make any demands and are never even in a position to have strong passions like love, or hate. They just keep on being miserable. Insofar as this has to do with today—

Int.: In the film, the gas explosion appears to be an accident. In your script was Maria's accident consciously caused?

Märthesheimer: Yes, she wants to end her life and Hermann's, who did this to her with this contract with Oswald. One can surmise from this ending that Maria is only now confronted with the reality of her love for Hermann. Up until then she was happy, as long as she and this man were kept apart.

Int.: Would a Maria Braun have contributed something to the reconstruction of the Bundesrepublik if she had not accidently encountered Oswald?

Märthesheimer: Not at all.

Int.: She would have had no motivation?

Märthesheimer: No.

Int.: How was your working relationship with Fassbinder?

Märthesheimer: Unfortunately, there was no working relationship. Instead, he read the scenario and said, it's wonderful just as it is.

A Letter to the Editor

Peter Märthesheimer

To better understand the variations between the script and the film, perhaps I should mention the following: *Maria Braun* was my first script and therefore has the distinguishing feature of all first works. Out of sheer enthusiasm to master the material and the characters, one can lose control of the words—the script became too long. With the perspective of a few weeks afterward, I realized this myself and I wanted to do a revised version. But Fassbinder would have no part of that. Instead, he wanted to film this "quite wonderful" script "just as it was," just as it lay before him.

I had known him long enough to know that he didn't mean that, and that, in actuality, he wanted to rework the script himself in order to add his own material. Since I agreed, and since there was no getting anywhere with Fassbinder once his mind was made up about something, we stuck with our original version.

Even though we stayed with this original script, there was something I didn't anticipate. Fassbinder began—but not until after the first day of shooting—to shorten the scenes and write new dialogue for the transitions, at night, in the breaks during shooting, and at lunch!

I might have expected it after *Despair* (his first script by someone other than himself). When he got *Despair*, also a script that was quite obviously much too long, he swore up and down to the author, Tom Stoppard, and myself (at that time I was his [Fassbinder's] producer) that he needed to direct the film from just exactly this script (also a "first version"!)—and that he'd do it very quickly and fast paced, something like a boulevard comedy. If you know the film, you can see what Fassbinder was up to at night after the first day of shooting.

But that's just how he worked—enthusiastically, spontaneously, and with complete confidence in the validity of his dreams—once he started to dream about something (I mean, the first day on location). (Otherwise, with *Lola* and *Veronika Voss*, film and script correspond pretty closely, except for, in each case, a significant reinterpretation of the characterizations. But this may simply have to do with the fact that I had learned more in the meantime.)

As for the ending of the film [*Maria Braun*]—we actually talked it over for quite some time. We were both in favor of Maria, when she realizes that her idea of love didn't correspond with the reality of this love, consciously putting an end to this love and this life. Even now, I find this type of ending preferable to the film's, as it were, inadvertent accident. Unfortunately, all that occurred to me at the time was this weak resolution with the automobile accident. Compared to my ending, the ending with the exploding house is, of course, much more impressive and significant. And, anyway, Fassbinder was always of the opinion that seemingly inadvertent things signified more about people's true motivations than their superficial, conscious actions. And there, ultimately, he was right.

(22 October 1983)

Interview with Rainer Werner Fassbinder: The Decline of the BRD

Hans-Jürgen Jagau

Int.: A little while ago, you had definitely decided to emigrate. Is your new maxim, "Stay in this country and keep up the fight"? How did you come to revise your plan?

Fassbinder: My plans to leave the Federal Republic of Germany haven't changed at all, but I never had any specific deadline. I was actually expressing the feeling that the climate in this country was heading noticeably, day by day, in a direction that frightened me more and more. So I think sooner or later the time will come when I won't be living here anymore. To put it simply, I just hope I never see the time when it's not possible for me just to leave.

Anyway, there were several obligations that I still had to take care of. And then all of a sudden this "Berlin Alexanderplatz" project came to me, and the nearly two years of work on this project made it seem more sensible to stay here. I did take one small, but still important step though, when I left Munich to live in Berlin; since Munich goes along with this trend in the German Federal Republic, which, in my opinion, is clearly regressive—in a frighteningly uncritical and almost too familiar way. Whereas Berlin still has a climate that, at least outwardly, permits a critical position that opposes this trend.

Besides—although what I'm about to say may merely be self deception—the form this West German democracy is taking, which, in my opinion, is a particularly subtle and sophisticated form of totalitarianism, is evolving much more slowly than it seemed to be doing so clearly in Fall, 1977. So, apart from expecting your dreams to come true, as long as you can still do something about this, then you should stay and do it.

Int.: Fascism and decadence seen from a very personalized perspective is the theme of *Despair*. Is your film *The Marriage of Maria Braun* similarly oriented?

Fassbinder: It wasn't my intention to make fascism and decadence the theme of

"Die BRD macht eine rückläufige Entwicklung durch. Gespräch mit Rainer Werner Fassbinder," *Zitty* (Berlin), May 1979, p. 32. Translated by Joyce Rheuban.

Despair. Rather it was the flight of an individual into a kind of utopia, from a feeling which he couldn't put into words but which, in fact, was the encroachment of fascism. This utopia of madness was the sure hope that insanity offered the chance, for always, to live happy and free, not in so-called reality, but, shall we say, in another country.

Obviously, this kind of utopia can only work for someone who isn't all caught up in the daily routine of making a living. It has to be somebody who is privileged enough to afford this madness. You may call that decadent, though I don't.

Of course the film *The Marriage of Maria Braun* is similar to this. But then *Maria Braun* is a film by me, and the films I make all relate to one another. Then again, the narrative style of *The Marriage of Maria Braun* is quite different from that of *Despair*. But like *Despair*, it has to do with a woman in this case, who is able to afford certain things which the majority of people are not able to afford. But unlike *Despair*, where the factory owner is independent from the beginning—at least outwardly—Maria wins her independence very slowly. She isn't privileged from the outset like Hermann [Hermann Hermann in *Despair*]. Her independence is quite clearly a hard won independence. So the film *The Marriage of Maria Braun* is similar to the film *Despair* and yet very different—as much as the works of one director can be different.

Int.: The portraits of the West German chancellors form a sequence in the last few moments of the film. Only Willy Brandt is missing, although during his term as chancellor the work bans came into effect as well as the anti-terrorist legislation, which limited the freedom of citizens even further.

Fassbinder: No, we talked this over for a long time. In that instance, fascist technocrats prevailed against him, as it were. He was still a symbol of the reform movement, and despite his failure—and that's another story—there is still a difference between him and the other chancellors.

Int.: You went from a German distributor to a "major company." Was that in order to gain greater financial freedom or was there another reason?

Fassbinder: Your question must be based on misinformation. It's not true that I turned to a major company. I made a film with German production companies for the Filmverlag der Autoren. The Filmverlag der Autoren is an enterprise in whose founding I was rather significantly involved. And I have, shall we say, a moral agreement with the Filmverlag der Autoren that they distribute all my films, even when, at the present time, I wouldn't do as well with them as I would with another distributor. The fact that this film [*Maria Braun*] is coming out under the auspices of a major company is completely opposed to my wishes and is the result of the shady tactics of the producer Michael Fengler and his moneyman, Eckelkamp. But this story still hasn't come out even now. I have nothing against a major company because I know that, naturally, a major company can do more for a film, at least at the moment. But, and this may sound sentimental, I'm too attached to the Filmverlag der Autoren.

Int.: Does success have any significance for you? One would like to think that Fassbinder would make films no matter what.

Fassbinder: Success only meant something to me, or was important to me when it enabled me to keep on working, and that's how it still is. It's not true at all that I'd keep on making films no matter what. Every film is a struggle. With each film you find yourself—or I find myself—in situations that could also turn out to be catastrophies for me personally.

Int.: What have you read recently?

Fassbinder: I've read Bakunin's *Statism and Anarchism*; Thomas's *The Ritual of Drugs*; Sigmund Freud's *Moses and Monotheism*; *Arsenic Blossoms*, by the girl who supposedly killed herself in Paris at seventeen. I've read Aloys [sic] Mario Simmel's *Hurrah, We're Still Alive*, and I'm reading, or am trying constantly to read Schopenhauer's *The World as Will and Idea*, and I'm always reading Vesper's *The Journey* and sado-masochistic pornos on a regular basis.

Int.: In two or three sentences, could you summarize what *In a Year of Thirteen Moons* is about?

Fassbinder: Let's say—as simply as possible—it's about a person who does something totally irrational in order to be loved. He undergoes an operation to be changed from a man into a woman. Until he ultimately kills himself, he is unable to free himself from: 1. his role as a woman, and 2. his amiable indifference toward an environment so caught up in superficially important things.

Responding to What You Experience:
An Interview with the Film Directors
Douglas Sirk and Rainer Werner Fassbinder

Ernst Burkel

Int.: Mr. Fassbinder, it's often observed that your own personality is always rather obviously apparent at the center of your films . . .

Fassbinder: I've always made them that way, but you only see it when you look back on them—that's the way it is with these so-called "studio directors" from Hollywood. If you look at their films now, you can see that these films could only have been made by a certain director. The fact that it's still a bit more personalized with us has to do with the fact that we don't have this studio system and can therefore involve our own personality more openly and easily. But even with this studio system, where there's always something hindering that freedom, you can clearly see that a certain film can only be by Douglas Sirk, another only by Raoul Walsh. In spite of the studios, in spite of the fact that these directors sometimes had to deal with actors they didn't want to work with, there is still a very personal view of the world conveyed there.

Int.: Is this your conception of film?

Fassbinder: I say what I'm experiencing, and what I then recount to people in an honest way must also apply to them, since, though I'm sure I look at things from a different perspective than most people, in the end, the experiences are the same. By that I mean, when I tell a story in a very personal way, it applies to more people than if I try to tell it in a way that's supposed to speak to everyone. But in this "Filmland" that he [Sirk] was in, this personalized vision occupied such an important place that individual oeuvres arose there too.

The only difficulty is finding out what it is that is personal and unique about them. A Jean Paul sentence is always recognizable as a Jean Paul sentence—and ultimately a Douglas Sirk sequence is always recognizable as a Douglas Sirk sequence, in spite of the film industry and its restrictions. The fact that now we

"Reagieren auf das, was man erlebt. Ein Gespräch mit den Filmregisseuren Douglas Sirk und Rainer Werner Fassbinder," *Süddeutsche Zeitung* (Munich), 8 March 1979, p. 11. Translated by Joyce Rheuban.

are a trace more personal has to do with the fact that we are able to be—at the moment. It could change again, maybe one of these days I'll go with some other system, but you'll always see a personal expression there. And this is what I saw concretely for the first time in Sirk—that, despite working under the conditions of a different kind of system that was based on profit, something quite unique and personal still came out of it.

Sirk: Rainer has hit upon the central issue of all filmmaking there. The most important thing to any filmmaker should be, what is his image of reality. I know that with Beckmann, for example, it can only be Beckmann's, Nolde is Nolde, and with Rainer I know it's got to be Rainer's. He has an unmistakable signature, an inimitable signature.

Fassbinder: It would be difficult to imitate my style. But there are actually people that do imitate things, who just try to copy some formal element because it's something they like, and they don't try to transform it in any way. In the first film I made after seeing his [Sirk's] films—that was *Merchant of Four Seasons*—I was also in danger that I would just copy *All That Heaven Allows*. Then I tried to do a remake, so to speak, of what I had seen—that was *Fear Eats the Soul*. But when you do something like this you have to try to let what you have seen come through and tell your story with the film experience you have, but you can't just make something over again just because you liked it. This relates to the scene with the television in my film. It's different than in *All That Heaven Allows*, where the children give a television instead of having the typical Christmas scene. My film takes place in a more base and brutal world. The same story takes place in his film in an American small town, where things are more under control than in the world of my story. But this is his point—to give a television instead of a man, within this whole small town context is much more sinister than the impulsive act that takes place in my film. That's the type of little thing that you can't just imitate, but need to transpose.

Sirk: Rainer, you're exactly right. My wife and I saw *Fear Eats the Soul* together and we think it's one of your best and most beautiful films, and unmistakably bears your mark. My wife, who obviously knows my films, never thought there was any connection between what she was watching and *All That Heaven Allows*.

Fassbinder: My way of making films is different from his [Sirk's]. He worked within the system, and was given a certain time to complete a film. I respond through my films to how I experience things, how I feel about them. But that doesn't mean that there has to be a difference. The difference may be that I'll make a hundred films and he's made thirty-nine. But that doesn't mean a thing. It only means that I have made films more directly and more radically, in a different kind of situation—that I've reacted differently and more spontaneously to reality than he has. He had the whole system behind him. That's why it's even more incredible that anyone managed to create such a personal world within this rigid American studio system. Not too many people succeeded in doing this. A lot of them gave in and made formula films, got hung up on success and sold out their innermost selves. To sell yourself isn't necessarily so bad—it's socially accept-able. But so many people sold out, right down to their deepest self, right down to the core of their perception, that I always rejoice over the few people and the few American oeuvres in which I experience something about life and time, about thoughts, about the possibilities of thinking, about perceptual possibilities, about narrative possibilities. And among these few directors is Douglas Sirk; I feel very close to him for this reason, and on a personal level too, because he's a German.

He was completely different than I had imagined a Hollywood director to be. In fact, he was just the way I hoped one would be. What I really wanted some-body who made Hollywood films to be was definitely not somebody who just read Mickey Mouse comic books and chewed gum, but somebody you could talk with about Arnolt Bronnen and Brecht, and who succeeded in complying with the conditions of the system, and yet made personal films. After I had made ten films which were very personal, the time came when we said, we have to find a way to make films for the public—and then came my encounter with his films, and then with Douglas Sirk himself. That was tremendously important for me. And then—to come back to this supposed father-son relationship—it was, and is not the same thing, because most father-son relations are usually relations of conflict. I found a person who makes art in a way, as I've said, that was bound to change something in me. I'm making something—and maybe he sees this—that takes what he made the next step. And now here we are, making this film to-gether and enjoying it very much. But we have too little time, and the film's too short, and any one film isn't enough. But I think he's gotten to know me better from my films, and I know more about him from his films than from this collaboration.

Sirk: The big difference is, he's making films, and I'm not anymore . . . Before I got to know Rainer, I could tell there was something about him. And then when I saw him, I could see with my own eyes that this was the filmmaker in whom I had sensed a personality of such great originality.

Int.: Herr Fassbinder, can you forsee a point where you too won't be making films any more?

Fassbinder: That, I really can't say. I'll probably always make films, as I see it now—but things could change. I can't imagine a point where I'm no longer able to make films—I just do it, and then it so happens that these films are treated like works of art.

I have to try to establish my own priorities in order to protect myself from being sucked up into other people's priorities. I have to try to arm myself against these rigid schemas from which I'd rather just be excluded entirely. . . . Isn't it art—to try to use what you create to sensitize your public for life, for the good of the world? It's a process of sensitizing, which you undertake on your own and then have to convey to your audience—that's all it is.

Sirk: I said to Rainer while we were discussing his role in this student production, just imagine that all of a sudden for some reason or other, you weren't able to make films any more—well, that's the way this character feels who is no longer able to write. And Rainer immediately understood—he *has to* make films. I can't imagine him not making films any more. I have the feeling that he's just starting on another, even greater career.

Fassbinder: It doesn't matter in the least whether you actually write, or whether you just create through your own fantasies—like this Chekov character I'm playing in the Tennessee Williams story we're doing. When he engages in his fantasy with such intensity that he's just as successful in bringing it into being as someone who writes it, then it's just the same as someone who really is a successful writer. Thomas Mann said, "I'd rather participate in life than write a hundred stories"— you can't always be so sure which is more important. Participating makes me feel very uncomfortable. There also has to be the option of not participating directly in life, but participating through some kind of process of mediation. And you don't have to look at this as if it were: either make films, or live life, or what have you—that's going a little too far. Why can't I live for people and still do my work? And then, you have to understand, my filmmaking takes a lot of my energy—but I'm not doing work that is alien to me. When you do work you don't care about, then you don't use as much energy and you live ten or twenty years longer—but those are sad years. That's why I think it's better to make films and not live like that—even though it takes more out of you.

Six Films by Douglas Sirk

Rainer Werner Fassbinder

"Film is like a battleground" Sam Fuller, who once wrote a script for Douglas Sirk, said in a film by Jean-Luc Godard, who, shortly before he made *A Bout de Souffle*, wrote a rhapsody on Douglas Sirk's *A Time to Love and a Time to Die* ["Des Larmes et de la Vitesse," *Cahiers du Cinéma*, no. 94]. But not one of us, Godard or Fuller or me or anybody else, can touch Douglas Sirk. Sirk has said: "Cinema is blood, is tears, violence, hate, death, and love." And Sirk has made films with blood, with tears, with violence, hate—films with death and films with love. Sirk has said: you can't make films about things, you can only make films with things, with people, with light, with flowers, with mirrors, with blood, in fact with all the fantastic things which make life worth living. Sirk has also said: a director's philosophy is lighting and camera angles. And Sirk has made the tenderest films I know, they are the films of someone who loves people and doesn't despise them as we do. Darryl F. Zanuck once said to Sirk: "They've got to like the movie in Kansas City and in Singapore." America is really something else.

Douglas Sirk had a grandmother, she wrote poems and had black hair. In those days Douglas was still called Detlef and lived in Denmark. As it happened the Nordic countries around 1910 produced their own films, specializing particularly in big human dramas. And so little Detlef and his poetry-writing grandmother went to the tiny Danish cinema and cried their eyes out, over and over again, at the tragic death of Asta Nielsen and many other beautiful ladies with pale, pale make-up. They could only go secretly, because Detlef Sierck was supposed to be brought up in the German tradition, have a proper classical education, and so one day his love for Asta Nielsen gave way to a love for Clytemnestra. He worked in the theatre in Germany: in Bremen, Chemnitz, Hamburg, Leipzig; he was an educated man who was also cultured. He counted Max Brod among his friends, got to know Kafka and so on. He seemed to be embarking on a career which could have led to the directorship of the Munich Residenztheater. But no, in

This article was first published as "Imitation of Life. Rainer Werner Fassbinder on the Films of Douglas Sirk" in *Fernsehen und Film* (Hannover) 2 (February 1971):9–13. Translated by Thomas Elsaesser and published in *Douglas Sirk*, ed. Laura Mulvey and John Halliday (Edinburgh: Edinburgh Film Festival, 1972).

1937, having made a few films in Germany for UFA, Detlef Sierck emigrated to America, became Douglas Sirk and made films which, among people of his sort of background in Germany, would merely raise a smile.

All That Heaven Allows

So it happens that you can meet a man in Lugano, in Switzerland, who is so alert, and so intelligent—unlike anyone else I have ever met, who can say, with a hardly perceptible, happy smile "sometimes I really loved the things I did—very much." What he loved, for example, was *All That Heaven Allows* (1956). Jane Wyman is a rich widow, Rock Hudson prunes trees for her. In Jane's garden a love tree is in flower, which only flowers where love is, and so, out of Jane's and Rock's chance meeting grows the love of their lives. But Rock is fifteen years younger than Jane and Jane is completely integrated into the social life of her small American town. Rock is a primitive and Jane has something to lose: her friends, her status which she owes to her late husband, her children. At the beginning Rock is in love with Nature, Jane at first doesn't love anything because she has everything.

It's a pretty abysmal start for the love of one's life. She, he and the world they live in. Basically that's how it seems. She has a motherly touch, she looks as though she might be able to soften at the right moment: we can understand what Rock sees in her. He is a tree trunk. He is quite right to want to be inside her. The world around is evil. The women all talk too much. There are no men in the film apart from Rock, in that respect arm chairs and glasses are more important. After seeing this film small town America is the last place in the world I would want to go. What it amounts to is that somewhere along the line Jane tells Rock that she is going to leave him, because of her idiotic children and so on. Rock doesn't protest too much, he still has Nature, after all. And there Jane sits on Christmas Eve, her children are going to leave her anyway and they've brought her a television set for Christmas. It's too much. It tells you something about the world and what it does to you. Later on, Jane goes back to Rock because she has headaches, which is what happens to us all if we don't fuck once in a while. But now she's back there's still no happy ending. If anyone has made their love life that complicated for themselves they won't be able to live happily ever afterwards.

This is the kind of thing Douglas Sirk makes movies about. People can't live alone, but they can't live together either. This is why his movies are so desperate.

All That Heaven Allows opens with a long shot of the small town. The titles appear across it. Which looks very sad. It is followed by a crane shot down to Jane's house, a friend is just arriving, bringing back some crockery she has borrowed. Really sad! A tracking shot follows the two women and there, in the background, stands Rock Hudson, blurred, in the way an extra usually stands around in a Hollywood film. And as her friend has no time to have a cup of coffee with Jane, Jane has her coffee with the extra. Still only close-ups of Jane Wyman, even at this stage. Rock has no real significance as yet. Once he has, he gets his close-ups too. It's simple and beautiful. And everybody sees the point.

Douglas Sirk's films are descriptive. Very few close-ups. Even in shot-countershot the other person doesn't appear fully in the frame. The spectator's intense feeling is not a result of identification, but of montage and music. This is why we come out of these movies feeling somewhat dissatisfied. What we have seen is something of other people. And if there's anything there which concerns you personally, you are at liberty to acknowledge it or to take its meaning with a laugh. Jane's children are something else. There's an old guy to whom they are superior in every way, in youth, in knowledge, and so on, and they think he would make an ideal match for their mother. Then there's Rock, who is not much older than they are, better looking, and not that stupid either. But they react to him with terror. It's fantastic. Jane's son offers them both, Rock and the old guy, a cocktail. Both eulogize the cocktail. In one case, when it's the old guy, the children beam with delight. But when it's Rock, the tension in the room is ready to explode. The same shot both times. The way Sirk handles actors is too much. If you look at Fritz Lang's later films which he made at that time, in which incapacity is everywhere in evidence, you can surely see what Sirk is all about. Women think in Sirk's films. Something which has never struck me with other directors. None of them. Usually women are always reacting, doing what women are supposed to do, but in Sirk they think. It's something that has to be seen. It's great to see women think. It gives one hope. Honestly.

Then, in Sirk, people are always placed in rooms already heavily marked by their social situation. The rooms are incredibly exact. In Jane's house there is only one way in which one could possibly move. Only certain kinds of sentences could come to mind when wanting to say something, certain gestures when wanting to express something. When Jane goes to another house, to Rock's, for instance, would she be able to change? That would be grounds for hope. Or, on the other hand, she may well be so hung-up and stereotyped already that in Rock's house she will miss the style of life she is used to and which has become her own. That's why the happy ending is not one. Jane fits into her own home better than she fits into Rock's.

Written on the Wind

Written on the Wind (1957) is the story of a super-rich family. Robert Stack is the son, who was never as good, in any way, as his friend, Rock Hudson. Robert Stack knows how to spend his money: he flies aeroplanes, drinks, lays girls; Rock Hudson is his constant companion. But they are not happy. There's no love in their lives. Then they meet Lauren Bacall. Naturally she is different from all other women. She's straightforward, works for her living, is practical, she's tender and understanding. And yet she chooses the bad guy, Robert, although the good guy, Rock, would suit her much better. Rock has to work for his living too, is practical, understanding and big-hearted, like her. She picks the one with whom things can't possibly work out in the long run. When Lauren Bacall meets Robert Stack's father for the first time she asks him to give Robert another chance. It's disgusting the way the kind lady kicks the good guy in the balls to set things up for the bad guy. Yes indeed, everything is bound to go wrong. Let's hope so. Dorothy Malone, the sister, is the only one who is in love with the right person, i.e. Rock Hudson, and she stands by her love which is ridiculous, of course. It has to be ridiculous when everyone else thinks their surrogate actions are the real thing, it is quite clear that everything she does, she does because she can't have the real thing.

Lauren Bacall is a surrogate for Robert Stack because he must know he will never be able to love her, and vice versa. And the father has an oil derrick in his hand which looks like a surrogate cock. And when Dorothy Malone at the end, sole surviving member of the family, has this cock in her hand it is at least as wretched as the television set which Jane Wyman gets for Christmas. Which is a surrogate for the fuck her children begrudge her just as Dorothy Malone's oil empire is a surrogate for Rock Hudson. I hope she won't make it and will go mad like Marianne Koch in *Interlude*. For Douglas Sirk, madness is a sign of hope, I think.

Rock Hudson in *Written on the Wind* is all in all the most pig-headed bastard in the world. How can he possibly not feel something of the longing Dorothy Malone has for him? She offers herself, goes after guys who look vaguely like him so as to make him understand. And all he can say is "I could never satisfy you." God knows, he could. While Dorothy is dancing in her room, dancing the dance of a corpse—maybe that's the moment her madness begins—her father dies. He dies because he is guilty. He has always fostered the belief in his real children that Rock Hudson was better than them, until in the end he really was. Because he could never do what he wanted himself and he had always thought Rock's father, who had never made any money and could go hunting whenever he wanted to go hunting, was better than he was. The children are just poor, dumb pigeons. Probably he understands his guilt and it kills him. In any case, the spectator understands it. His death isn't terrible.

Because Robert doesn't love Lauren he wants a child by her. Or because Robert has had no chance to achieve anything, he wants at least to father a child. But his efforts reveal a fatal weakness. Robert starts drinking again. Now it becomes clear that Lauren Bacall is no use to her husband. Instead of drinking with him, understanding something of his pain, she becomes nobler and purer than ever, she makes us feel more and more sick and we can see more and more clearly how well she would get on with Rock Hudson, who also makes us feel sick and is also noble. People who are brought up to be useful, with their heads full of manipulated dreams, are always screwed up. If Lauren Bacall had lived with Robert Stack, instead of living next to him, through him, and for him then he might have believed that the child she is expecting is really his. He wouldn't have had to suffer. But, as it is, the child belongs more to Rock in actual fact, although he never slept with Lauren.

Dorothy does something bad, she sets her brother against Lauren and Rock. All the same, I love her as I rarely love anyone in the cinema, as a spectator I follow with Douglas Sirk the traces of human despair. In *Written on the Wind* the good, the "normal," the "beautiful" are always utterly revolting; the evil, the weak, the dissolute arouse one's compassion. Even for the manipulators of the good.

And then again, the house in which it all takes place. Governed, so to speak, by one huge staircase. And mirrors. And endless flowers. And gold. And coldness. A house such as one would build if one had a lot of money. A house with all the props that go with having real money, and in which one cannot feel at ease. It is like the Oktoberfest, where everything is colorful and in movement, and you feel as alone as everyone. Human emotions have to blossom in the strangest ways in this house Douglas Sirk had built for the Hadleys. Sirk's lighting is always as unnatural as possible. Shadows where there shouldn't be any make feelings plausible which one would rather have left unacknowledged. In the same way the camera angles in *Written on the Wind* are almost always tilted, mostly from below, so that the strange things in the story happen on the screen, not just in the spectator's head. Douglas Sirk's films liberate your head.

Interlude

Interlude (1957) is a film which is hard to get into. To begin with everything seems false. The film takes place in Munich, which we know is not like that at all. Munich in *Interlude* is made up of monumental show pieces: Königsplatz, Nymphenburg, Herkulessaal. After a while we can see the point: this is Munich as it might look to an American. June Allyson comes to Munich to experience Europe. What she experiences is a great love, the love of her life. He is Rossano Brazzi, who plays a Karajan-like conductor. June Allyson is slightly atypical of Sirk's characters. She seems to be too naturalistic, too healthy. Too much in bloom. Although she's sick enough by the end. Rossano Brazzi is a conductor through and through, right down to the softest, tenderest whispers of love. The way he moves is a feat of direction: always like a cockerel, always putting on a show for others even when he seriously means what he says. Brazzi plays his part the way that Wedekind's *Musik* ought to be played.

Brazzi has a wife, Marianne Koch. And if one wants to understand Douglas Sirk's view of the world, this character is crucial. Marianne Koch is in love with Rossano Brazzi. He married her, she was always happy when she was with him, and her love for him destroyed her. She went mad. All Sirkian characters chase an ideal, a longing. The one character who got everything she wanted was destroyed by it. Does this mean that in our society people are only accepted if they are always chasing something, like the dog with its tongue hanging out? Just as long as they stick to the rules which allow them to remain useful. After seeing Douglas Sirk's films I am more convinced than ever that love is the best, most insidious, most effective instrument of social repression. June Allyson takes a lesser love back to the States with her. But they will not be happy together either. She will always be dreaming of her conductor and he will always be seeing signs of her dissatisfied longings. They will absorb themselves all the more in their work, which will naturally now be exploited in turn. Right.

The Tarnished Angels

The Tarnished Angels (1958) is the only black and white Sirk I have been able to see. It is the film in which he had most freedom. An incredibly pessimistic film. It is based on a story by Faulkner which unfortunately I do not know. Apparently Sirk has profaned it which becomes it well.

The film, like *La Strada*, shows a dying profession, only not in such an awfully pretentious way. Robert Stack has been a pilot in the First World War. He had never wanted to do anything but fly, which is why he now takes part in air-shows circling round pylons. Dorothy Malone is his wife; she demonstrates para-chute jumping. They can barely make a living. Robert is brave but he knows nothing about machines, so he has a mechanic, Jiggs, the third one of their team, who is in love with Dorothy. Robert and Dorothy have a son, who Rock Hudson meets when he is being teased by the other fliers: "Who's your old man today kid? Jiggs, or . . . ." Rock Hudson is a journalist who wants to write a fantastic piece about these gypsies of the air who have crankcase oil in their veins instead of blood. It happens that the Shumanns have nowhere to stay so Rock Hudson invites them to his place. During the night Dorothy and Rock get to know each other. We get the feeling that these two would have a lot to say to each other. Rock loses his job, one of the fliers crashes in the race. Dorothy is supposed to prostitute herself for a plane as Robert's has broken down. Rock and Dorothy haven't got that much to say to each other after all, Jiggs repairs a broken-down plane, Robert goes up in it and is killed.

Nothing but defeats. This film is nothing but an accumulation of defeats. Dorothy is in love with Robert, Robert is in love with flying, Jiggs is in love with Robert too, or is it Dorothy and Rock? Rock is not in love with Dorothy and Dorothy is not in love with Rock. When the film makes one believe for a moment that they are, it's a lie at best, just as the two of them think for a couple of seconds, maybe . . . ? Then towards the end Robert tells Dorothy that after this race he'll give up flying. Of course that's exactly when he is killed. It would be inconceivable that Robert could really be involved with Dorothy rather than with death.

The camera is always on the move in the film; just like the people it moves round, it pretends that something is actually happening. In fact everything is so completely finished that everyone might as well give up and get themselves bur-ied. The tracking shots in the film, the crane shots, the pans! Douglas Sirk looks at these corpses with such tenderness and radiance that we start to think that something must be at fault if these people are so screwed up and, nevertheless, so nice. The fault lies with fear and loneliness. I have rarely felt fear and loneliness so much as in this film. The audience sits in the cinema like the Shumanns' son in the roundabout: we can see what's happening, we want to rush forward and help, but, thinking it over, what can a small boy do against a crashing aeroplane? They are all to blame for Robert's death. This is why Dorothy Malone is so hysterical afterwards. Because she knew. And Rock Hudson, who wanted a scoop. As soon as he gets it he starts shouting at his colleagues. And Jiggs, who shouldn't have repaired the plane, sits asking "Where is everybody?" Too bad he never noticed before that there never really was anybody. What these movies are about is the way people kid themselves. And why you have to kid yourself. Dorothy first saw Robert in a picture, a poster of him as a daring pilot, and she fell in love with him. Of course Robert was nothing like his picture. What can you do? Kid yourself. There you are. We tell ourselves, and we want to tell her, that she's under no compulsion to carry on, that her love for Robert isn't really love. What would be the point? Loneliness is easier to bear if you keep your illusions.

There you are. I think the film shows that this isn't so. Sirk has made a film in which there is continuous action, in which something is always happening, and the camera is in motion all the time, and we understand a lot about loneliness and how it makes us lie. And how wrong it is that we should lie, and how dumb.

A Time to Love and a Time to Die

A Time to Love and a Time to Die (1958). John Gavin is on leave in Berlin from the Eastern Front in 1945. His parents' house has been bombed. He runs into Liselotte Pulver whom he had known when they were children. And as they are both desperate and alone they begin to fall in love. The film is rightly called *A Time to Love and a Time to Die*. The time is wartime. Quite clearly a time to die. And in Douglas Sirk where death is, and bombs and cold and tears, there love can grow. Liselotte Pulver has planted some parsley outside her window, the only living thing among the rubble. It's clear from the start that John Gavin will be killed in the end. And somehow it really all has nothing to do with war. A film about war would have to look different. It's about a state of being. War as a condition and breeding ground for love. If the same people, Liselotte Pulver and John Gavin met, say, in 1971, they would smile at each other, say how are you, what a coincidence and that would be it. In 1945 it could become a great love. It's quite true. Love isn't where the problem's at. The problems are all happening on the outside. Inside two people can be tender to each other.

An ordinary love and unexceptional people for the first time in Douglas Sirk. They watch what's happening around them with wide startled eyes. Everything is incomprehensible to them, the bombs, the Gestapo, the lunacy. In a situation like that love is the least complicated thing of all, the only thing you can understand. And you cling to it. But I wouldn't like to think about what would have happened to them if John had survived the war. The war and its horrors are only the decor. No one can make a film about war, as such. About how wars come about, what they do to people, what they leave behind, could well be important. The film is not pacifist, as there is not a second which lets us think: if it were not for this lousy war everything would be so wonderful or something. Remarque's novel *A Time To Live—A Time to Die* is pacifist. Remarque is saying that if it weren't for the war this would be eternal love. Sirk is saying if it weren't for the war this would not be love at all.

Imitation of Life

Imitation of Life (1959) is Douglas Sirk's last film. A great, crazy movie about life and about death. And about America. The first great moment: Annie tells Lana Turner that Sarah Jane is her daughter. Annie is black and Sarah Jane is almost white. Lana Turner hesitates, then understands, hesitates again and then quickly pretends that it is the most natural thing in the world that a black woman should have a white daughter. But nothing is natural. Ever. Not in the whole film. And yet they are all trying desperately to make their thoughts and desires their own. It's not because white is a prettier color than black that Sarah Jane wants to pass for white, but because life is better when you're white. Lana Turner doesn't want to be an actress because she enjoys it, but because if you're successful you get a better deal in this world. And Annie doesn't want a spectacular funeral because she'd get anything out of it, she's dead by then, but because she wants to give herself value in the eyes of the world retrospectively, which she was denied during her lifetime. None of the protagonists come to see that everything, thoughts, desires, dreams arise directly from social reality or are manipulated by it. I know of no other film in which this fact is formulated with such precision and with such desperation. At one point, towards the end of the film, Annie tells

Lana Turner that she has a lot of friends. Lana is baffled. Annie has friends? The two women had been living together under one roof for ten years by then, and Lana knows nothing about Annie. No wonder Lana Turner is surprised. Lana Turner is also surprised when her daughter accuses her of always having left her alone, and when Sarah Jane starts being stroppy to the white goddess, when she has problems and wants to be taken seriously, even then Lana Turner can only show surprise. And she's surprised when Annie dies. How could she simply lie down and die? It's not fair, suddenly to find yourself confronted with reality quite out of the blue. All Lana can do is be surprised throughout the second part of the film. The result is that she wants to play dramatic parts in future. Pain, death, tears—one can surely make something out of that. This is where Lana Turner's problem becomes the problem of the film-maker. Lana is an actress, possibly even a good one. We are never quite sure on this point. At first Lana has to earn a living for herself and her daughter. Or is it that she wants to make a career for herself? The death of her husband doesn't seem to have affected her that much. All she knows about him is that he was a good director. I think Lana wants to carve out a career for herself. Money is of secondary interest to her, success comes first. John Gavin is third in line. John is in love with Lana; for her sake, in order to support her, he has abandoned his artistic ambitions and got a job as a photographer in an advertising agency. Lana cannot understand how someone could give up their ambition for love. John is also rather dumb, he confronts Lana with a choice, either marriage or career. Lana thinks this is fantastic and dramatic and opts for her career.

Things are like this throughout the film. They are always making plans for happiness, for tenderness, and then the phone rings, a new part and Lana revives. The woman is a hopeless case. So is John Gavin. He should have caught on pretty soon that it won't work. But he pins his life on that woman all the same. For all of us it's the things that won't work that keep our interest. Lana Turner's daughter then falls in love with John, she is exactly what John would like Lana to be—but she's not Lana. This is understandable. Only Sandra Dee doesn't understand. It could be that when one is in love one doesn't understand too well. Annie, too, loves her daughter and doesn't understand her at all. Once, when Sarah Jane is still a child, it is raining and Annie takes her an umbrella at school. Sarah Jane has pretended at school that she is white. The truth comes out when her mother shows up at the school with the umbrella. Sarah Jane will never forget. And when Annie, shortly before her death wants to see Sarah Jane for the last time, her love still prevents her from understanding. It seems to her to be a sin that Sarah Jane should want to be taken for white. The most terrible thing about this scene is that the more Sarah Jane is mean and cruel the more her mother is poor and pathetic. But in actual fact, exactly the reverse is true. It is the mother who is brutal, wanting to possess her child because she loves her. And Sarah Jane defends herself against her mother's terrorism, against the terrorism of the world. The cruelty is that we can understand them both, both are right and no one will be able to help them. Unless we change the world. At this point all of us in the cinema cried. Because changing the world is so difficult. Then they all come together again at Annie's funeral, and behave for a few minutes as though everything was all right. It's this "as though" that lets them carry on with the same old crap, underneath they have an inkling of what they are really after, but they soon forget it again.

Imitation of Life starts as a film about the Lana Turner character and turns quite imperceptibly into a film about Annie, the black woman. The film-maker has turned away from the problem that concerns him, the aspect of the subject which deals with his own work, and has looked for the imitation of life in Annie's fate, where he has found something far more cruel than he would have either in Lana Turner's case or in his own. Even less of a chance. Even more despair.

I have tried to write about six films by Douglas Sirk and I discovered the difficulty of writing about films which are concerned with life and are not literature. I have left out a lot which might have been more important. I haven't said enough about the lighting: how careful it is, how it helps Sirk to change the stories he had to tell. Only Joseph von Sternberg is a match for him at lighting. And I haven't said enough about the interiors Douglas Sirk had constructed. How incredibly exact they are. And I haven't gone into the importance of flowers and mirrors and what they signify in the stories Sirk tells us. I haven't emphasized enough that Sirk is a director who gets maximum results out of actors. That in Sirk's films even zombies like Marianne Koch and Liselotte Pulver come across as real human beings, in whom we can and want to believe. And then I have seen far too few of Sirk's films. I would like to have seen them all, all thirty-nine of them. Perhaps I would have got further with myself, my life and my friends. I have seen six films by Douglas Sirk. Among them were the most beautiful in the world.

# Reviews and Commentaries

Reviews

German critics, who, generally, had been less tolerant of Fassbinder's earlier work than their American or French counterparts, tended to greet *The Marriage of Maria Braun* as a welcome surprise. Many viewed it as a return to the "realism" and "humanism" of *The Merchant of Four Seasons*, *Fear Eats the Soul*, and *Effi Briest*, and thus as a retreat from the self-centered eccentricity of *Satan's Brew* and *In a Year of Thirteen Moons* and the self-consciously "artistic" trappings of *Chinese Roulette* and *Despair*. Moreover, except for reviews in the most conservative papers (which brushed it off as "just melodrama") the majority of reviews approved of the film's presentation of postwar Germany. Nonetheless, some German critics—perhaps prompted by their general uneasiness with Fassbinder—felt obliged to surmise that the success of the film had less to do with Fassbinder's direction than with the fact that someone else wrote the script and with Hanna Schygulla's performance in the title role.

Some American critics—even Fassbinder's most ardent champion in the American press, Vincent Canby (in his *New York Times* review of *Maria Braun* at the 1979 New York Film Festival)—praised the film but were put off by the "confusion" of the ending. Most found a pleasure of the familiar in their recognition of the film's debt to American family melodramas of the 1940s and 1950s that they had not found in certain of Fassbinder's recent films. And they were, like the Germans, virtually unanimous in their praise of Hanna Schygulla.

The sampling of American and German reviews that follows is intended to present a variety of viewpoints.

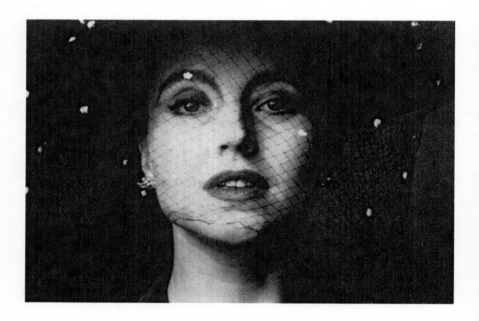

Philadelphia Inquirer

Douglas Keating

Maria Braun should enter the pantheon of great women of the screen, along with such characterizations as Marlene Dietrich's nightclub singer in *The Blue Angel* and Joan Crawford's Mildred Pierce.

Indeed there is much of both of them in Maria Braun. . . . [The film] is schmaltzy, soap operaish, and implausible, but Fassbinder and Miss Schygulla make it convincing. . . .

From the *Philadelphia Inquirer*, 22 December 1979.

Fassbinder's contrived unsatisfactory conclusion . . . seriously mars Fassbinder's otherwise excellent film. The question that arises naturally from the story is: when Maria and Hermann finally get together will their love survive?

Instead of providing an answer, Fassbinder opts for a gratuitously dramatic final scene that not only leaves the moviegoer unsatisfied but also prevents Miss Schygulla from bringing the character of Maria Braun to its logical conclusion within the context of the story.

Time

Frank Rich

One thing is certain about Rainer Werner Fassbinder, the most prolific of West Germany's New Wave film makers, his movies could not be mistaken for those of any other contemporary director. Who but Fassbinder would shoot a scene from the point of view of a character's ankles, or punctuate a film with shots of telephones? What is more, Fassbinder's idiosyncrasies are more skillfully performed with each film. . . .

Alas, Fassbinder is doing more than mere fooling around. Increasingly, he seems to be the '70s heir to such past camp masters as the '50s Hollywood director Douglas Sirk (*Magnificent Obsession*) and the '60s Warhol disciple Paul Morrissey (*Flesh*). But unlike his predecessors, Fassbinder does not recognize the limits of the form. Camp is fine for movies that want to trade exclusively in offbeat humor and florid emotions. In *Maria Braun*, Fassbinder makes the serious mistake of trying to convey ideas. . . .

There is nothing wrong with this familiar yet entertaining tale, or with Hanna Schygulla's finely shaded portrayal of the protagonist. The trouble stems from Fassbinder's belief that Maria can serve as a damning metaphor for modern Germany's Economic Miracle. Since his style expresses complex emotions and ambiguous political history in broad theatrical gestures, he never makes his case. Eventually the strain between form and content becomes irritating. The final shot is a portrait of Chancellor Helmut Schmidt, who is thus equated with the film's opening image of Hitler. No sale. If Fassbinder wants to take such dangerous stands, he will have to abandon his facile mannerisms and arm himself with the most powerful tools of his art.

From *Time* 17 (22 October 1979):85–86.

Women's Wear Daily

Christopher Sharp

There has been a lot of talk about the young vanguard of German filmmakers, but the fact remains that few people either in Germany or America are taking the trouble to see their films. There are even a few film experts who insist that directors like Rainer Werner Fassbinder, Werner Herzog and Wim Wenders are taken more seriously by Americans than they are by their fellow Germans.

The reason for all the yawning accompanying new German films is that the young directors are established nonconformists in the way they dress and talk, but tedious conformists when it comes to making movies. Directors, they say, should make movies for themselves, not for general movie audiences. This concept of filmmaking leads to the self-indulgent sameness so apparent in all of Herzog's movies, where ugly men and women interact violently through neurotic screenplays. The only benefit of this homogeneity to the average filmgoer is that we know what we are in for when seeing the latest angry young German movie.

For the past five years that has been the bad news about German films. The good news this year is that Fassbinder has finally come up with a film, "The Marriage of Maria Braun," that is fully cognizant of an audience. This treatment of a woman who picks herself up from the ashes of a war and national disgrace and becomes an efficient, modern businesswoman is a dramatic metaphor for a nation making a similar transition. The energy of this movie is generated by a luminous performance by Hanna Schygulla in the title role. Schygulla has a quality of complementing intriguing emotions with equally interesting restraints, but it is her feelings that finally prove to be even stronger than her formidable mind.

What is most surprising about this New York Film Festival entry is that while Fassbinder and his contemporaries previously have prided themselves on the lack of sentimentality in their cold films, this movie is an unabashed love story. The long and profound relationship between Maria Braun and the husband who goes

From *Women's Wear Daily*, 12 October 1979.

to prison for her crime is the thread to which everything else in the film is tied. It is refreshing to see that a director like Fassbinder is capable of breathing some fresh air. Perhaps someday he will even make a comedy.

Stuttgarter Zeitung

Hans-Dieter Seidel

Maria Braun—the very name suggests normality. And the fate to which Rainer Werner Fassbinder assigns this film figure is intended, above all, to be typical—as an invitation to identification. Even though the biography of this woman, in accordance with the conventions of melodrama, is exaggerated beyond the range of credibility, Fassbinder never loses sight of this play for audience identification. Maria Braun is a woman who, in her inimitable way, rises above the rubble, but she builds her world according to the rules of men. By her own definition, she is fulfilling the function of a stand-in. Despite the all-important title character, *The Marriage of Maria Braun* is therefore no apotheosis of the feminine, and no feminist film. It is indeed the story of a woman, but it is also the story of a time that was exclusively oriented around the man— first the man who was lost in the war, then the one who finally came home, regained his strength and reclaimed his power. It is only in pursuit of the ultimate goal of this takeover that

From *Stuttgarter Zeitung*, 30 March 1979. Translated by Joyce Rheuban.

the absurd marriage of Maria Braun can be justified. Only by defining her methods, emotions, and actions in terms of this takeover, is it possible for the disenfranchised Maria to carry on.

Detailed descriptions of what *The Marriage of Maria Braun* deals with have already been widely circulated following the opening of the Berlin Film Festival. The reader will therefore be spared another faithful rendering of the stations of a German life, which can be readily enjoyed by going to see the film at a Stuttgart cinema. However, besides the purely thematic level, there is a formal mastery in this film that can easily be missed on the first viewing because you become so involved with the exciting development of the character. Fassbinder practically tells his story "in stereo." In other words, while the impulse of Maria Braun's private story is perceived through one channel of our consciousness, the other channel is tuned to a flow of detailed information pertaining to the time period. And for those signals which the images can't convey, Fassbinder utilizes the level of sound in a significant way.

The background before which Maria Braun's fate is fulfilled is one of selected ambient sounds: radio reports, the monotonous reading of missing person notices, speeches by Adenauer, pop tunes of the day, at the end—Herbert Zimmermann's play-by-play of the finale in Bern, and throughout—the ever present pneumatic drill of prosperity which affirms the steady reconstruction of a destroyed country. Fassbinder's directorial skill achieves mastery in this stereophonic art form, where the spectator synthesizes in his head signals sent out on separate channels.

The dramatic structure of this film can only be compared to the sophisticated, intricate matrix of Fassbinder's *Despair*, except that here, the film is aimed much more directly at the viewer through a realistic mode of access. And never before has Fassbinder renounced his self-centered eccentricity so heroically. Never before has he told a story so concisely. Through its dramatic economy alone, the film constitutes a terse *Lehrstück*. A good example of this is the film's exposition in which the wartime marriage of Maria Braun, which only lasts for half a day and a night, is never confirmed in the visual images by even one shot.

And then there are the actors! Hanna Schygulla, through her grace and self-assurance, her devotion and simultaneous detachment, is overwhelming in the title role. Alongside her an impressive squad of character players lend much to the film's capacity to win us over: Gisela Uhlen and Elisabeth Trissenaar as two women caught up in the meshes of the male machinery, Ivan Desny in a virtuosic flip-flop between superiority and insecurity, Hark Bohm, drawing an incredibly comic aspect from the solemnity of his role, and Klaus Löwitsch, Gottfried John and Fassbinder himself in an accomplished articulation of a gallery of types. And for a director born in 1946 [sic], he handles the changing fashions of the late forties and early fifties with the requisite confidence—as seen in the interior decor, costumes, hair styles, and in people's overall bearing.

The jury of the Berlin Film Festival deemed *The Marriage of Maria Braun* worthy of a Silver Bear for Hanna Schygulla and another one for the technical crew. The joke was, the director left empty-handed. His recognition will have to come from the public. And his prospects have never been better for getting it.

Die Zeit

Peter W. Jansen

They have half a day and a night, and then it's all over. Hermann Braun has to return to the front. The film doesn't bother to show even one second of this thirty-six hour marriage. Afterward, Maria Braun sustains her marriage for ten more years, from 1944 to 1954, but *without* her husband.

During the marriage ceremony, there is an aerial strike, everybody runs out of the town hall, and, lying on the street in a hail of shrapnel and debris, Corporal Braun forces the registrar to sign the marriage certificate; he wets the stamp he took with him and sets it to the piece of paper. Maria enters an apartment wrecked by the war carrying an all-too-light rucksack. The building is destroyed; doors aren't needed anymore. She's been out bartering and manages to bring home a few potatoes. There are many women standing around the war-torn train station; among them is Maria. She wears a sign around her neck and there's a photo of Hermann stuck to the sign which says, "Who knows

From *Die Zeit* (Hamburg), 23 March 1979. Translated by Joyce Rheuban.

about Hermann Braun?" Former German soldiers and released prisoners of war are getting off the train.

With these three scenes, Fassbinder has set the tone for his film, *The Marriage of Maria Braun*. It is at once laconic and explicit, realistic and eccentric, cool and melodramatic. Meanwhile, we've already heard for some time and will continue to hear something called "the wanted register," that warm, solicitous, monotonous voice that reads long lists of names—the names of the missing; a people searching for its scattered children; a people searching for itself. The film is inundated with ambient sounds—radio broadcasts, pop tunes by Rudi Schuricke and Catarina Valente, speeches by Adenauer, the noise of construction machinery, the Herbert Zimmermann broadcast of the final game of the soccer world championship of 1954 in Bern.

As concretely as these sounds invoke their sources, they are also deployed so subjectively, as part and parcel of the film's subjectivity so to speak, they intone what lies beyond the perception of the characters who are on the scene. (They hear nothing of the women's humming or the fist-fight at the train station.) Yet the sounds are part of their consciousness. They've heard these sounds (or their neighbor has) at some time. They're in the air they breathe; the sounds belong to them, and they belong to those sounds.

The form and content of this sound montage, with its essayistic appeal, brings about a remarkable reversal of the field of meaning and its consequences. Although the images are loaded with various accoutrements of the period and, historically speaking, are convincing in their accuracy as far as the furniture, rubble, carpets, rucksack, costumes, hair styles, and mannerisms are concerned, these images nevertheless come across as the most private observations from that time. This is because the sounds—arbitrarily, but not accidentally blended in independently of the images, and from a detached perspective—simply render all this as the everyday status quo. These sounds are the acoustic assertion of the history of that time, which rolls on, uninfluenced by the events and sensations of the mise-en-scène and the dialogue, as a kind of macro-event. The assertion of this macro-level makes all private motivations, emotions, and resolutions seem almost meaningless and arbitrary—like the exertion of

dwarfs compared to the march of the spirit of the time through history.

This sound strategy is a decisive outgrowth of the function of speaking as developed in the work of Rainer Werner Fassbinder (and taken a step further in *In a Year of Thirteen Moons*, which appeared after *Maria Braun*). Fassbinder's breakthrough soundtrack gives the tearjerking melodramatic dramaturgy the coolness of marble sculpture he requires. This goes for the eccentric mannerisms as well, which close the spectator off from the escape route of sentimentality or aestheticism. Fassbinder's next step—altering the nature of filmed speech—will be at least as important as the wide open cosmos of his "stories."

Semi-prostitution as a "B-girl" for the Americans came after the war and lasted as long as Hermann Braun was considered dead. Then there was the death blow for the well-meaning black Bill when Hermann stands in the door one day. Then Hermann takes the blame and goes to jail for Maria, who, in the meantime, becomes involved in the economic miracle. Her beauty and her intelligence, her warmth and her coldness, her emotion and her calculation suit her for becoming rich and acquiring a house for herself and Hermann. By plan and persuasion and because she needs to, she becomes the mistress of an industrialist—or rather, she takes the industrialist as her lover and makes herself his private secretary. She understands better than the man how to separate the desk and the bed.

When Hermann finally returns to her, as if only a day had passed, he returns to the nest she has prepared for him; and Maria makes a mistake with the gas stove. The smoker who never has a match causes the gas stove to explode and brings the history of her rise to its proper end. Proper when considered objectively as well, since what also ended in the mid-fifties was the participation of women in the reconstruction (and also their entry into the prevailing power structure)—the beginning, at least, of a new kind of life. But scarcely had the rubble been cleared for their men, than the men came back, and returned to power.

The Marriage of Maria Braun is simultaneously the story [*Geschichte*] of a woman and the history [*Geschichte*] of the time in which she lived. It is a time of absence—of the material and of the ideal, and definitely of the men. It is a time in which the women, though in the clear majority, were nevertheless building for a male-oriented society. The German

chancellor of those years was nothing other than a kind of father figure, elected and supported by women. Maria Braun could even have been one of those who voted for him. Thus everything she lived for was to bring about the takeover of power by the men, even though she chose freely and her choices were dictated by the needs of her mind and body. Yet these were *her* needs and *her* decisions—experienced and resolved upon by her, independently of a man. And as meaningless as this all may seem, as arbitrary as the accident is that brings an end to all this—this life stands as a symbol that another kind of life is possible. And the fact that this life has to end in no way proves that this new kind of life is unattainable. Rather, her death is the seal of authenticity of her endeavor to live this different kind of life.

Fassbinder, who was born just after the war, has recorded and interpreted the history of the German restoration. *The Marriage of Maria Braun* is the film of a son about his parents' generation. It is a film in which someone has finally begun to define what this means and what we have become— the republic of money and purchased feelings.

Cineaste

Ruth McCormick

The *Marriage of Maria Braun* is well on its way to becoming R. W. Fassbinder's most popular film to date in this country. The prolific and controversial German director is by now well-known to people knowledgeable about film, but *Maria Braun* may become his breakthrough film to mass audiences in the U.S. His films have ranged from the beautifully clear *Ali: Fear Eats the Soul* to the well-nigh incomprehensible *Chinese Roulette*; *Maria Braun* definitely belongs to the former category. It is all political satire and human drama, the story of modern Germany and of a woman determined to have her way.

Maria Braun, played by Hanna Schygulla, is a modern Mother Courage, with a touch of Polly Peachum and Pirate Jenny. Fassbinder makes her a human metaphor for postwar Germany, as well as a strong and believable, although flawed, female character.

The film begins with a picture of Adolf Hitler and ends with photos of Adenauer, Erhardt, Kiesinger and Schmidt (significantly, Brandt is not

From *Cineaste* 2 (Spring 1980): 34–36.

included in the line-up). These portraits bracket the story of Maria and her beloved Hermann, whose marriage begins amid the explosions of bombs, and ends with that of a gas stove. It is a marriage that lasts, in the physical sense, half a day and one night before Hermann is shipped to the Russian Front. When he does not return at the end of the war, she remains convinced that he is alive simply, as she says, because she loves him and wants him back. She is already displaying the kind of will that will one day take her to the top of society.

Maria, in fact, comes to personify the triumph of the will, although she is no philosopher, not much of a patriot, and totally apolitical. She knows how to use all situations to her advantage. When she learns from her brother-in-law, who does return from the front, that Hermann is dead, she takes up with Bill, a black American sergeant—not a handsome youth, but a stolid, kindly man several years her senior. Hermann is *not* dead, however, and he returns to Maria's apartment just as she and Bill are about to make love. A fight ensues, and Maria, trying to protect Hermann, accidentally kills her American lover. Hermann confesses to the crime, and is sentenced to a long prison term. Maria promises to wait for him, and to do all in her power to prepare a good life for them when he is released.

Maneuvering her way into the First Class compartment on a train, Maria meets Karl Oswald, a sixty-ish French industrialist who owns large business interests in Germany. She charms him so completely that he not only falls in love with her, but also gives her a high position in his firm. She becomes his mistress, but she insists that their business and personal lives be kept separate. Through her hard work and innovative ideas, the company prospers more than ever, and Maria becomes rich and powerful. She tells Hermann everything. Karl, whom Maria has refused to marry, learns about Hermann and Maria's dedication, and is so impressed that he wills all his worldly goods to the couple. In the end, Hermann is finally reunited with Maria. Karl has died, and they are rich. But Maria has changed. Her love of life has weakened. She has become tired, cynical, and, for the first time in her life, careless.

The Marriage of Maria Braun is one of Fassbinder's longest films (two hours), yet it is so full of dramatic and cinematic vitality, arresting characters, and often very amusing dialogue and situations, that its pace never slackens. The script, by Peter Märthesheimer and Pea Fröhlich, with additional dialogue by Fassbinder (who usually writes his own scripts), is witty and sharp and, for those who don't understand German, the English subtitles are especially good. Michael Ballhaus, one of Germany's best cinematographers who has often worked with Fassbinder, once again shows his special talent for dramatic framing devices. Here, his camera is more free-wheeling than usual—this is one of the least "claustrophobic" of Fassbinder's films—as if we are being allowed to see that there are a multiplicity of possibilities open to Maria not enjoyed by many of Fassbinder's more oppressed characters. It is only at the end of the film, when Maria and Hermann are finally reunited in their "dream" house, that the camera narrows its perspective to an imprisoning tightness—restating the director's view that the family, as a microcosm of the state, entraps almost all of us.

There are some marvelous moments: the opening bombing sequence; a mirror shot of Maria having her hair upswept and putting on makeup; a family picnic; a sensitive love scene between Maria and Bill (sexual scenes are rarely warm in Fassbinder's films); a stuffy restaurant; the mother's raucous birthday party; Maria bluffing her way through a crowded train station by searching for a nonexistent child; a close-up, as Maria is told of Hermann's death while washing her hands, of one hand frozen under the tap, water flowing down her arm like tears, and the immediately following sequence in which Maria, her face immobilized by sorrow, crosses the crowded dance floor of the *hofbrau* where she works to the table where Bill, until now only a casual friend, sits. As when she first met him, she asks, "Mr. Bill, will you dance with me?" In his arms she tells him, almost breaking down, "My Hermann [sic] is dead." Never again will she display her feelings so openly, but it is here that she conquers the audience, as well as poor Bill. The sequence is brilliant. Ballhaus' low-angle camera follows her across the room to Bill's table (while the jukebox plays "In the Mood," a song that seems to crop up at one point or another in every Japanese, Italian and German film about the Occupation) so as to make her tower above the dancers, like a goddess of tragedy.

Throughout the film, the radio brings contact with the outside world, with local news interspersed with speeches by Adenauer and other politicians about peace, prosperity and the state of the nation.

As usual, Fassbinder knows how to choose actors; in fact, even his weaker films cannot be faulted on this count. Klaus Löwitsch is a stoic, almost melancholy Hermann, a man whose sufferings are etched upon his face, a not-so-young Werther. Ivan Desny as Oswald, the ageing tycoon, is urbane and sensitive, a liberal humanist who, in representing a dying *haute bourgeois* culture, can say of postwar Germany, "I live in a country called Insanity." Hark Bohm, a talented director himself, gives a witty performance bordering on, but never quite descending into, caricature, as Senkenberg, Oswald's accountant, a Prussian martinet with (as his boss notes) no imagination. Rabidly anti-labor, thoroughly sexist and probably an unregenerate fascist, he weeps in a drunken moment when he recalls how Oswald deserted the Fatherland during the war.

In smaller parts, Gisela Uhlen as Maria's pleasure-loving mother, George Byrd as the dignified, affable Bill, Claus Holm as Maria's philosophical, drug-addicted doctor, and lanky Gottfried John as Maria's socialist brother-in-law, all contribute to a stunning group portrait. Anton Schirsner never utters a word as Maria's senile grandfather, but he hums the Horst Wessel Lied with gusto, is adept at snitching food, and is always first into the family's only bathroom.

Maria, as played by Schygulla, is

heroine and anti-heroine—one of the strongest female characters in recent cinema, but certainly no feminist ideal, nor is she meant to be since, on a straight narrative level, she uses rather than questions the patriarchal system in her quest for a better life. As a metaphor, of course, she is Germany, hoping to liberate herself after a taste of what the Americans (and Russians) have told her is "democracy," only to fall for the lie and then slip back into her old habits of authoritarianism. The usually absent Hermann signifies for Maria a shining, almost metaphysical ideal of love and happiness—the kind of transcendence yearned for by all the great German idealists and transformed by their early admirer and later critic, Karl Marx, into a scientific theoretical framework by which human beings might truly achieve a happier existence. However, her marriage is, dialectically, Maria's commitment to the bourgeois ideals of family, property and social position. Maria at one point jokingly tells Senkenberg, who is uneasy about her warm camaraderie with her militant brother-in-law, that she is the muse of the "German economic miracle"—a capitalist tool by day, but an agent of the masses by night.

To Fassbinder and his scenarists, Maria Braun represents the best and the worst in the German character.

She is disciplined, hard-working, beautiful, intelligent and, at least in the beginning, a person with high ideals. She is also, however, compulsive, assured by her superiority, competitive, conniving and, though rigid, easily able to unconsciously compromise herself. Maria sees herself as strong, moral, dutiful and *nice*. She never deliberately injures others (people sometimes just happen to be in her way), is supportive of her family (and their differing political views), and is scrupulously honest with everyone (except herself).

Fassbinder, true to his interest in Freud, Reich and Marcuse (he once said that in a revolutionary society everyone should have the right to free psychoanalysis), locates the reason for the failure of Maria (and Germany) to achieve her dreams in her need for a father (a leader). At the very beginning of the film, after Germany's defeat, Maria consoles her mother by pointing out that "Father is dead, but we're still alive!" When she wants something, she gets it from men by innocently being sexy. When a group of Americans comment on her looks, she tells them off; not only do they apologize profusely, but they give her their cigarettes. She gets bargains from the local black marketeer (Fassbinder in an amusing cameo) with whom she is so prettily prim that he offers her the works of Kleist rather than a night on the town. When she gets a job at the off-limits-for-Germans bar, she wins the respect of the middle-aged owner. She tells her elderly doctor, to whom she is daughterly even in the nude, that she will sell only beer at the bar, not herself. She is true to her principles—a nice German girl. Only three men share her bed—Hermann is obviously ten years her senior, as is Bill, who is in any case a "fatherly" type. She is as much daughter as lover or business partner to Karl Oswald. She is cool, efficient, friendly and, most of all, pure. To her two lovers, it is her purity that is appealing; to Maria, it is their capacity to protect her that is consoling. To Fassbinder, Maria's need for a paternal figure reflects the Germans' need for a *Führer*.

Despite Maria's hard work and material success, she has learned nothing new; her rise becomes her fall from happiness. The woman who once believed in miracles finds herself incapable of feeling; more than once, she declares that the times are bad for emotions. Despite her strength and seeming independence, she never really liberates herself. In the long run, she has given too much of herself to a system oriented toward competition, performance and pollution (signified by Maria's becoming a chain smoker) to be capable of fulfilling her desire for love and transcendence.

She has betrayed her own commitment to life, grown materially but not spiritually. When the "big moment" comes that she might fall ecstatically into Hermann's arms and move on to a happy, new life, she destroys everything.

While *The Marriage of Maria Braun* may be seen as a simple narrative on the ability of power to corrupt, Fassbinder's political message is clear. All of his best films are as much political parables as human dramas. *Beware the Holy Whore* is as much about authoritarianism and the misuse of political power as it is about the making of a film; *Merchant of the Four Seasons* says as much about the destruction of the German petty bourgeoisie as it does about a "born" loser; *Fox and His Friends* depicts the continuing betrayal of the working class by the bourgeoisie as much as it portrays gay life in Munich; *Ali: Fear Eats the Soul* and *Mother Küsters Goes to Heaven* are stories of German working-class life as well as pessimistic allegories about the inability of oppressed people to change their condition.

Maria Braun demonstrates all these concerns. Germany (and Fassbinder may well be talking as much about the East as the West) has been built up by the Great Powers since its defeat to become the most prosperous nation in Europe. This has been due, also, to the German work ethic and perhaps to a national self-confidence that, since Germany's original unification, has been both the country's great strength and weakness. Germany is rich, powerful, with a thriving nuclear industry; yet, there is a great sense of malaise among its youth, its intellectuals, and its underprivileged. The political activism of the 60s and early 70s is dead in the West, and there is no viable workers' movement. The Communist Party is weak and conservative (East Germany is one of the most productive, but also one of the most conservative countries in the Soviet bloc). Gone is much of the hope, enthusiasm and desire for a new and better society that prevailed as Germany was recuperating from its defeat. There has been no new, meaningful, revolutionary theory coming out of Germany for years.

What has this to do with Maria Braun? Hermann represented to her these same high hopes for a new life. By killing Bill, who may well represent genuine democracy, and bringing about Hermann's imprisonment, Maria Braun's fall from grace has already begun. In allying herself with the liberal, bourgeois Oswald, and eventually with the reactionary Senkenberg, she gains wealth, but loses her ideals. The joyful, willful girl becomes a snappish, compulsive woman who is sexually cold and politically an opportunist. The final blast in the film may well be a comment on the proliferation of nuclear power in Germany.

Fassbinder is not a pamphleteering director. He insists upon the intimate relation between the personal and the political. His pessimism about his own country and, by extension, the rest of the world, is obvious, and it has turned a lot of people off. There is also a disturbing coldness in most of his films that, for many, works against his professed humanist concerns. Still, at their best, Fassbinder and his talented associates make films that are not only politically probing and insightful, but also exciting works of art. *The Marriage of Maria Braun* is one of those films.

Commentaries

The two essays included in this section—Sheila Johnston's "A Star is Born: Fassbinder and the New German Cinema" and Thomas Elsaesser's "Primary Identification and the Historical Subject: Fassbinder and Germany"—offer complementary approaches to Fassbinder's work in general and to *The Marriage of* *Maria Braun* in particular. Johnston places *Maria Braun* within the context of Fassbinder's achievement as a leading figure of the "New German Cinema." Elsaesser offers a view of Fassbinder's films about the postwar Bundesrepublik that is representative of new currents in contemporary film scholarship and criticism.

A Star is Born:
Fassbinder and the New German Cinema

Sheila Johnston

F assbinder is one of the leading lights of the New German Cinema. A figure who has succeeded in attracting popular attention, critical acclaim and academic scrutiny,[1] he now enjoys the status of an international star whose image as a kind of contemporary *poète maudit* has been further enhanced by his remarkable, "obsessive" productivity.

It is tempting to account for his spectacular career in terms such as "talent" or even "genius," and indeed I have argued elsewhere[2] that the institutional/ideological framework of the New German Cinema promotes precisely this kind of picturesque myth. I should like here to pursue this line of inquiry a little further. If concepts like talent or dedication are not adequate to explain the Fassbinder phenomenon, what in fact were the qualities called for in West Germany's aspiring auteurs and to what extent does he in particular answer to these requirements? To map the changing contours of the New German Cinema and to locate Fassbinder's position within it can afford a revealing perspective on this bumpy terrain where state and culture intersect.

* * *

Two kinds of misconceptions about the New German Cinema can be found in the various histories of its origins. The popular press favors the myth, referred to above, of the handful of young visionaries who changed the face of Germany's film culture virtually overnight.[3] More sophisticated accounts point to the crucial role played by government legislation and detail the impressive panoply of public organizations ready and willing to provide unlimited encouragement, opportuni-

From *New German Critique* 24–25 (Fall/Winter 1981–1982):57–72.
1. Including Judith Mayne, "Fassbinder and Spectatorship," *New German Critique* 12 (Fall 1977), and two collections of essays: Peter W. Jansen and Wolfram Schütte (eds), *Rainer Werner Fassbinder* (Munich, 1974) and Tony Rayns (ed), *Fassbinder* (London, 1976).
2. Sheila Johnston, "The Author as Public Institution," *Screen Education* 32–3 (1979–80).
3. For numerous examples of this view, see ibid.

ties and, most important of all, money on the table for independent productions.[4] Yet even here little indication is given of the powerful motives and often conflicting interests at work. Implicitly or explicitly, a scenario is constructed along the following lines: A group of determined young lobbyists published a manifesto at the 1962 Oberhausen Short Film Festival in which they declared their intention to "create the New German Film" and demanded to be given a chance to do so in relative freedom from commercial constraints.[5] The state then promptly acknowledged and acceded to their requests, releasing massive funds to finance these plans into being.

It was, I would suggest, not quite that straightforward. To investigate in detail the complex interplay of political, economic and cultural forces that propelled the New German Cinema to its present prominence lies beyond the scope of this study. The main point here is to bring out a fact that has tended to remain hidden: that the pleas, both at Oberhausen and elsewhere, for public aid for the cinema constantly met (and indeed to this day continue to meet) with vigorous resistance in many quarters. It is the aim of this article to investigate the reasons for that resistance and to show, with particular reference to Fassbinder, how it shaped the face of the New German Cinema.

This long-standing aversion to the very idea of "subsidies" for the film industry is cited, in a report on this subject submitted to the *Land* [state] of North Rhine-Westphalia in 1966,[6] as one of the reasons for the virtual absence of any measures to protect the domestic film industry in the 1950s—an absence which was a major contributing factor in its steady and seemingly relentless decline. The writer described as a euphemism the term "guaranteed credits" (*Ausfallbürgschaften*) used to designate the only short-lived official aid plan. That term, which referred to a scheme whereby the government stood surety for bank loans to distributors, disavowed the fact that this was in effect a subsidy system, since the films which came out of it almost invariably lost large sums of money.

In the 1960s, other elaborate circumlocutions were employed to justify what amounted to a U-turn in public policy towards the cinema. This same report

4. An article which typifies this sort of misrepresentation is John Sandford, "The New German Cinema," *German Life and Letters*, XXXII, 3 (1979).

5. The now celebrated "Oberhausen manifesto" has been reproduced in a number of places, e.g., Rayns, op. cit., and Sandford, op. cit.

6. Hans-Peter Herringer, *Die Subventionierung der deutschen Filmwirtschaft* [The subsidizing of the German film industry]. Forschungsbericht des Landes Nordrhein-Westfalen nr. 1637 (Cologne and Opladen, 1966).

contained a striking image that depicted the proposed subsidies as "the oil . . . which temporarily prevents the finely-tuned motor of the 'market economy' from overheating." In the often heated debates, the requests for aid were habitually formulated and defended as a "help towards self-help," a provisional measure needed in order to strengthen the industry sufficiently so that it could thenceforth stand on its own two feet. Lawyers and government officials connected with these negotiations were at pains to point out that such legislation would "entail no dirigisme . . . and . . . safeguard private initiative,"[7] obsessively attempting to banish the anathema of concepts like "state intervention" or, even worse, "protectionism."

In certain quarters, these arguments were motivated by compelling vested interests. The existing film industry, in particular, as represented by the various organs of the trade press and by its own official body, the SPIO (*Spitzenorganisation der deutschen Filmwirtschaft*), was conspicuously concerned to nip in the bud any potential challenge to its hegemony. The anti-aid alliance was, however, far more broadly based than this observation suggests. To understand the reasons behind it, we need to recall that, at the time of Oberhausen, Konrad Adenauer had been Federal Chancellor at the head of various CDU/CSU [Christian Democrat/Christian Social] dominated coalitions for over a decade. The unprecedented prosperity and stability enjoyed by the country during this administration appeared to endorse its predominantly *laissez faire* policies. The manifesto was one tiny symptom of the imminent changes in the political climate—it was perhaps more than coincidental that it appeared in the year of the infamous *Spiegel* affair, an event which ushered in a period of crisis for Adenauer's leadership. But the consensus opinion that the cinema, as an industry, should survive on its own merits in a market economy was deeply entrenched and not to be quickly or easily displaced.

The arguments mobilized to change these attitudes were couched accordingly and are typified by an article by Norbert Kückelmann, a lawyer and founder member of the very first public funding agency, the *Kuratorium junger deutscher Film*. In order to justify the financing of this organization from the *Länder* purse, Kückelmann pointed out that, as a result of the growing recession in the film industry during the 1950s, the number of production, distribution and exhibition companies had gradually dwindled to the point where "the pluralism of the film

7. From an interview with Berthold Martin, the (CDU) politician who was largely responsible for devising the 1967 Film Subsidy Bill, in *Filmecho/Filmwoche*, 93–94 (1962).

supply" was placed in jeopardy. The collapse of the UFA, the major German production company and theater chain, in 1961 had seemed to set the seal on this trend. The only chance of reversing it, Kückelmann maintained, was to abandon the principle of non-intervention and actively work to promote a climate favorable to the flourishing of small film enterprises: this course of action would, he felt, have to be endorsed even by "committed defenders of absolute state neutrality."[8]

It was polemics like this that shifted the public consensus toward a recognition that some form of legislation was essential to preserve a varied and healthy cinema culture. The ideals of economic self-sufficiency and free market competition persisted, however, in coloring the complexion of the subsidy system and the kind of film-making (and -makers) predicated by it.

It has been necessary to sketch in this background in order to understand the extraordinary virulence of certain reactions to the Oberhausen manifesto when it first appeared. The trade press, predictably, voiced strident disapproval of the very notion of state aid, condemning the accompanying request by the signatories for five million DM as an "unrealistic demand for a blank cheque . . . a real pipe-dream."[9] The fact that the "old guard" had itself, as mentioned above, swallowed up large sums (about thirty million DM) in guaranteed credits in the course of the 1950s somewhat takes the edge off its criticism. But similar attacks also issued from other, more disinterested camps. For instance, an article published in (conservative, Axel Springer-owned) *Die Welt* and provocatively entitled "Demands are easy, achievements more difficult" poured scorn on the manifesto's "new model of freedom" which was to be financed by the taxpayer and which would "eliminate every form of risk" for the beneficiaries.[10] Another writer was even more emphatic, calling on the newcomers to "get down to work without waiting for public funding and subsidy" and holding up as a paradigm the established independent producer Artur Brauner who was "an astute and flexible film businessman . . . a self-made man." On the other hand, he maintained, "most of the young men from Munich unfortunately give the impression of waiting until Fortune showers them from her horn of plenty and they can realize the brilliant ideas of their dreams."[11]

8. Norbert Kückelmann, "Filmkunstförderung unter sozialstaatlichem Aspekt" [Film subsidy in a socialized context], *UFITA*, 59 (1971), 123.

9. Quoted, along with a number of other press comments in "Pressespiegel," *Filmkritik*, 4 (1962).

10. Kurt Joachim Fischer, "Fordern ist leicht, etwas zu leisten ist schwieriger," *Die Welt*, 23 June 1962.

11. Kurt Habernoll, "Was ist mit Opas Kino?," *Film-Telegramm*, 17 (1962).

At first sight these responses are unremarkable, the kind of disapprobation of state aid for the arts (particularly for less accredited artforms or artists) that can be found in almost any western country. Closer inspection, however, reveals the writers to be incensed not simply by the principle of subsidy but also, and perhaps to an even greater extent, by the lobbyists' alleged aim to eliminate totally any personal risk. This finds its expression in the special praise reserved for Brauner and the demand that the filmmakers also be businessmen, creating opportunities and fending for themselves, rather than unworldly artists who deserve and need public patronage.

What is perhaps most surprising (and impressive) about the Oberhausen manifesto is the sensitivity it betrays to this climate of opinion. The authors' explicit statement that they were prepared as a collective to "bear the economic risks" seems aimed at preempting objections such as those quoted above, and their request for five million DM was rationalized as a carefully calculated business proposition. In return for this relatively small amount, they undertook to produce ten feature films, calculating that if only one was a big success and if three others did moderately well, the receipts from these four alone would offset the losses from six failures.[12] The thinking behind this was a radical departure from the established practice of the lavish, star-studded productions which had by then brought the industry to the verge of disaster,[13] in favor of a more modest, low-budget style. The Oberhausen group presented themselves as small-scale entrepreneurs, able by keeping down their overheads to balance the books: the five million DM were to be no more than an "initial booster," after which, they expected, the project would pay for itself. An important corollary of this approach was that it allowed, indeed, in a sense obliged a single individual to take control over all the major aspects of the film-making process. The *auteur* cinema (or *Autorenkino*) which eventually emerged was thus shaped not only by cultural and political factors[14] but also by economic imperatives.

It now becomes easier to perceive part of the logic behind one of the most curious and often remarked on features of the film aid system in the Federal Republic. Multiple finance is the rule, not the exception, and it is not unusual for a production to be funded from five or six sources. Clearly, one of the reasons for this is that certain organizations, particularly the Kuratorium, have only meager resources which they understandably prefer to spread around. Elsewhere, how-

12. Quoted by Enno Patalas, "Die Chance," *Filmkritik*, 4 (1962).
13. For a spirited attack on this practice of "thinking big," see Joe Hembus, *Der deutsche Film kann gar nicht besser sein* [German film just can't get any better] (Bremen, 1961).
14. For a more detailed account of these, see Johnston, op. cit., and below in this article.

ever, different motives may be inferred. The Film Subsidy Board (*Filmförde-rungsanstalt*) is not permitted to put up more than 50% of a film's total budget (only 40% before the first renewal of its mandate in 1971);[15] the fact that the provision is based on a percentage rather than on an absolute figure suggests a deliberate strategy to enforce applicants to "sell" their projects to other potential patrons. Similarly, although it was originally possible for the same person to win several awards from the Ministry of the Interior for the same film (Alexander Kluge got two prizes for *Abschied von Gestern/Yesterday Girl* in his dual capacity as scriptwriter and director), this loophole was closed in 1972 by a governmental decree.[16] Television finance, particularly when granted under the terms of the 1974 co-production agreement, also expects the director to go elsewhere to meet the budget.[17]

Many a frustrated film-maker has complained that the average award made by one of these funding bodies was on its own inadequate to produce something of an acceptable standard, feeling, like Johannes Schaaf, that the "discrepancy between the original concept and what is economically possible" had a "fatal" effect on the quality of the end product. Indeed, his interviewers concluded from their conversations with Schaaf and with sixteen other "new" German directors that "the ideal film of the director's imagination cannot be realized under the economic conditions which in fact obtain in the film industry."[18]

What these observers have failed to perceive is that the insufficiency of individual loans and premiums is not an unfortunate accident. It has been built into the very system which requires directors to hawk around each new product rather than basking in the assured largesse of automatic and total subsidies. In practice, of course, established *auteurs* are preferred over newcomers on the strength of their reputations and past achievements,[19] but, as will be seen, even someone of Fassbinder's stature is not always certain of public funds. Based on the free market principle that finance be "earned" on merit rather than bestowed as an artist's

15. For this provision as currently formulated see *1979 Filmförderungsgesetz* [Film subsidy bill], Par. 26, Sec. 1.4.

16. For details of this case (and indeed an extremely comprehensive account of the West German film industry) see Georg Roeber & Gerhard Jacoby, *Handbuch der filmwirtschaftlichen Medienbereiche* [film media handbook] (Pullach, 1973).

17. Paragraph 3b of this agreement requires that a minimum of 25% of total production costs be found by the producer.

18. Barbara Bronnen and Corinna Brocher, *Die Filmemacher* (Munich, 1973), pp. 137, 262.

19. See in particular the constant polemics in *Filmfaust*, a publication launched in 1976 to represent the interests of debutant directors.

privilege, the system seems to effect an odd and uneasy reconciliation between the twin poles of private enterprise and public patronage.

Through this fusion, film-makers become emblems of, simultaneously, economic and political liberalism. On the one hand, they are to exemplify the entrepreneurial spirit—an assignment which, paradoxically, the long-term structural weaknesses of the West German film industry make virtually impossible to fulfill. The ascendancy of the American majors and of large, downtown theater chains over a fragmented and vulnerable network of independent distributors and exhibitors means that New German films, once made, stand very little chance of ever being given the right kind of promotion or exposure. The problem has been aggravated by a government policy which has been heavily concentrated on the "creative," production-end of the industry, turning out movies which then get blocked in the bottleneck further down the line. More recent legislation has, it is true, attempted to redress the balance, but the dream of eventual economic self-sufficiency will almost certainly remain well out of reach. Though this failure to find consistent box-office success is largely due to factors beyond their control, the hapless cineastes have constantly been subjected to criticism (and indeed also contrite self-criticism) for being unable to break out of what is habitually described as a state-funded "art-ghetto" or "nature preserve."

On the other hand, their quasi-official status as living testimony to the tolerance and pluralism of West German democracy, though to some extent common to all "free" artists, is, in the case of the New German Cinema, brought intriguingly to the fore by the peculiar circumstance that here the film culture industry is generated and sustained directly by the state. A brief glance back to those debates of the early 1960s reveals a surprising candor in the recorded statements of key politicians and legislators about the ideological function of the planned revival of German film culture.

Kückelmann, for example, pointed out that the current crisis threatened not only economic competition but also the liberal ideal of "free artistic activity and development." Instead of clinging blindly to the precept of passive non-interventionism, the government needed, he argued, to take active measures to preserve this freedom.[20] To appreciate what was at stake here, we need to remember that the events of all-too-recent history, the effects of centralized state control over the arts, and especially the cinema during the Third Reich, were another argument, and, for many people, a weighty one against legislation or subsidy.

20. Kückelmann, p. 137.

Warnings, especially in the trade press, that this might lead to a kind of *Bundesfilmkammer* (the term is highly emotive, evoking the spectre of the Nazi *Reichsfilmkammer*) played upon these fears, and thus Kückelmann's article is implicitly concerned to demonstrate that state intervention and individual self-expression are not incompatible but, in this instance, closely intertwined.

The Social Democratic Party, in opposition since 1949 and solicitous not to present too startling an alternative cultural program, had been formulating its policy along similar lines. Its purpose, according to Willy Brandt at a 1960 party conference on this theme, was "to define the parameters of the space within which freedom can evolve" and other speakers noted the importance of culture in general and (above all in the Third World "where illiteracy is still widespread") of the cinema in particular for enhancing West Germany's national prestige, disseminating its values and combatting the "distorted and falsified image of contemporary (Federal) German problems" being projected by "Eastern propaganda." [21]

The speeches are not without Cold War overtones (this was, after all, only one year after the party's Godesberg program signalled a decisive break with Marxism), overtones which become even more pronounced as we move further to the right of the political spectrum.

In 1961, the Ministry of the Interior had introduced prizes of 200,000 DM for films which "especially enhance the prestige of Germany abroad" and "are likely to contribute to an appreciation of the free democratic way of life." [22] Even more explicit is a government report which appeared in 1962 and stated that "to maintain the vitality of the German cinema is essential to our political and cultural activity abroad. The Federal Republic needs the German film to convey views and opinions from one people to another, as a national ambassador and, last but not least, to ward off the extraordinarily strong cultural offensive from the Eastern block almost everywhere in the world." [23] It should be mentioned here that the GDR cinema had for some time been attracting interest abroad; the invariable comparisons with West Germany's desolate film scene were a constant source of humiliation. Significantly, in the parliamentary debates that preceded

21. See the speeches by Willy Brandt, Heinz Kühn and Winfried Böll in *Kultur und Politik in unserer Zeit*, Dokumentation der SPD am 28. und 29. Oktober 1960 in Wiesbaden.
22. Quoted by Enno Patalas, "Prämien für die Braven" [Bonuses for the deserving] *Filmkritik*, 10 (1961).
23. "Bericht der Bundesregierung über die Situation der deutschen Filmwirtschaft" [Report of the Federal Government on the status of the German film industry] dated 25 April 1962, in *Deutscher Bundestag 4. Wahlperiode*, Drucksache LV/366.

the passing of the 1967 Film Subsidy Bill, the speakers for all three parties referred to the activities of the DEFA (the state production board of the GDR), which was seen either (by the CDU speaker) as another invidious agent of Communist propaganda or (by the SPD and FDP delegates) as a successful example that the West should try to follow.[24]

No doubt a case could be made in support of the theory that little had changed since the 1950s, when censorship was widely practised, particularly on films imported from Warsaw Pact countries, and Bonn had taken an active and attentive interest in productions financed with the aid of guaranteed credits: one, *Stresemann*, the last film to benefit from the system, was known in the trade as *Stresenauer*, because its portrait of the politician as elder statesman and its theme of European unity were regarded as thinly disguised propaganda for Adenauer's foreign policy.

It would, however, be mistaken to dismiss the New German Cinema, as have some observers,[25] as being under the sign of direct state control. The official statements quoted above and indeed the films themselves suggest that, rather than being required to keep to a narrow and rigidly-defined path, directors were allowed a certain leeway which was able to accommodate an (admittedly limited) range of ideological positions.

The characteristic malaise of West German intellectuals at their innocuous "court jester" function, which allowed criticism and satire (provided it was entertaining), but with no real political bite, takes on a new and acute immediacy for these film-makers. Their heavy dependence on public funds combined with, in most cases, an intention to produce some form of social critique placed, and continued to place them in a delicate position. Some took refuge in anarchic or broadly anti-establishment stances, declaring a rejection of "that art and culture shit" that squared ill with the hopes of the organizations backing their work. Others, particularly those with a declared left-wing alignment, were constantly aware of the precariousness of their institutional status, wondering "whether the bourgeois state is prepared in the long term to subsidize anti-bourgeois films."[26] Their sense of disquiet and insecurity is a sobering reminder that, though the system is the envy of film-makers everywhere in the world, it is a house of cards

24. For transcripts of these speeches, see *UFITA*, 51 (1968), 193–201.
25. For an extreme example of this position see Klaus Kreimeier, *Kino und Filmindustrie in der BRD* (Kronberg, 1973).
26. For the former position, see the statements by Werner Schroeter and Volker Vogeler, and for the latter position, Christian Ziewer, all in Bronnen & Brocher.

painfully vulnerable to the chill winds of economic recession and right-wing reaction.

*   *   *

Let us now consider how the "test case" of Fassbinder fits into the general pattern. The match is, as will be seen, by no means perfect: the "case" is exemplary but also, in important ways, exceptional.

The most immediately striking aspect of Fassbinder's activity is the remarkable extent to which it conforms to the free enterprise ethic. Thus, even at the very beginning of his career, he could be found voicing his contempt for colleagues dependent on grants and subsidies and claiming that he could complete a film in the time that it took others to read the small print on the Kuratorium's application forms. Statements like this were to earn him much approving comment in the German press, where the "generation of 'Oberhausener'" was contrasted unfavorably with such bright young people who worked on their own initiative "without the Kuratorium, without a script premium and without papa's producers."[27]

What are the material conditions that enable him to do this? An answer is suggested by an interview given shortly after his first feature, *Liebe ist kälter als der Tod/Love Is Colder Than Death*, had been greeted with "mocking laughter and pitying smiles" at its premiere at the 1969 Berlin Film Festival. Denying the need for either critical or financial success, he announced with studied nonchalance that he had succeeded in securing a distributor's guarantee (a rare achievement for a "new" director, for reasons detailed above) and that the next film was already on its way.[28]

Crucial here is an ability to keep down costs. Johannes Schaaf who, as noted already, felt himself to be hamstrung by inadequate resources, had estimated the cost of making a film on a par in artistic terms with a work by "Fellini, Rosi, or Truffaut" as "at the least" 600,000 DM to 800,000 DM; the budgets for his own two previous productions had been 750,000 DM (for *Tätowierung/Tattoos*) and 1,200,000 DM (for *Trotta*). These were, it should be stressed, not inordinately

27. This comment was taken from an article, representative of many others, by Ingeborg Weber, "Gegen den Missbrauch aller Gefühle" [Against the abuse of Emotion], *Der Tagesspiegel*, 29 June 1969.

28. A detailed account of Fassbinder's early career is provided by Ekkehard Pluta, "Die Sachen sind so, wie sie sind" [Things are the way they are], *Fernsehen und Film*, 12 (1970). The interview referred to is in *Filmkritik*, 8 (1969).

large sums compared with those quoted by some other directors. Fassbinder, in contrast, was coming up with international successes at around this time which were, literally, made on a shoestring: *Der Händler der vier Jahreszeiten/The Merchant of Four Seasons* (1971), *Die bitteren Tränen der Petra von Kant/The Bitter Tears of Petra von Kant* (1972) and *Angst essen Seele auf/Ali: Fear Eats the Soul* (1973). Their budgets were, respectively, 178,000 DM, 325,000 DM and 260,000 DM—an achievement all the more astonishing if we recall that these movies were shot on 35mm color stock (independent productions often cut costs by working on 16mm and/or in black-and-white). Even these are princely sums after Fassbinder's first two full-length films which were made for 95,000 DM and 80,000 DM.[29]

Speed and efficiency are essential in order to work this cheaply. Fassbinder produced his early features at a breakneck pace: the shooting time of his first thirteen films averages out at about seventeen days (*Katzelmacher*, completed in three days holds the record). Film crews were kept to a minimum: *Love Is Colder Than Death* was, according to Fassbinder, shot with only one cameraman and one lighting engineer. Gradually a small nucleus of actors and technicians formed, whose regular collaboration would streamline the production process still further. More pertinently, many of them would be family, friends or fans prepared to work for little or no payment, or for back-paid wages: deferment of fees until the film had been released and, with luck, was beginning to make money.

This extremely widespread practice is only possible because of the relative absence of union regulations on the size and composition of film crews, enabling directors to use the cheap labor without which the New German Cinema would be virtually inconceivable. A glance at a few production credits reveals that similar "teams" of non-professionals have also gathered around other figures such as Alexander Kluge, Werner Herzog, Wim Wenders, Werner Schroeter and Jean-Marie Straub, making a valuable contribution to the final "look" of their films. The speed and distinctiveness of Fassbinder's work, both in the theater and in the cinema, would undoubtedly never have been achieved without his team; even when, as in *Despair*, he moved outside this original circle, it is the speed and authority acquired from his apprentice films that enable him to do so.

In addition to producing quickly, competently and on risibly low budgets, Fassbinder also exemplifies the director who is able to sell his projects to very

29. These figures are taken from information supplied by Bronnen and Brocher, and from the filmography in Jansen & Schütte.

diverse kinds of sponsors. Lack of this ability has had, as we shall see, fatal results for some of his contemporaries; at this stage I want simply to note that Fassbinder's fabled versatility, the eclectic range of his source material (from a literary classic, for *Effi Briest* to "an idea by the 35-year-old housewife Asta Scheib," for *Angst vor der Angst/Fear of Fear*) both determines and depends on his successful salesmanship. The various government organizations have all been milked by him to this purpose, and he has worked extensively for television, most recently and spectacularly completing the fourteen-part serialization of Alfred Döblin's novel *Berlin Alexanderplatz*.

It is worth briefly enlarging on this point, because it vividly brings out the ideological function of figures like Fassbinder and the process by which they are installed in a licensed, authorial space. West German television is composed of a network of public service corporations (*Anstalten des öffentlichen Rechts*) entrusted with the official mandate of embodying "the principle of a representative democracy." This principle is inscribed in the system of *Proporz* (proportional representation) under which the party-political composition of supervisory boards and key program staff in a particular station is to reflect that of the government of the *Land* or *Länder* it services. The mandate of television was originally interpreted as the duty to provide dissenting views, a variety held to be essential to preserve flexibility and to enable growth and change. Simultaneously, however, the broadcasting companies were pushed in the opposite direction by pressures (mainly from the right) to maintain political balance, reflecting safe, consensus opinions of all and not just their current affairs programs. The extensive use of creative freelancers has been an overt strategy to evade these pressures and to provide controversial and provocative television without threat of reprisals. The status of freelancers outside the institution and, particularly in cases such as Fassbinder, a flamboyant persona which would be equated in the public mind with an intensely subjective worldview, help to immunize the networks, which tend to present their role here as that of neutral transmitting agents, against criticisms of imbalance.[30] Publicity is thus concerned to promote a close identity between author and work: a striking example is the *Spiegel* cover story on Fassbinder's adaptation of *Berlin Alexanderplatz*.[31] Quite apart from the magnitude of the TV companies' contribution to the New German Cinema in purely monetary terms, the fact that, here, the debates around accountability and the place of art within a public institution have always been conducted in West Germany on an

30. See Johnston, op. cit., for a fuller argument and details of sources.
31. "Der Biberkopf, das bin ich" [This Biberkopf is me] (the very title is symptomatic), *Der Spiegel*, 42/1980.

unusually explicit level makes the example of television especially significant for my general argument. From the liberalism of the 1960s to the increasing economic and political retrenchment of the 1970s the shifting attitudes of the broadcasting networks towards independent film-makers are a sensitive index of other changes which have affected the New German Cinema: changes within the social formation as a whole which are more sweeping and therefore more complex and difficult to assess.

One of the reasons why Fassbinder has been able to survive these changes is the fact that he has wisely never allowed himself to become dependent on any single source of finance. Part of his strategy has been to attract investment from the private sector—individual patrons and distribution companies and, at the other end of the scale, tax-shelter organizations like the Geria: *Despair* must be the only New German film to have enjoyed the favor of this circumspect and frugal "Maecenas." This, combined with an immense prolificness that allows him to hedge his bets, means that, (here too the intrepid entrepreneur) he can underwrite if necessary a declared emotional or intellectual commitment with his own personal capital and unpaid labor.

Witness the case of *Die dritte Generation/The Third Generation* where initial offers of sponsorship from the Berlin Senate and the *Westdeutsche Rundfunk* were abruptly withdrawn. The reasons, inevitably, remain hidden, but Fassbinder infers a plausible connection with the film's theme of the interdependence of capital and terrorism, commenting: "In the end, the WDR withdrew its offer for clear political reasons. The producer responsible said to me that in the film an opinion is put forward which he is unable to share and did not feel he could defend to the broadcasting house. The representative of the Berlin Senate also backed off, after an initial and spontaneous agreement, once they had begun to consider the theme of the film. . . . When they called it off, we were already in the first week of shooting. The only thing that's changed is that I'm perhaps 300,000 DM deeper in debt. . . . I could still have stopped production—then I wouldn't have had as many debts, but I wouldn't have had the film either. . . . Only by piling up debts without knowing how they are to be repaid could films be made that might one day result in an industry. I can't imagine it any other way because I don't find it such a good idea to try to build up an industry through committees and lobbies—in the end you have to make too many compromises. You just have to do it the capitalist way, on speculation and risk." [32]

32. From an interview with Wolfram Schütte, "Nur so entstehen bei uns Filme: indem man sie ohne Rücksicht auf Verluste macht" [That's the way we make films—by not worrying about our losses], *Frankfurter Rundschau* 43/1979.

I have dwelt on this little incident in some detail because it raises a number of interesting points about Fassbinder and his peers. Firstly, it indicates the growing reluctance within television stations to take potentially explosive projects. Many observers feel that a film like Volker Schlöndorff and Margarethe von Trotta's *Die verlorene Ehre der Katharina Blum/The Lost Honour of Katharina Blum*, already exceptional when it first appeared in 1975, could almost certainly not be made under the same conditions today:[33] funded by the Film Subsidy Board and the WDR, co-produced by the German subsidiary of an American company, distributed in West Germany by one of the American majors and awarded a quality rating by the Film Evaluation Board (*Filmbewertungsstelle Wiesbaden*).

This again suggests that the tendency is not confined to television, but that a similar reluctance may also be found elsewhere, in the other public financing agencies. Though in theory the sheer number of different patrons might be supposed to enable a wide variety of work to be produced, in practice the need to please (or rather, not to displease) them all can too easily impose homogeneity and the aesthetics and politics of compromise. That uniquely West German genre, the notorious "committee film" (*Gremienfilm*), conceived for the needs of the selection boards where the lowest common denominator is often a script based on the classroom classics with minimal popular appeal, is undoubtedly part of this development.

Which brings me to my second point. For practically any other film-maker working in West Germany today, these setbacks and the peremptory withdrawal of aid would have ensured that *The Third Generation* would never have got past the planning stage. That the project was realized demonstrates just how unusual Fassbinder is in not being entirely dependent on public sponsorship in one form or another. It is his unique method of working that allows him to undertake in the same year both a generously bankrolled and commercially attractive film like *Die Ehe der Maria Braun/The Marriage of Maria Braun* and also privately produced works like *The Third Generation* which might be too thematically hazardous and/or aesthetically forbidding to be eligible for state or television support.

Thus he has repeatedly affirmed his belief that the laws of the jungle are vastly preferable to a safe, government protected nature preserve: a "completely commercial system" opened up, he felt, the possibility of temporary disjunctures between the interests of capital and the state into which radical artists of varying

33. This view has been articulated in a survey of the New German Cinema: Hans Günther Pflaum and Hans Helmut Prinzler, *Film in der Bundesrepublik Deutschland* (Munich, 1979), pp. 45–7.

hues could insinuate themselves.[34] The paradigm here is, of course, the Hollywood of the studio era, within which the work of directors like Douglas Sirk is seen by Fassbinder (and by some British film theorists)[35] as possessed of a keen cutting edge.

Thirdly, however, and despite this capacity to produce privately on a modest scale, he is clearly still in no way autonomous. The self-image projected in the above quotation of a lonely pilgrim on the capitalist road, a small-time entrepreneur able, because of a national economic independence, to withstand intervention and censorship, is a telling sign of the illusion of self-sufficiency fostered, as I have argued, by the apparatus of sponsorship.

This leads us straight to a question at the core of the Fassbinder phenomenon, that of his political impact. Is he, as he repeatedly maintains, a truly subversive voice? Or is he a harmless court jester, consolidating the very social order he believes himself to undermine? The growing ambivalence, or in some cases downright disenchantment with which his recent work has been greeted by the German left would seem to suggest the latter, but some discretion is called for in evaluating the weight of these criticisms. The accusals, noted by one journalist not unsympathetic to Fassbinder, that he has allowed himself to become "the pampered pet of the established media, the alibi . . . of the culture industry"[36] are tinged with a distinct flavor of sour grapes. In one sense, all these filmmakers find themselves caught up in the classical no-win situation: success attracts the odium of left-wing critics, who view it with deep suspicion as an automatic symptom of selling out, whereas failure brings censure from the right for squandering tax-payers' money.

With Fassbinder, though, there are other elements in play. Much of the disillusion with his work grew up in the early 1970s, in the wake of his move away from the shoestring budgets and fringe aesthetic of the *anti-theater* film and stage productions, and his gradual turn to a new strategy: collaboration with the "culture industry," use of conventional outlets and sources of finance and the exploitation of the art-form *par excellence* of (in the words of Wim Wenders) "U.S. imperialism." His "discovery" of Sirk, announced in a now celebrated article[37]

34. See the uncredited interview "Lieber Strassenkehrer in Mexiko sein . . ." [I'd rather be a street sweeper in Mexico], *Der Spiegel* 29/1977.
35. For instance in *Screen*, Vol. 12, no. 2/1971 (a special number on Sirk); and Laura Mulvey & Jon Halliday (eds), *Douglas Sirk* (Edinburgh, 1972).
36. Wolf Donner, "Der Boss und sein Team," *Die Zeit* 31/1970.
37. Fassbinder, "Imitation of Life. Über die Filme von Douglas Sirk," *Fernsehen und Film* 2/1971; translated in Mulvey & Halliday and included in this volume.

and subsequent nostalgic infatuation with Hollywood came more than coincidentally at a moment of widespread reaction against the impenetrably elitist-esoteric
work coming out of the New German Cinema.[38] It was thus in many ways a
necessary gambit (Fassbinder was by no means alone in reappraising the tactics
of an oppositional art by that time), but a gambit that was inevitably seen by the
left and the avant-garde as signalling opportunism and compromise.

His function has been further complicated by a persistent refusal to align himself with any political party or faction, or even with a minority group, a refusal
that has at various moments exposed his work to charges of anti-communism
(*Mutter Küsters Fahrt zum Himmel/Mother Küsters' Trip to Heaven*), misogy-
nism (*Die bitteren Tränen der Petra von Kant/The Bitter Tears of Petra von Kant*,
Martha), or anti-gay sentiments (*Faustrecht der Freiheit/Fox*). A policy of constant provocation from a non-sectarian position has tended to isolate him, laying
him open to attacks on every flank.

Appearing bent on pursuing a career as his country's bad conscience, Fassbinder has consistently done his best to outrage and offend, in a seemingly non-
stop series of scandals far too numerous to detail here. In this respect, too, he
could be (and indeed has been) seen as trapped in an especially invidious double
bind: however many wounds he manages to inflict, the very fact that he is allowed
to continue to hit out is, one might feel, *ipso facto* proof of his failure to do any
real or lasting damage. It is easy, then, to dismiss him as the ineffectual angry
young man, desperately trying to smash through the liberal consensus, only to be
continually reabsorbed within it. Yet there is increasing evidence to suggest that
his practices have become embarrassing or even, finally, unacceptable, rather
than mildly amusing. The storm which broke over the alleged anti-semitism of
his 1976 play *Der Müll, die Stadt und der Tod/The Refuse, the City and Death*
indicated that in the Jewish question he had succeeded in locating an issue that
was still very much a raw nerve (as the emotional reactions to *Holocaust* when it
was broadcast on West German television in 1979 and the lengthy debates on
whether to suspend the statute of limitations, due shortly to expire, for Nazi war
crimes, were both later to bear out). The "Rich Jew" affair was regarded at the
time by some observers as portending a general swing to the right which was also
manifesting itself in hostile criticism of other controversial writers.[39]

The point here is not that Fassbinder himself has become more *outré*, but that

38. See Johnston, op. cit.
39. For examples of reactions to the play, see the five contributions to *Die Zeit* 16/1976 and Hellmuth Karasek, "Shylock in Frankfurt?", *Der Spiegel* 15/1976.

it is the climate of opinion which has changed since he began making films. To adopt and adapt Willy Brandt's metaphor, the "space within which freedom can evolve," especially when as in this case it was largely cleared by government decree, is highly elastic, expanding when circumstances allow and rapidly contracting when pressures are brought to bear.

There are, one suspects, conclusions to be drawn from all this about the origins and future of the New German Cinema and the story of Fassbinder's success. It is clear that although his career could be explained in terms of astutely anticipating and occupying a gap in the market, such a view would obscure the extent to which he stands out as a quite remarkable figure. His colorful personality, the extreme visibility of the authorial inscription in his films, his inexhaustible and much-admired capacity for hard work and his entrepreneurial willingness to take financial risks all combine to make him, in every sense of the word, *exceptionally* compatible with the requirements of the system within which he has worked.

He is remarkable also, we should remember, in his international stardom which, like that of the rest of the tiny elite who dazzle at foreign film festivals, depends on a galaxy of lesser lights (directors and, just as importantly, their teams of collaborators) which are only dimly discernible to audiences abroad.

But, prodigious as he might be, Fassbinder is still a child of his times, whose activities call for certain optimum conditions. The opportunities for freelance production have always been to a high degree contingent on reasonable economic prosperity and low unemployment; and public indulgence of provocation presupposes an atmosphere of political stability and détente. Though initially allowed to testify to "the principle of a representative democracy," those on the fringes of acceptability are particularly vulnerable when this space begins to contract. As an established director, with finance (in most cases) assured by his reputation for cost effectiveness, and tolerance (usually) conceded because of his national and international prestige, he will doubtless survive the passing of the conjuncture which originally enabled his work to come to fruition. Which leaves poignantly unanswered the question of what would happen to Fassbinder (and the other unknown ones like him) if he were standing at the beginning of his career today.

Primary Identification and the Historical Subject: Fassbinder and Germany

Thomas Elsaesser

The entire cinematographic apparatus is aimed at provoking . . .
a subject-effect and not a reality-effect.

— J. L. Baudry

Film studies returns to the question of identification[1] in the cinema, which used to be one of the main concerns of mass media studies in the 40s and 50s, with a symptomatic ambivalence. American social psychologists like Martha Wolfenstein and Nathan Leites[2]—indebted to Siegfried Kracauer and, at one remove, the Institute for Social Research—represented the very type of approach from which film theory dissociated itself in order to establish a "theory of the visible." And yet, by a completely different route, Baudry and Metz seem to confirm a fundamental insight of media psychology: the cinema as an institution confines the spectator in an illusory identity, by a play of self-images, but whereas media psychology sees these self-images as social roles, for Baudry they are structures of cognition.

Two kinds of determinism seem to be implied in the perspectives opened up by Baudry's description of the "apparatus": a historical one, where the development of optics and the technology of mechanical reproduction produce the cinema, as a specific visual organization of the subject, and an ontogenetic one, where the cinema imitates the very structure of the human psyche and the forma-

From *Cine-Tracts* 11 (Fall 1980):43–52.
1. The reader is asked to forgive a rather large assumption made here. In the context of the conference it was necessary to pre-suppose the audience's familiarity with three essays that discuss (primary/secondary) identification, the "apparatus" and "subject-effect": Jean Louis Baudry, "Ideological Effects of the Basic Cinematographic Apparatus," *Film Quarterly* 28, no. 2 (Winter 1974–75); Christian Metz, "The Imaginary Signifier," *Screen*, vol. 16, no. 2 (1975); Jean Louis Baudry, "The Apparatus," *Camera Obscura*, vol. 1, no. 1 (1976).
2. Martha Wolfenstein/Nathan Leites, *Movies—A Psychological Study* (New York: Atheneum, 1970).

tion of the ego. The "apparatus" seems to be locked into a kind of teleology, in which the illusionist cinema, the viewing situation and the spectator's psyche combine in the concrete realization of a fantasy that characterizes "Western man" and his philosophical efforts towards self-cognition.

While in Baudry's writing, one can still make out a historical argument which, however remotely, underpins his ideas about the condition of a contemporary epistemology, Metz has used Baudry in "The Imaginary Signifier" in order to establish a classification system rather than an ambivalently evolutionary ontology. With this, the historical determinants seem to be entirely displaced towards other parts of the "institution-cinema," and the question of identification—in the concept of primary identification—is recast significantly, so as to make as clear a distinction as possible between his work and work concerned with role definition, stereotyping and role projection.

Metz's and Baudry's arguments have several important implications for film studies. For instance, part of the aim of auteur—or genre-studies and close textual analysis—has been to identify levels of coherence in a film or a body of films. In the light of "The Imaginary Signifier" one might be better advised to speak of a "coherence-effect," and to call the very attempt to establish coherence a displaced subject-effect. The task of analysis or interpretation comes to an end at precisely the point where the spectator-critic has objectified his or her subjectivity, by fantasmatizing an author, a genre, or any other category, to act as a substitute for the "transcendental subject" that Baudry talks about. The perversity of this conclusion can only be mitigated, it seems, if one reminds oneself that Metz's distinction between primary and secondary identification is a procedural one, defining a certain logic operation. Or as Alan Williams put it: "The first and most fundamental level of meaning in cinema is . . . that of the coherence of each film's overall surrogate 'subject.'"[3] This leaves open the possibility that the surrogate subject is differently constituted from film to film.

The more immediately apparent consequence of accepting Metz's position affects independent or avant-garde film-making practice.[4] Baudry's argument implicitly and explicitly designates the cinema as "idealist" in the philosophical sense, not because of a specific historical or ideological practice, such as Hollywood classical narrative, but by its "basic cinematographic apparatus." An un-

3. Alan Williams, *Max Ophuls and the Cinema of Desire* (New York, 1980).
4. See Constance Penley, "The Avant-garde and Its Imaginary," *Camera Obscura*, vol. 1, no. 2 (1977).

bridgeable subject/object division renders the object forever unknowable, and consciousness grasps the outer world only in terms of its own unconscious/linguistic structure. The cinema, in this respect, is an apparatus constructed by a Kantian epistemologist. Metz's distinction of primary identification amplifies this point. The filmic signifier is an imaginary one because perception in the cinema always involves between spectator and image the presence of a third term which is hidden: the camera. It is the repression of this absence and deferment in the act of perception that turns the subject/object relation into an imaginary one. Primary identification designates the unperceived and unrecognized mirroring effect that such a constellation produces for the viewer, with the consequence that all possible identifications with the characters in particular are modelled on and circumscribed by a structure of narcissism which inflects the viewer-screen relationship at any given moment.

Perception in the cinema is voyeuristic not because of any particular kinds of representations or points of view. It is not the implied hidden spectator which a scene sometimes addresses, but the always hidden camera which the scene cannot exist without that turns all object-relations in the cinema into fetishistic ones. They hold the subject in a position of miscognition or self-estrangement, regardless of whether the film in question is representational or not, avant-garde or narrative-illusionist. A film either fetishizes the characters or it fetishizes the apparatus. According to Metz, there is no escape from this closed circle.[5] In this respect, the cinema is indeed an "invention without a future" because it systematically ties the spectator to a regressive state, in an endless circuit of substitution and fetishization.

Such pessimism has been questioned, not least because it seems to invalidate the political and cognitive aims of radical avant-garde film-making. Suspecting a logical flaw, Geoffrey Nowell-Smith[6] has challenged Metz's distinction, by arguing that it is difficult to see how one can talk about primary and secondary identification, if one means by this an anteriority, in a process that is essentially simultaneous and dynamic. Consequently, Nowell-Smith wants to argue that "pure specularity," the transformation of Freud's secondary narcissism into the imaginary reintegration of the subject's self-image, is an abstraction, and no more than a misleading theoretical construct. In any concrete act of viewing, the spectator is involved in identifications which are "primary" and "secondary" at

5. See Interview with Christian Metz, *Discourse* 1 (1979).
6. Geoffrey Nowell-Smith, "A Note on History—Discourse," *Edinburgh Magazine*, no. 1 (1976), pp. 26–32.

the same time (if only by the metonymization of shots), and every fragmenta-
tion, be it montage, point of view shots or any other principle of alternation,
breaks down primary identification.

The very fact that something is posited as primary should make us instantly
suspicious. To say something is primary is simply to locate it further back in
the psychic apparatus. It does not, or should not, invite any conclusions about
its efficacy. I would argue, therefore, that the so-called secondary identifications do tend to break down the pure specularity of the screen/spectator relation in itself and to displace it onto relations which are more properly intra-
textual, relations to the spectator posited from within the image and in the
movement from shot to shot.[7]

Metz might well reply that he is not talking about a perceptual anteriority, but a
conceptual a priori, and that he is not interested in concrete acts of viewing as
much as in a classification of distinct categories. However, much of Metz's argument is buttressed by Baudry's essays, whose Platonic ontology of the cinema is
historicized only at the price of turning it into a negative teleology. At times, it
appears that Metz accepts or is indifferent to the suggestion that the cinema is
inescapably idealist. Confronted with the question whether "primary identification" is coextensive with the cinematic apparatus as analyzed by Baudry and to
that extent, unaffected by textual or historical production, Metz conceded, without much enthusiasm or conviction, that conceivably, if the nature of the family
were to change radically, so might the cinematic apparatus.[8]

Film studies has responded to these problems not only by a renewed interest in
theory. Equally significant is the attention given to alternative or deviating practices in the history of cinema regarding the relationship of spectator to film, and
the kind of "materialism" or "specularization" which it undergoes. The Japanese
cinema (Ozu, Oshima, Mizoguchi) has become a privileged area for such inves-
tigations, in terms of narrative space, point of view shots, or culturally different
codes of representation and identification.[9] This paper is an attempt to isolate
another deviating practice, within the European context, which has developed as
closely as the Japanese cinema in a reciprocity and rivalry with the "dominant"

7. Ibid., p. 31.
8. Interview, *Discourse* 1 (1979).
9. See, for instance, Kristin Thomson and David Bordwell, "Space and Narrative in the Films of
Ozu," *Screen*, vol. 17, no. 2 (1976); Edward Branigan, "Formal Permutations of the Point of View
Shot," *Screen* vol. 16, no. 3 (1975); Stephen Heath, "Narrative Space," *Screen* vol. 17, no. 3
(1976); Noel Burch, *To the Distant Observer* (London, 1979).

practice of classical narrative. The recent German cinema seems to me to represent both a confirmation of Baudry's and Metz's arguments, and at the same time offers a textual practice which might make apparent a dimension elided or repressed in "The Imaginary Signifier." In particular, I am wondering whether the mirroring effect of cinema, the specularization of all subject/object relations, their rigid division (which is the "other scene" of primary identification), and the return of a transcendental subject may not point to internalized social relations whose dynamic has been blocked, a blockage that Metz and Baudry have theorized and systematized.

In choosing the films of Fassbinder, I am guided by the fact that his work has given rise to the most widespread discussions about spectator-positioning and types of identification/distanciation. Thus, a certain familiarity can be assumed for the terms of the argument and the examples cited.

Most of Fassbinder's films are centered on interpersonal relationships and problems of sexual and social identity, in a way that is recognizable from classical Hollywood cinema; and yet, even on casual inspection, his work seems to confirm quite strongly a heavy investment in vision itself and a concentration on glance/glance, point of view shots and seemingly unmotivated camera movements that foreground the processes of filmic signification. Accordingly, one finds two Fassbinders in the critical literature: a) the German director who wants to make Hollywood pictures and whose audience-effects keep a balance between recognition and identification through genre-formulae and the use of stars, while at the same time distancing the spectator, placing him/her elsewhere through stylization and artifice. Tony Rayns, for instance, sums up some of these points when he argues that "Sirk taught Fassbinder how to handle genre, which became an important facet of his audience-getting strategies." [10] b) the modernist in Fassbinder, whose cinema is self-reflexive to the point of formalism, and whose deconstruction of narrative involves him in fetishizing the apparatus. Cathy Johnson writes:

> Fassbinder's highly visible cinematic signifier points to a fetishization of cinematic technique. Because all fetishism is an attempt to return to the unity of the mirror stage, one suspects Fassbinder of indulging in the very pleasure he withholds from his audience. Fassbinder is finally a director who approaches the Imaginary by means of a powerful attachment to and manipulation of cinematic technique as technique, while simultaneously barring

10. Tony Rayns, ed, *Fassbinder* (London: British Film Institute, 1980), p. 4.

entry to those of his audience who seek the Imaginary in the invisible cinematic signifier.[11]

I think one needs to argue that these positions contradict each other only insofar as they see audience-getting and audience-frustrating as opposite aspects of a basically unproblematic category, namely the spectator. It seems to me that Fassbinder's highly systematic textuality is not so much a fetishization of technique as the result of inscribing in his films and addressing a historical subject and a subjectivity formed by specific social relations. What is historical, for instance, in films like *Despair*, *The Marriage of Maria Braun*, or *Germany in Autumn* is the subject as much as the subject-matter.

In West Germany, the "spectator" is a problematic category first of all in a sociological sense. Given that most film-production is state–and tv–financed, the audience does not recruit itself through box-office mechanisms but via diverse cultural and institutional mediations. And yet, film-makers want to create an audience for themselves, not only by being active in restructuring the distribution and exhibition machine of cinema, but also by trying to bind potential audiences to the pleasure and habit of "going to the cinema." Paradoxically, however, the most common form of binding in the commercial cinema, through character identification, is almost completely and consistently avoided by directors like Fassbinder, Herzog, Wenders, Syberberg or Kluge as if somehow in the absence of a genre tradition, or an indigenous commercial cinema, audiences needed to be addressed at a different level.

It has been argued that the German cinema, and Fassbinder in particular, show in this respect the influence of Brecht: characters do not embody their parts but enact roles. But it seems to me that the viewer/film relation and the relation of the characters to the fiction which they enact is considerably more complex. In one sense, the two structures mirror each other infinitely and indefinitely, yet—as I shall argue—there is built into them an asymmetry, an instability that brings the relations constantly into crisis. Where Fassbinder seems to differ from both classical narrative and from modernist, deconstructive cinema is in his attitude to voyeurism and fascination. It is rarely fetishized in the form of action or spectacle, and does not seem to derive from primal scene or castration fantasies, as in the suspense or horror genre. Yet neither is it ascetically banished, not even in the long frontal takes of the early films. Instead, the awareness of watching marks both the entry-point of the spectator into the text, and the manner in which

11. Cathy Johnson, "The Bitter Tears of Petra von Kant," *Wide Angle*, vol. 3, no. 4 (1980), p. 25.

characters interact and experience social reality. One is tempted to say that in Fassbinder's films all human relations, all bodily contact, all power-structures and social hierarchies, all forms of communication and action manifest themselves and ultimately regulate themselves along the single axis of seeing and being seen. It is a cinema in which all possible subject-matter seems to suffer the movement between fascination and exhibitionism, of who controls, contains, places whom through the gaze or the willingness to become the object of the gaze. It is as if all secondary identifications were collapsed into primary identification, and the act of seeing itself the center of the narrative.

Faithful to a persistent Romantic tradition, German directors seem to be pre-occupied with questions of identity, subjectivity, estrangement, Foundlings, orphans, abandoned children, social and sexual outsiders wherever one looks. Yet narrativization of these quests for identity are almost never coded in the classical tradition of conflict, enigma, complication, resolution. Instead of (Oedipal) drama, there is discontinuity, tableau, apparent randomness and fortuity in the sequence of events. One might say that in Fassbinder, but it is also true of Wenders and Herzog, there is a preference for paratactic sequencing, with little interest in action-montage. Identity is a movement, an unstable structure of vanishing points, encounters, vistas and absences. It appears negatively, as nostalgia, deprivation, lack of motivation, loss. Characters only know they exist by the negative emotion of anxiety—the word that in the German cinema has become a cliché: *Angst vor der Angst*, the title of one of Fassbinder's films, and also an important line in both *Alice in the Cities* and *The American Friend*. As in *Die Angst des Tormanns beim Elfmeter*, it almost graphically marks the place, the position where the ego, the self, ought to be, or used to be, but isn't. It is the empty center, the intermittent, negative reference point which primarily affects the protagonists, but which in another movement, is also the empty place of the spectator; and one of the most striking characteristics of the films of Wenders, Fassbinder and Herzog are the ingenious strategies employed to render the position of the camera both unlocalizable and omnipresent, de-centered and palpably absent.

"I would like to be what someone else once was" is the sentence uttered by Kaspar Hauser, the foundling, when he was first discovered standing in the town square. The historical phrase appears in Herzog's *Enigma of Kaspar Hauser* as "I want to be a horseman like my father once was." As an attempt to formulate one's identity, such a project is symptomatic in its contradiction and impossibility. It tries to inscribe an Oedipal supercession in a temporal—historical succession:

I/someone else, I/my father is the unthinkable equation, immersed in the Heraclitean flux of identity, difference, deferment. In Wim Wenders' *Alice in the Cities*, the same impossibility articulates itself in terms peculiar to the cinema. Traveling through America in search of himself, the hero takes pictures with his Polaroid. But by the time he looks at them, they never show what he saw when he saw it. Delay and difference as functions of an identity mediated by the presence/absence of the camera. Visiting a former girl friend in New York, the hero has to agree with her when she says: "You only take pictures so you can prove to yourself that you exist at all." The cinema as mirror confirming an illusory identity, in the form of a double matrix of estrangement. Film and subjectivity find a common denominator in the German word *Einstellung*, whose polysemic etymology is often drawn on by Wenders in his writings. In film-making, the term applies both to the type of shot (i.e. the distance of camera from object) and the take itself (e.g. a long take). But outside film-making it means "attitude, perspective, moral point of view," and is literally derived from "finding oneself or putting oneself in a particular place." Language here anticipates the image of a spatial and specular relation, which only the cinema can fully realize.

In Fassbinder's *Merchant of Four Seasons*, Hans, the hero—another outcast seeking an identity by trying to take the place where someone else once was—explains how he lost his job. "The police had to sack me from the force for what I did. If I couldn't see that, then I wouldn't have been a good policeman. And I was a good policeman. So they had to fire me." Such double-binds, where identity is coextensive with its simultaneous denial, fatally flaw all attempts at reintegration in Fassbinder, and they form the basis for a structure of self-estrangement that in other films appears as a social problem before it becomes a definition of cinema. In Margareth von Trotta's film, *Sisters*, or *The Balance of Happiness* one finds the line: "It's not me that needs you, it's you who needs me needing you." The story concerns a woman who systematically tries to turn her younger sister into a double and idealized self-image of herself, until the weaker one commits suicide in order to punish the stronger one. As a symptom of the split subject, the configuration described here has much in common with recent trends in the commercial cinema, especially as reflected in sci-fi and horror thrillers. To find the same material in the German cinema reminds one of its origins in German Romanticism and expressionist cinema. The situation where a character seeks out or encounters an Other, only to put himself in their place and from that place (that *Einstellung*) turn them into an idealized, loved and hated self-image, is of course the constellation of the Double, analysed by Freud in terms of castration-anxiety and secondary narcissism. If one can agree that, especially in the light of Metz's and Baudry's use of Lacan's mirror-phase, the problematic of Other and Double has emerged as the cinematic structure par excellence, then its predominance in the representation as the cinematic theme par excellence of German films seems to demand further exploration. In classical narrative, the double and the split subject make up the repressed structure of primary identification. It appears that in the German films, because this structure is actually represented on screen, it points to a repression elsewhere, which in turn might serve to "deconstruct" primary identification.

Fassbinder's filmic output is instructive in that a certain line of development becomes clear in retrospect. What gives the impression of continuity despite the change of genres—gangster parody, melodrama, international art-film—is that an obsession with mirroring, doubling, illusory self-images evolves from being a generalized cinematic theme to becoming a specifically German theme, or at any rate, the occasion for historicizing the obsession.

In the early gangster films (*Gods of the Plague, American Soldier*) the heroes' desire revolves not around the acquisition of money or women, but is a completely narcissistic desire to play their roles "correctly." Both men and women have a conception of themselves where their behavior is defined by how they wish to appear in the eyes of others: as gangsters, pimps, tough guys, prostitutes, femmes fatales. They play the roles with such deadly seriousness because it is the only way they know how of imposing an identity on aimless, impermanent lives. What authenticates these roles is the cinema itself, because it provides a reality more real, but it is a reality only because it implies spectators. The characters in *Katzelmacher* are passive not because they are marginals and spectators of life. Their endless waiting wants to attract someone to play the spectator, who would confirm them as subjects, by displaying the sort of behavior that would conform to the reactions they expect to elicit. The audience is inscribed as voyeurs, but only because the characters are so manifestly exhibitionist. Substantiality is denied to both characters and audience, they de-realize each other, as all relations polarize themselves in terms of seeing and being seen. Except that to this negative sense of identity corresponds an idealism as radical as that of Baudry's "apparatus": to be, in Fassbinder, is to be perceived, *esse est percipi*. To the imaginary plenitude of classical narrative, Fassbinder answers by showing the imaginary always constructing itself anew.

The sociological name for this imaginary is conformism. The melodramas seem to offer a social critique of pressures to conform and the narrow roles that prejudice tolerates. But what if conformism was merely the moral abstraction applied to certain object-relations under the regime of the gaze? An example from *Fear Eats the Soul* might illustrate the problem. Ali and Emmi suffer from social ostracism because of a liaison that is considered a breach of decorum. But the way it presents itself is as a contradiction: the couple cannot be "seen together," because there is no social space (work, leisure, family) in which they are not objects of extremely aggressive, hostile disapproving gazes (neighbors, shopkeepers, bartenders). Yet conversely, they discover that they cannot exist without being seen by others, for when they are alone, the mutually sustaining gaze is not enough to confer or confirm a sense of identity. Love at home or even sex is incapable of providing the pleasure that being looked at by others gives.

The final scene resolves the contradiction. At the hospital where Ali is recovering from an ulcer, a doctor keeps a benevolent eye on the happily reunited couple. It is a look which only we as spectators can see, in a mirror placed on a parallel plane to the camera. The need which is also an impossibility of being perceived by others and nonetheless remain a subject produces both the sickness and the cure (in this case, a wishfulfilling regression to a mother-son, nurse-invalid relationship under the eyes of an institutionally benevolent, sanitized father figure). Only the spectator, however, can read it as such, because the mirror inscribes the audience as another—this time, "knowing" gaze.

It is a configuration strongly reminiscent of *Petra von Kant*. As the drama of double and Other unfolds between Petra and Karin, the spectator becomes ever more aware of Marlene as his/her double within the film. Instead of adopting the classical narrative system of delegating, circulating and exchanging the spectator's look, via camera position, characters' points of view and glances off, Fassbinder here "embodies" the spectator's gaze and thus locates it, fixes it. Marlene's shadowy presence in the background seems to give her secret knowledge and powers of mastery. Yet this other character virtually outside or at the edge of the fiction is offered to the spectator not as a figure of projection, merely as an increasingly uncanny awareness of a double. But to perceive this means also to perceive that Marlene only appears to the puppeteer who holds the strings to the mechanism called Petra von Kant. As soon as we recognize our double, we become aware of the camera, and in an attempt to gain control over the film, fantasmatize an author, a coherent point of view, a transcendental subject. We are plunged into the abyss of the *en abyme* construction: Marlene is inscribed in another structure, that of the camera and its point of view, which in turn stands apart from the structure in which the spectator tries to find an imaginary identity.

Petra von Kant is dedicated to "him who here becomes Marlene": who, among the audience, realizing that the dedication addresses them, would want to become Marlene?

Fassbinder's characters endlessly try to place themselves or arrange others in a configuration that allows them to re-experience the mirror phase, but precisely because the characters enact this ritual of miscognition and dis-placement, the spectator is not permitted to participate in it. Explicitly, this is the subject of *Despair*, in which the central character, attempting to escape from a particular sexual, economic and political identity, chooses as his double a perfect stranger, projecting on him the idealized nonself, the Other he wishes to be. When this surrogate structure collapses, the hero addresses the audience by a look into the camera, saying: "don't look at the camera—I am coming out." If in Metz's term, the screen becomes a mirror without reflection, in Fassbinder's films we see characters act before a mirror, but this mirror is not the screen, except insofar as it coincides with the place where the camera once was. A dimension of time, of delay and absence is inscribed, in such an insistent way as to make it impossible for the spectators to use the screen as the mirror of primary cinematic identification.

Instead, one constantly tries to imagine as filled the absence that provokes the characters' self-display. The paradox which I have been trying to describe is that in Fassbinder's films the protagonists' exhibitionism is only partly motivated by the action, however theatrical, and does not mesh with the spectators' voyeurism, because another, more urgent gaze is already negatively present in the film. Another Fassbinder film, in which this absent gaze is both named and erased, is *The Marriage of Maria Braun*. Hermann, Maria's husband, has a role similar to that of Marlene in *Petra von Kant*. His disappearance, coinciding with the fall of Hitler, becomes a necessary condition for the fiction to continue. The idée fixe of true love, on which Maria bases her career, is only disturbed by the periodic return of the husband, from the war, from prison, from making his fortune in Canada. It is for him that she does what she does, but only on condition that his place remains empty—reduced to the sign where someone once was. Absence turns her object-choice into an infatuation, which—expelled and fatasmatized into an idée fixe—becomes a transcendental but alienated self-image. Maria represses the return of the source of idealization, thereby also repressing the knowledge of the source of her economic wealth. Her life and identity appear under the sign of a marriage whose consummation is forever postponed and deferred.

The apparent perfunctoriness and lack of plausibility that strikes one so disagreeably about motive and motivation in characters like Maria or the hero of *Despair* render palpable that not only is the visual space centered elsewhere, but so is the narrative. The characters, motivated by attracting a confirming gaze and simultaneously repressing it, display a symptomatically "paranoid" behavior. An ambiguity arises from the fact that the split corresponds to a repressed desire, where the anxiety of knowing oneself to be observed or under surveillance is overlaid by the pleasure of knowing oneself looked at and looked after: Fassbinder's cinema focuses on the pleasure of exhibitionism, not voyeurism.

Increasingly, and explicitly, this exhibitionism is identified with German fascism. In *Despair*, for instance, Nazism appears as both the reverse side and the complementary aspect of the protagonist's dilemma: to escape the sexual and social demands made on him. Hermann's personality splits—into a paranoid and a narcissistic self, and he dresses up in someone else's clothes. Meanwhile, in the subplot, the personality split is metonymically related to economics, the change from small-enterprise capitalism to monopoly capitalism, and the proletarianization of the middle classes, who believe in the world-Jewish-Bolshevik conspiracy as a way of relieving anxiety about the future. The white-collar supervisor Müller, who works in Hermann's family firm, resolves his identity crisis also by dressing up: one morning he appears at the office wearing the brownshirt uniform of the SA. The exhibitionist-narcissist of practically all of Fassbinder's films here assumes a particular historical subjectivity: that of the German petit bourgeois, identifying himself with the State, and making a public spectacle of his good behavior and conformism. Compared to Müller, Hermann's paranoia is sanity itself and to narcissism as repressed paranoia in Hermann corresponds exhibitionist aggression in Müller. Conformism appears as the social side of the Imaginary which breaks down and constructs itself always anew in Fassbinder's films. To vary Brecht's poem *The Mask of Evil*, one might say that Fassbinder's films, optimistically, show how painful and difficult it is to fit in, to conform.

The structures of self-estrangement, of mirroring and miscognition, of positionality and identification with the Other, the double binds, structures that have habitually been interpreted as coinciding with the construction of the basic cinematic apparatus: might they not here be equally amenable to a historical reading? For instance, in terms of fascism, or more generally, as the need even today of binding a petit bourgeois audience in the "social imaginary" of secondary narcissism. What, Fassbinder seems to ask, was fascism for the German middle—and working—class which supported Hitler? We know what it was for Jews, for those actively persecuted by the regime, for the exiles. But for the apolitical Germans who stayed behind? Might not the pleasure of fascism, its fascination have been less the sadism and brutality of SS officers, but the pleasure of being seen, of placing oneself in view of the all-seeing eye of the State. Fascism in its Imaginary encouraged a moral exhibitionism, as it encouraged denunciation and mutual surveillance. Hitler appealed to the *Volk* but always by picturing the German nation, standing there, observed by "the eyes of the world." The massive specularization of public and private life, diagnosed perhaps too cryptically by Walter Benjamin, as the "aestheticization of politics": might it not have helped to institutionalize the structure of "to be is to be perceived" that Fassbinder's cinema problematizes? But what produces this social imaginary, once one conceives of the Imaginary outside of cinema or the individual psyche? And conversely, what or whom does the cinema serve by reproducing in its apparatus socially paranoid and narcissist behavior?

Such questions raise the political context in which Fassbinder works, what is usually referred to as the "repressive climate," the "counter-revolution" that has taken over in West Germany. As the government perfected its law-and-order state in overreaction to terrorist acts and political kidnapping, the experience of the semi-politicized student movement and many of the intellectuals was a massive flight into paranoia. In the face of a bureaucratic surveillance system ever more ubiquitous, Fassbinder toys with another response: an act of terrorist exhibitionism which turns the machinery of surveillance—including the cinema—into an occasion for self-display. For in his contribution to the omnibus-film *Germany in Autumn*, he quite explicitly enacts the breakdown of authority, the paranoid narcissistic split which he sees as the subjective dimension of an objectively fascist society. In this film—structured around the question of the right to mourn and to bury one's dead, of letters sent by dead fathers to their sons, of sons of the Fatherland forced by the state to commit suicide so their bodies can return home for a hero's funeral, of children who kill father-figures and father-substitutes, and then commit suicide inside state prisons—Fassbinder concentrates single-mindedly on himself. Naked, in frontal view, close to the camera, he shows himself falling to pieces under the pressure of police sirens, house searches, and a virtual news blackout in the media. During the days of Mogadishu, when German soldiers carried out an Entebbe-style raid to recapture a hijacked plane, he enacts a spectacle of seedy, flamboyant paranoia: that of a left-wing, homosexual, drug-taking artist and film-maker (the Jew of the 70s?) hiding out in his apartment, while his mother explains to him the virtues of conformism in times of political crisis and why she wishes the state was ruled by a benevolent dictator whom everyone could love. Fassbinder makes the connection between paranoia and narcissistic object choice by a double metaphor, boldly cutting from his mother saying that she wishes Hitler back to himself helplessly embracing his homosexual lover, as they roll on the floor, just as in *Despair* the employee Müller puts on a Nazi uniform, while Hermann goes off in search of a double.

What becomes problematic for Fassbinder is ultimately the question of sexual and social roles and the impossibility of deriving stable role-models from a "normal" Oedipal development. In the absence of constructing identity within the family (Fassbinder always demonstrates the violence and double binds that families impose on their members), the need to be perceived, to be confirmed, becomes paramount as the structure that regulates and at the same time disturbs the articulations of subjectivity. This means that the cinema, spectacle, the street, as places where the look is symbolically traded, become privileged spaces that actually structure identity outside the family, and in effect replace the family as an identity-generating institution. A film like *The Marriage of Maria Braun* on one level depicts a socialization process that enforces identity not through Oedipal conflict, substituting an object choice to escape the threat of castration, but through a structure modelled on the reaction formation to the loss of a particularly extreme substitution of the ego by an object. And under these conditions, the individual's most satisfying experience of subjectivity may be paradoxically as an exhibitionist, a conformist, in the experience of the self as object, not for anyone in particular, but under the gaze of the Other—be it history, destiny, the moral imperative, the community peer-groups: anyone who can be imagined as a spectator. What may once have been the place of the Father, the Law, Authority and its castrating gaze,[12] here manifests itself as the desire to identify with a lost object, the benevolent eye of the "mother" as we know it from the mirror phase. It would therefore be wrong to say that the palpaple absence of the camera marks necessarily the place of the Father.

Conformism was once a central subject of American schools of sociology and ego-psychology. David Riesman's idea of "inner-directed—other directed" (*The Lonely Crowd*), Erik Erikson's "approval/disapproval by a significant other," Melanie Klein's "good/bad object" in various ways all used Freud's papers on narcissism or his *Mass Psychology and the Ego* to conceptualize changes in social behavior in the face of a weakening family structure. In Germany, two

12. See *Cahiers du Cinéma*'s reading of "Young Mr. Lincoln," *Screen*, vol. 13, no. 3 (1972).

books by the director of the Sigmund Freud Institute in Frankfurt, Alexander Mitscherlich, discuss the social psychology of German fascism and the post-World War II reconstruction period. In *Society Without the Father*, for instance, Mitscherlich argues that fascism, in its appeal to Germans of all classes, represents a regressive solution to the "fatherlessness . . . in a world in which the division of labor has been extended to the exercise of authority." [13] Instead of assuming that Hitler figured as the Father, one has to imagine him fulfilling the role of a substitute for the primary love-object:

> (The mass leader), surprising as it may seem, . . . is much more like the image of a primitive mother-goddess. He acts as if he were superior to conscience, and demands a regressive obedience and the begging behaviour that belongs to the behaviour pattern of a child in the pre-Oedipal stage. . . . The ties to the Führer, in spite of all the protestations of eternal loyalty, never reached the level (i.e. Oedipal) so rich in conflict, where the conscience is formed and ties with it are established. [14]

According to Mitscherlich, this helps to explain why Hitler vanished so quickly from the minds of Germans after 1945 and why the collapse of the Third Reich did not provoke the kinds of reactions of conscience, of guilt and remorse that "the world" had expected. In *The Inability to Mourn* he writes:

> Thus, the choice of Hitler, as the love-object took place on a narcissistic basis; that is to say, on a basis of self-love. . . . The possibility of any dissociation from the object is lost; the person is in the truest sense of the term "under alien control." . . . After this symbolic state has been dissolved, the millions of subjects released from its spell will remember it all the less clearly because they never assimilated the leader into their ego as one does the model of an admired teacher, for instance but instead surrendered their own ego in favor of the object. . . . Thus, the inability to mourn was preceded by a way of loving that was less intent on sharing in the feelings of the other person than on confirming one's own self-esteem. Susceptibility to this form of love is one of the German people's collective character traits. The structure of the love-relation of the Germans to their ideals, or the various human incarnations of those ideals, seems to us to underlie a long history of misfortune. . . . Germans vacillate all too often between arrogance and self-abasement.

13. Alexander Mitscherlich, *Society Without the Father* (1969), p. 283.
14. Ibid., p. 284.

But their self-abasement bears the marks not so much of humility, as of melancholy. . . .[15]

The West German economic miracle was sustained psychologically by defense mechanisms. The work-ethic, ideologies of effort, the performance principle took on such ferocious proportions because of the "self-hatred of melancholia." [16] Why did West Germans rebuild such a conservative and conformist society? Democracy came to them imposed from without, and once again "under alien control," they reconstructed their Imaginary in the image of American consumer-capitalism. In parabolic fashion, this is the story of *The Marriage of Maria Braun*, whose heroine's ambiguous strength lies precisely in her "inability to mourn." Benevolent eyes, such as those of Chancellors Adenauer or Schmidt, gaze in ghostly fashion out of portraits whose frame once contained that of Hitler.

To support a film-analysis, however cursory, with such metapsychological observations courts many risks: can complex social and historical developments be reduced to and modeled on psychoanalytical concepts derived from clinical practice with individuals? Are generalizations about the national character not bound to remain at best abstractions, at worst mystifications that involve a mysteriously collective unconscious? Implicitly analogizing capitalism and the family structure as Mitscherlich does runs counter to the work, say, of R. D. Laing, or Bateson, where it is the family that becomes the place of contradictions specifically produced by capitalism. More serious still is the danger of collapsing a particular form of textual production such as the cinema, with a naive reflection theory so favored by sociologists of film or literature.

What is different between the Freud of Riesman, Erikson, Klein on the one hand, and that of Lacan, Metz, or Baudry on the other, is that the latter emphasize over and over again, the *specularity* of relations which for the former are somehow substantial, physical, like the symptoms displayed by Freud's hysterical patients. Lacan's insistence on the image, the eye in the deformation of the self—however incomplete this would be without his notion of textuality—shows the extent to which he has in fact read Freud in the light of concrete historical and social changes. Conversely, what separates Fassbinder from Mitscherlich, and what makes me risk speaking of a "social imaginary" without fear of getting it confused with some "collective unconscious" is Fassbinder's commitment to the

15. Alexander Mitscherlich, *The Inability to Mourn* (1975), pp. 60–61, 63–64.
16. Ibid., p. 63.

primacy of vision and the representation of interaction and action in terms of fascination and specular relations.

If fascism is then only the historical name given to the specularization of social, sexual and political life, then the concepts of Freudian psychoanalysis can indeed be pertinent, once Lacan has taught us how to read them. But by the same token, it suggests itself that Metz's primary identification partakes, as a theoretical construct or a descriptive category, in a historical development: call it, for the sake of the argument, the specularization of consciousness and social production—which his categories do not adequately reflect. In particular, to talk about primary and secondary identification as if it were a closed system risks conflating important distinctions, and, in the case of Fassbinder, and other "deviant" cinematic practices, tends to institutionalize a deconstructive, overly theoretical reading, where a historical reading might also be essential.

This said, it can be argued that in the case of the New German Cinema, we may actually have an interesting example of a productive misreading. One of the problems of the New German Cinema is that it is only slowly and against much resistance finding the audience inscribed in its texts—German intellectuals and the middle-class. The major successes have been in the capitals of Western Europe and on American university campuses, i.e., with an audience who, ignoring the peculiar historical inscriptions that the texts might carry, have been happy to appropriate the films on the basis precisely of a familiarity with models of narrative deconstruction, modernist self-reflexivity, whether of the kind typical for certain European films, or of the critical readings that film-scholars have produced for the classical Hollywood narrative. In turn, the popularity which the films of Fassbinder, Herzog, Wenders have achieved abroad, and above all the critical attention given to them by magazines, at conferences or in seminars, have, in a considerable way, strengthened their directors' chances of gaining more financial support in their own country from the government. This repeats the structure (on the level of production) which I tried to indicate is present in the texts themselves: the Germans are beginning to love their own cinema because it has been endorsed, confirmed and benevolently looked at by someone else: for the German cinema to exist, it first had to be seen by non-Germans. It enacts, as a national cinema, now in explicitly economic and cultural terms, yet another form of self-estranged exhibitionism.

Filmography and Bibliography

Fassbinder Filmography, 1965–1982

Complete filmographies of Rainer Werner Fassbinder are available in several titles listed in the bibliography. These sources also include Fassbinder's numerous theatrical productions and acting appearances. The citations in the list that follows include only the script writer and script source for each film. Fassbinder's productions on film for television and for theatrical release are included here, as well as his television productions on video. Productions in which Fassbinder participated in a capacity other than that of director and/or screenwriter are not included. The director is Fassbinder unless otherwise indicated.

1965

Der Stadtstreicher (The Bum)
Script: Rainer Werner Fassbinder.

1966

Das kleine Chaos (A Little Chaos)
Script: Rainer Werner Fassbinder.

1969

Liebe ist kälter als der Tod (Love Is Colder Than Death)
Script: Rainer Werner Fassbinder.

Katzelmacher
Script: Rainer Werner Fassbinder, based on his play of the same name, produced by the Action Theater in April 1968, and directed by Fassbinder and Peer Raben.

Fernes Jamaica (Far Jamaica)
Script: Rainer Werner Fassbinder. An anti-teater production directed by Peter Moland.

Götter der Pest (Gods of the Plague)
Script: Rainer Werner Fassbinder.

Warum läuft Herr R amok? (Why Does Herr R Run Amok?)
Improvisational situations suggested by Michael Fengler and Rainer Werner Fassbinder. Directed by Michael Fengler and Rainer Werner Fassbinder.

1970

Rio das Mortes
Script: Rainer Werner Fassbinder, based on an idea by Volker Schlöndorff.

Das Kaffeehaus (The Coffee House)
Television adaptation on video by Rainer Werner Fassbinder, based on the Italian comic play of 1750, *La bottega del caffè*, by Carlo Goldoni. The stage production was presented at the Stadttheater in Bremen in September 1969, and directed by Peer Raben and Rainer Werner Fassbinder.

Whity
Script: Rainer Werner Fassbinder.

Die Niklashauser Fahrt (The Niklashauser Journey)
Script: Rainer Werner Fassbinder, Michael Fengler. Directed by Rainer Werner Fassbinder and Michael Fengler.

Der amerikanische Soldat (The American Soldier)
Script: Rainer Werner Fassbinder, based on his play of the same name, produced by the anti-teater in

December 1968, and directed by Fassbinder and Peer Raben.

Warnung vor einer heiligen Nutte (Beware of a Holy Whore)
Script: Rainer Werner Fassbinder.

Pioniere in Ingolstadt (Pioneers in Ingolstadt)
Script: Rainer Werner Fassbinder, based on the play of the same name by Marieluise Fleisser, originally produced in Dresden in 1928. A version of the play, titled *Zum Beispiel Ingolstadt*, was presented by the Action Theater at the Büchner Theater in Munich in February 1968 under the direction of Fassbinder and Peer Raben. A new production, titled *Pioniere in Ingolstadt*, was presented in Bremen in January 1971, under Fassbinder's direction.

1971

Der Händler der vier Jahreszeiten (The Merchant of Four Seasons)
Script: Rainer Werner Fassbinder.

1972

Die bitteren Tränen der Petra von Kant (The Bitter Tears of Petra von Kant)
Script: Rainer Werner Fassbinder, based on his play of the same name, presented by the anti-teater at the Frankfurt "Experimenta," in June 1971, and directed by Peer Raben.

Wildwechsel (Jail Bait)
Script: Rainer Werner Fassbinder,
based on the play of the same name
by Franz Xaver Kroetz, originally
produced in Dortmund in 1968.

*Acht Stunden sind kein Tag (Eight
Hours Are Not a Day)*
Script: Rainer Werner Fassbinder.

Bremer Freiheit (Bremen Freedom)
Television adaptation on video by
Rainer Werner Fassbinder, based on
the play of the same name by Rainer
Werner Fassbinder. The stage production was presented by the anti-teater
at the Bremen Stadttheater in December 1971, directed by Fassbinder.

1973

Welt am Draht (World on Wires)
Script: Fritz Müller-Scherz, Rainer
Werner Fassbinder, based on the novel
of the same name by Daniel F.
Glouye.

Nora Helmer
Television adaptation on video by
Rainer Werner Fassbinder of the play,
"A Doll's House" by Henrik Ibsen, as
translated by Bernhard Schulze.

*Angst essen Seele auf (Fear Eats
the Soul)*
Script: Rainer Werner Fassbinder.

Martha
Script: Rainer Werner Fassbinder.

1974

Fontane Effi Briest (Effi Briest)
Script: Rainer Werner Fassbinder,
based on the novel of the same name
by Theodor Fontane, originally
published in 1895.

*Faustrecht der Freiheit (Fox and His
Friends)*
Script: Rainer Werner Fassbinder,
Christian Hohoff.

*Wie ein Vogel auf dem Draht (Like
a Bird on the Wire)*
Script: Rainer Werner Fassbinder,
Christian Hohoff. Lyrics: Anja
Hauptmann. On video.

1975

*Mutter Küsters' Fahrt zum Himmel
(Mother Küsters' Trip to Heaven)*
Script: Rainer Werner Fassbinder,
in collaboration with Kurt Raab.

Angst vor der Angst (Fear of Fear)
Script: Rainer Werner Fassbinder,
based on an idea by Asta Scheib.

*Schatten der Engel (Shadows of
Angels)*
Script: Daniel Schmid, Rainer Werner
Fassbinder, based on Fassbinder's
unproduced play, "Der Müll, die Stadt
und der Tod, oder Frankenstein am
Main" ("Garbage, the City and
Death, or Frankenstein on the Main").
Directed by Daniel Schmid.

1976

Ich will doch nur, dass Ihr mich liebt
(*I Only Want You to Love Me*)
Script: Rainer Werner Fassbinder,
based on an actual case study from
the book *Lebenslänglich* (*Life Term*)
by Klaus Antes and Christiane
Ehrhardt, published in 1972.

Satansbraten (*Satan's Brew*)
Script: Rainer Werner Fassbinder.

Chinesisches Roulette (*Chinese Roulette*)
Script: Rainer Werner Fassbinder.

1977

Bolwieser (*The Stationmaster's Wife*)
Script: Rainer Werner Fassbinder,
based on the novel *Bolwieser—
Roman eines Ehemanns* (*Bolwieser—
Story of a Married Man*) by Oskar
Maria Graf, originally published
in 1931.

Frauen in New York (*Women in
New York*)
Television adaptation on film by
Rainer Werner Fassbinder, based on
his Hamburg Schauspielhaus production of the 1936 Broadway play, *The
Women*, by Claire Boothe Luce, as
translated by Nora Gray. The stage
production was presented in September 1976, directed by Fassbinder.

Eine Reise ins Licht—Despair
(*Despair*)
Script: Tom Stoppard, based on the
novel of the same name by Vladimir
Nabokov. Written in Berlin in Russian
as *Otchayanie* in 1932, it first appeared two years later in a Parisian
emigré review. Nabokov's English
translation was published in 1936;
a revised English version appeared
in 1965.

1978

Deutschland im Herbst (*Germany
in Autumn*)
Script: Heinrich Böll, Peter
Steinbach, and the directors. A
collaborative film directed by Alf
Brustellin, Rainer Werner Fassbinder,
Alexander Kluge, Maximiliane
Mainka, Edgar Reitz, Katja Rupé/
Hans Peter Cloos, Volker Schlöndorff,
and Bernhard Sinkel. Script of the
Fassbinder episode: Rainer Werner
Fassbinder.

Die Ehe der Maria Braun (*The
Marriage of Maria Braun*)
Script: Peter Märthesheimer, Pea
Fröhlich, based on an idea by
Fassbinder. Dialogue: Pea Fröhlich,
Rainer Werner Fassbinder, Peter
Märthesheimer.

In einem Jahr mit 13 Monden
(*In a Year of Thirteen Moons*)
Script: Rainer Werner Fassbinder.

1979

Die Dritte Generation (The Third Generation)
Script: Rainer Werner Fassbinder.

1980

Berlin Alexanderplatz
Script: Rainer Werner Fassbinder, based on the novel of the same name by Alfred Döblin, originally published in 1929.

Lili Marleen
Script: Manfred Purzer, Rainer Werner Fassbinder, in collaboration with Joshua Sinclair, based on the autobiography of Lale Andersen, *Der Himmel hat viele Farben (The Sky Has Many Colors)*, originally published in 1972.

1981

Lola
Script: Peter Märthesheimer, Pea Fröhlich. Dialogue: Rainer Werner Fassbinder.

Theater in Trance
Script: Rainer Werner Fassbinder, including texts from Antonin Artaud's *Le Théâtre et son double (The Theater and Its Double)*, originally published in 1938.

Die Sehnsucht der Veronika Voss (The Longing of Veronika Voss)
Script: Peter Märthesheimer, Pea Fröhlich.

1982

Querelle—Ein Pakt mit dem Teufel (Querelle)
Script: Rainer Werner Fassbinder, Burkhard Driest, based on the novel *Querelle de Brest* by Jean Genet, originally published in 1953.

Selected Bibliography

Altman, Rick. "A Semantic/Syntactic Approach to Film Genre." *Cinema Journal* 3 (Spring 1984): 6–18.

Baer, Harry, with Maurus Pacher. *Schafen kann ich, wenn ich tot bin. Das atemlose Leben des Rainer Werner Fassbinder*. Cologne: Kiepenheuer & Witsch, 1982.

Brooks, Peter. *The Melodramatic Imagination: Balzac, Henry James, Melodrama, and the Mode of Excess*. New Haven: Yale University Press, 1976.

Collins, Richard, and Vincent Porter. *WDR and the Arbeiterfilm: Fassbinder, Ziewer and others*. London: British Film Institute, 1981.

Comolli, Jean-Luc, and Paul Narboni. "Cinema/Ideology/Criticism." Susan Bennett, trans. *Screen* (London) 1 (Spring 1971): 27–36. Originally published in *Cahiers du Cinéma* (Paris) 216–217 (October–November 1969).

Corrigan, Timothy. *New German Film. The Displaced Image*. Austin: University of Texas Press, 1983.

Craig, Gordon A. *The Germans*. New York: Putnam, 1982.

Eckhardt, Bernd. *Rainer Werner Fassbinder*. Munich: Wilhelm Heyne Verlag, 1982.

Elsaesser, Thomas. "Tales of Sound and Fury: Observations on the Family Melodrama." *Monogram* (London) 4 (1972): 2–15.

Fassbinder, Rainer Werner. *Filme befreien den Kopf*. Michael Töteberg, ed. Frankfurt am Main: Fischer Taschenbuch Verlag, 1984.

Feinstein, Howard, "BRD 1-2-3: Fassbinder's Postwar Trilogy and the

Spectacle." *Cinema Journal* 1 (Fall 1983):44–56.

Hayman, Ronald, *Fassbinder, Film Maker*. New York: Simon & Schuster, 1984.

Hughes, John, and Brooks Riley. "A New Realism: Fassbinder Interviewed." *Film Comment* 6 (November–December 1975):14–17.

Iden, Peter, et al. *Fassbinder*. New York: Tanam Press, 1981. Originally published in German as *Reihe Film 2. Rainer Werner Fassbinder*, by Carl Hanser Verlag in 1974.

Kaes, Anton. "History, Fiction, Memory: Fassbinder's *The Marriage of Maria Braun*." *Persistence of Vision* 2 (Fall 1985): 52–60.

Kaplan, E. Ann. "Integrating Marxist and Psychoanalytical Approaches in Feminist Film Criticism." *Millennium Film Journal* 6 (Spring 1980):8–17.

———, ed. *Women and Film: Both Sides of the Camera*. New York: Methuen, 1983.

———, ed. *Women in Film Noir*. London: British Film Institute, 1980.

Klinger, Barbara. " 'Cinema/Ideology/Criticism'-Revisited: The Progressive Text." *Screen* 1 (January–February 1984):30–44.

Krütnik, Frank. "*The Shanghai Gesture*. The Exotic and the Melodramatic." *Wide Angle* 2 (1980):36–42.

Lehman, Peter. " 'Thinking with the Heart': An Interview with Douglas Sirk." *Wide Angle* 4 (1980):42–47.

Limmer, Wolfgang. *Rainer Werner Fassbinder, Filmemacher*. Hamburg: Spiegel Verlag, 1982.

Mayne, Judith. "Fassbinder and Spectatorship." *New German Critique* 12 (Fall 1977):61–74.

Merritt, Russell. "Melodrama: Postmortem for a Phantom Genre." *Wide Angle* 3 (1983):24–31.

Mulvey, Laura. "Notes on Sirk and Melodrama." *Movie* (London) 25 (Winter 1977–1978):53–56.

———. "Visual Pleasure and Narrative Cinema." *Screen* 3 (Autumn 1975):6–18.

———, and John Halliday, eds. *Douglas Sirk*. Edinburgh: Edinburgh Film Festival 72, 1972.

New German Critique. "Special Double Issue on New German Cinema." 24–25 (Fall/Winter 1981–82).

Nichols, Bill. *Ideology and the Image*. Bloomington: Indiana University Press, 1981.

Nowell-Smith, Geoffrey. "Minnelli and Melodrama." *Screen* 2 (Summer 1977):113–118.

October. "Rainer Werner Fassbinder. A Special Issue." 21 (Summer 1982).

Orr, Christopher. "Closure and Containment. Marylee Hadley in *Writ-*

ten on the Wind." Wide Angle 2 (1980):29–35.

Pflaum, Hans Günther, and Rainer Werner Fassbinder. *Das bisschen Realität, das ich brauche. Wie Filme entstehen.* Munich: Carl Hanser Verlag, 1976.

Pipolo, Tony. "German Filmmakers Seldom Focus on the Legacy of Nazism." *New York Times,* 1 August 1982, pp. 1, 15.

Quarterly Review of Film Studies. "West German Film in the 1970s," special issue. Eric Rentschler, guest editor. 2 (Spring 1980).

Raab, Kurt. "My Life with Rainer." *Village Voice,* 3 May 1983, pp. 43–45.

———, and Karsten Peters. *Die Sehnsucht des Rainer Werner Fassbinder.* Munich: C. Bertelsmann Verlag, 1982.

Rayns, Tony, ed. *Fassbinder.* London: British Film Institute, 1980.

Rentschler, Eric. *West German Film in the course of time.* Bedford Hills, N.Y.: Redgrave Publishing Co., 1984.

Sirk, Douglas. *Sirk on Sirk.* John Halliday, ed. New York: Viking Press, 1972.

Sparrow, Norbert. " 'I Let the Audience Feel and Think': An Interview with Rainer Werner Fassbinder." *Cineaste* 2 (Fall 1977):20–21.

Zwerenz, Gerhard. *Der langsame Tod des Rainer Werner Fassbinder. Ein Bericht.* Munich: Münchener Edition/Schneekluth, 1982.

———. *Die Ehe der Maria Braun, Roman.* (A novelization of the film.) Munich: Wilhelm Goldmann Verlag, 1979.

Jan 18/08

Printed in the United States
68577LVS00003B/49-57